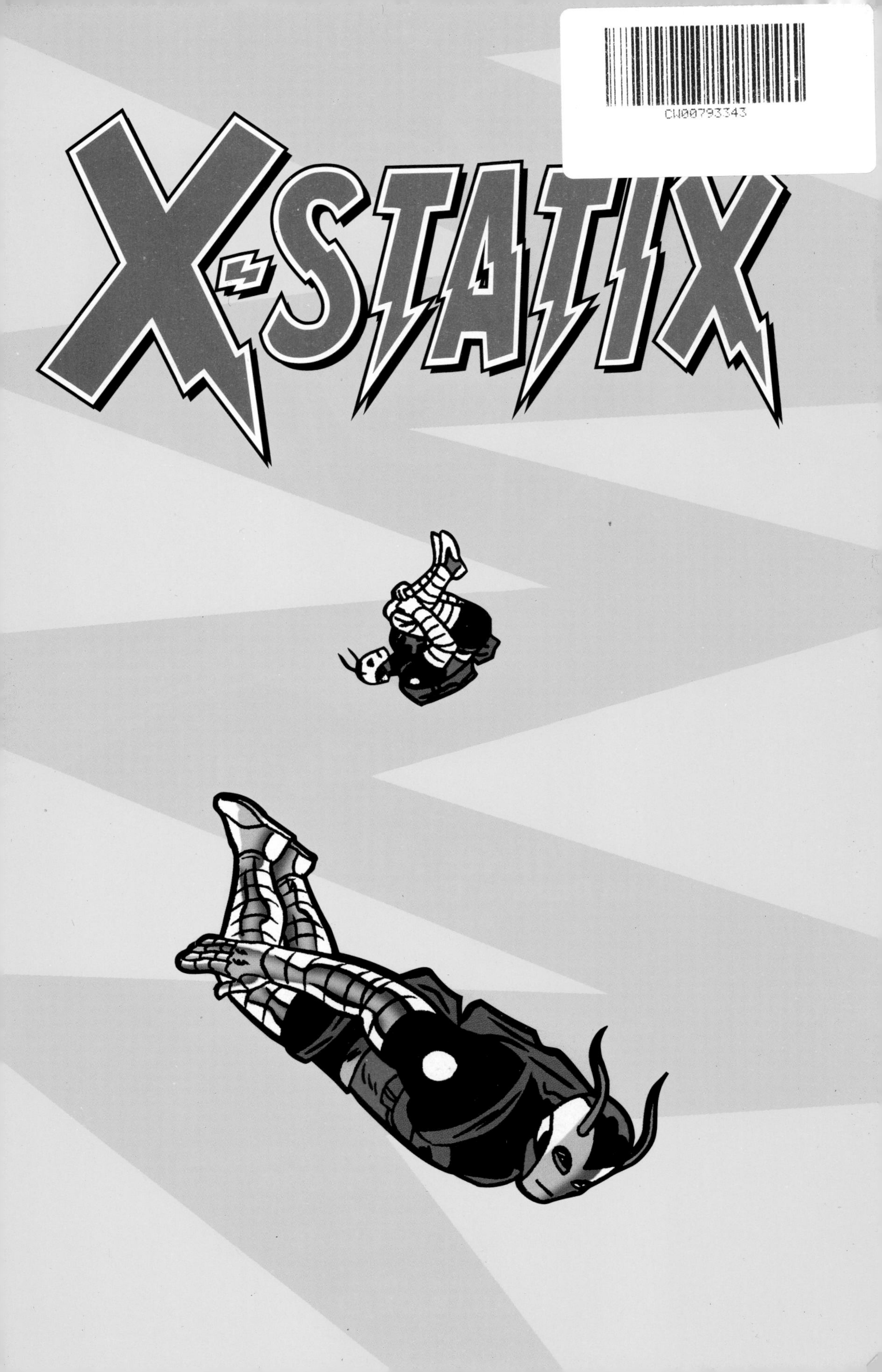
X-STATIX

Peter Milligan
WRITER

Mike Allred
with Darwyn Cooke & Paul Pope
ARTISTS

Laura Allred
COLORIST

Doc Allred & Blambot's Nate Piekos
LETTERS

Axel Alonso
EDITOR

John Miesegaes & Warren Simons
ASSISTANT EDITORS

Joe Quesada
EDITOR IN CHIEF

Bill Jemas
PRESIDENT

GOOD
OMENS

X-STATIX VOL. 1: GOOD OMENS. Contains material originally published in magazine form as X-Statix #1-5. First printing 2003. ISBN# 0-7851-1059-3. Published by MARVEL COMICS, a division of MARVEL ENTERTAINMENT GROUP, INC. OFFICE OF PUBLICATION: 10 East 40th Street, New York, NY 10016. Copyright © 2002 and 2003 Marvel Characters, Inc. All rights reserved. $11.99 per copy in the U.S. and $19.25 in Canada (GST #R127032852); Canadian Agreement #40668537. All characters featured in this issue and the distinctive names and likenesses thereof, and all related indicia are trademarks of Marvel Characters, Inc. No similarity between any of the names, characters, persons, and/or institutions in this magazine with those of any living or dead person or institution is intended, and any such similarity which may exist is purely coincidental. **Printed in Canada.** STAN LEE, Chairman Emeritus. For information regarding advertising in Marvel Comics or on Marvel.com, please contact Russell Brown, Executive Vice President, Consumer Products, Promotions and Media Sales at 212-576-8561 or rbrown@marvel.com

10 9 8 7 6 5 4 3 2 1

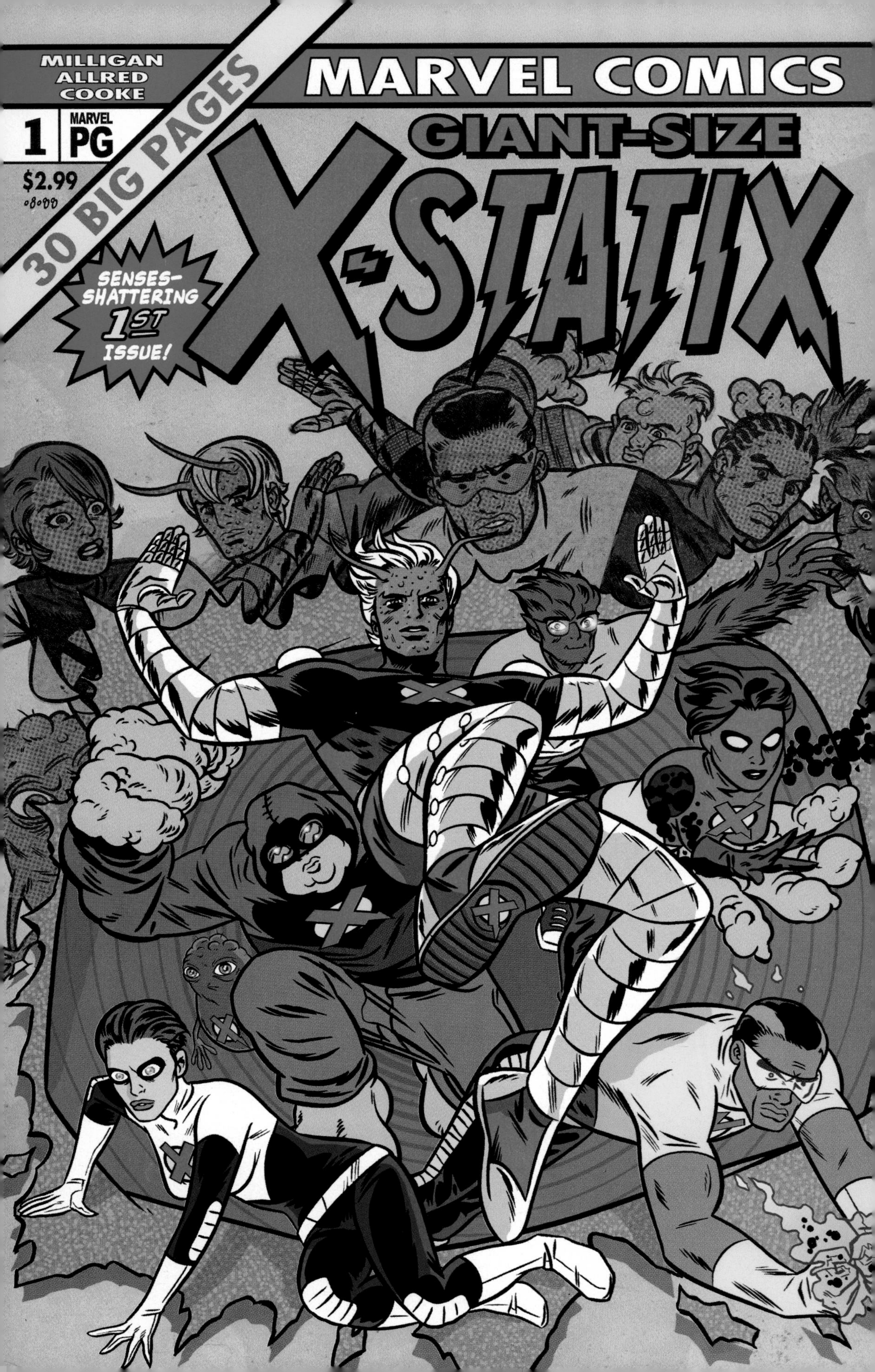

MILLIGAN
ALLRED
COOKE
30 BIG PAGES
MARVEL COMICS
1
MARVEL
PG
$2.99
GIANT-SIZE
X-STATIX
SENSES-SHATTERING 1ST ISSUE!

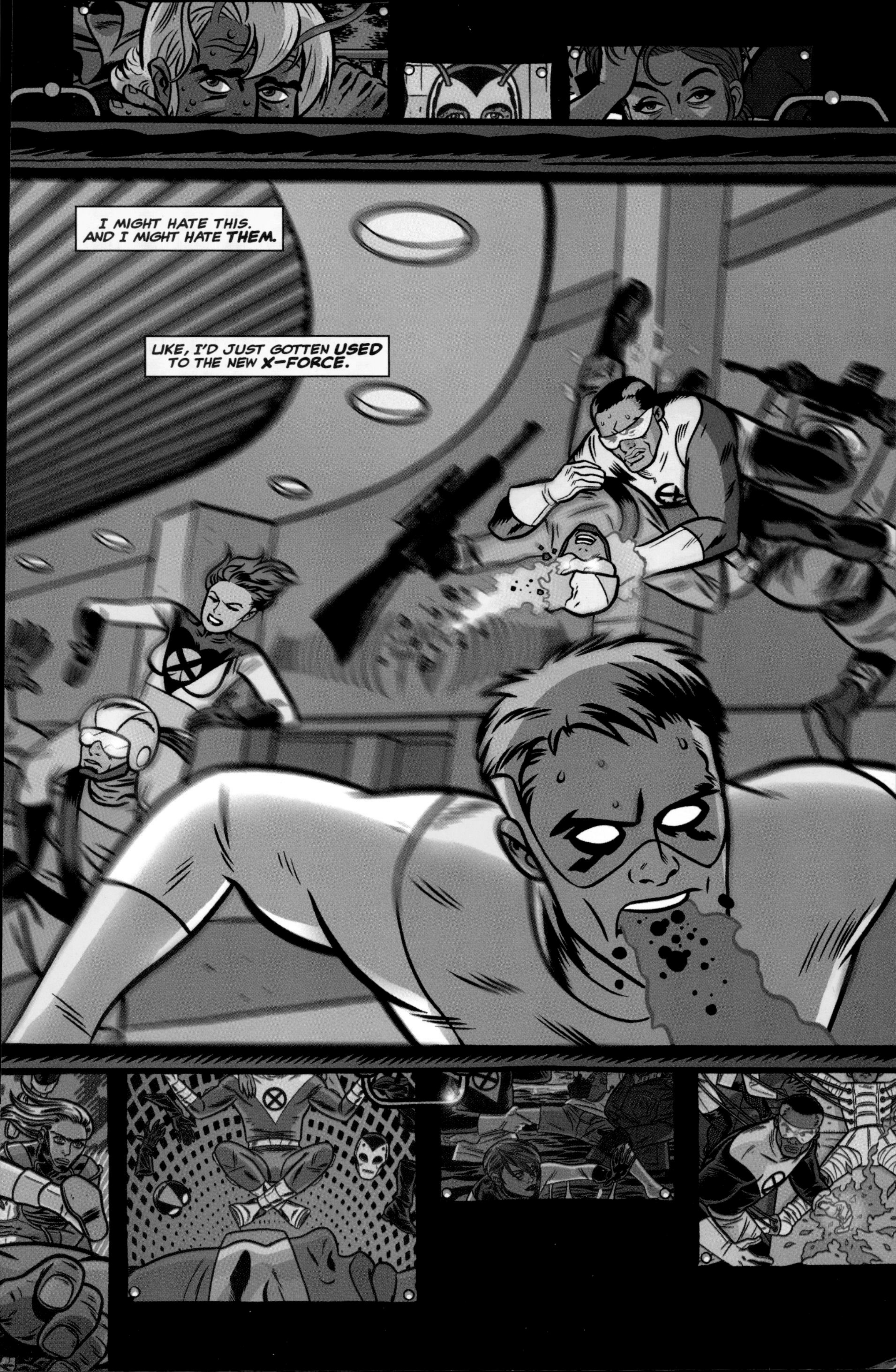
I MIGHT HATE THIS. AND I MIGHT HATE THEM.
LIKE, I'D JUST GOTTEN USED TO THE NEW X-FORCE.

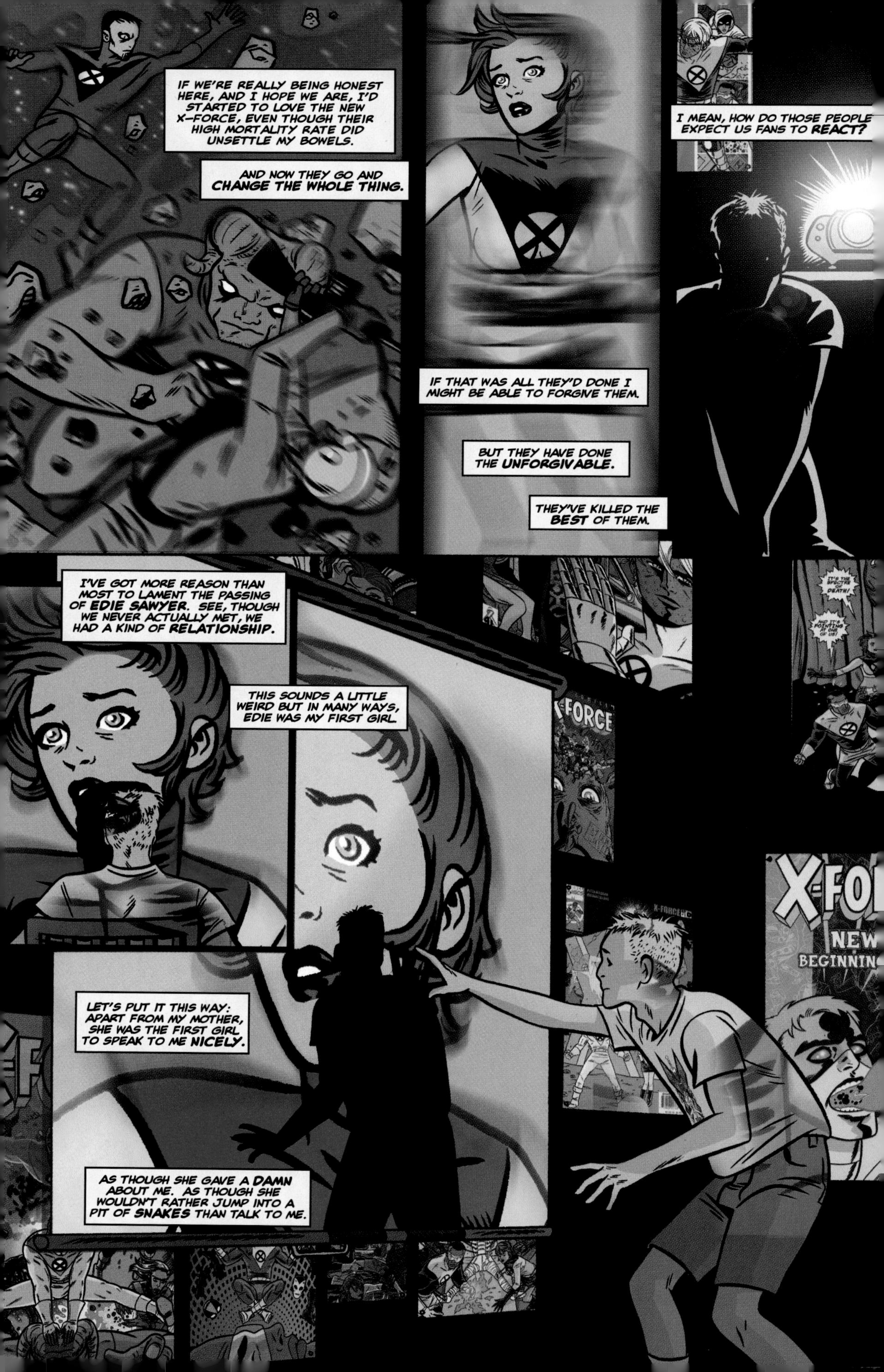
IF WE'RE REALLY BEING HONEST HERE, AND I HOPE WE ARE, I'D STARTED TO LOVE THE NEW X-FORCE, EVEN THOUGH THEIR HIGH MORTALITY RATE DID UNSETTLE MY BOWELS.
AND NOW THEY GO AND CHANGE THE WHOLE THING.
IF THAT WAS ALL THEY'D DONE I MIGHT BE ABLE TO FORGIVE THEM.
BUT THEY HAVE DONE THE UNFORGIVABLE.
THEY'VE KILLED THE BEST OF THEM.
I MEAN, HOW DO THOSE PEOPLE EXPECT US FANS TO REACT?
I'VE GOT MORE REASON THAN MOST TO LAMENT THE PASSING OF EDIE SAWYER. SEE, THOUGH WE NEVER ACTUALLY MET, WE HAD A KIND OF RELATIONSHIP.
THIS SOUNDS A LITTLE WEIRD BUT IN MANY WAYS, EDIE WAS MY FIRST GIRL.
LET'S PUT IT THIS WAY: APART FROM MY MOTHER, SHE WAS THE FIRST GIRL TO SPEAK TO ME NICELY.
AS THOUGH SHE GAVE A DAMN ABOUT ME. AS THOUGH SHE WOULDN'T RATHER JUMP INTO A PIT OF SNAKES THAN TALK TO ME.
X-FORCE
X-FO
NEW
BEGINNIN

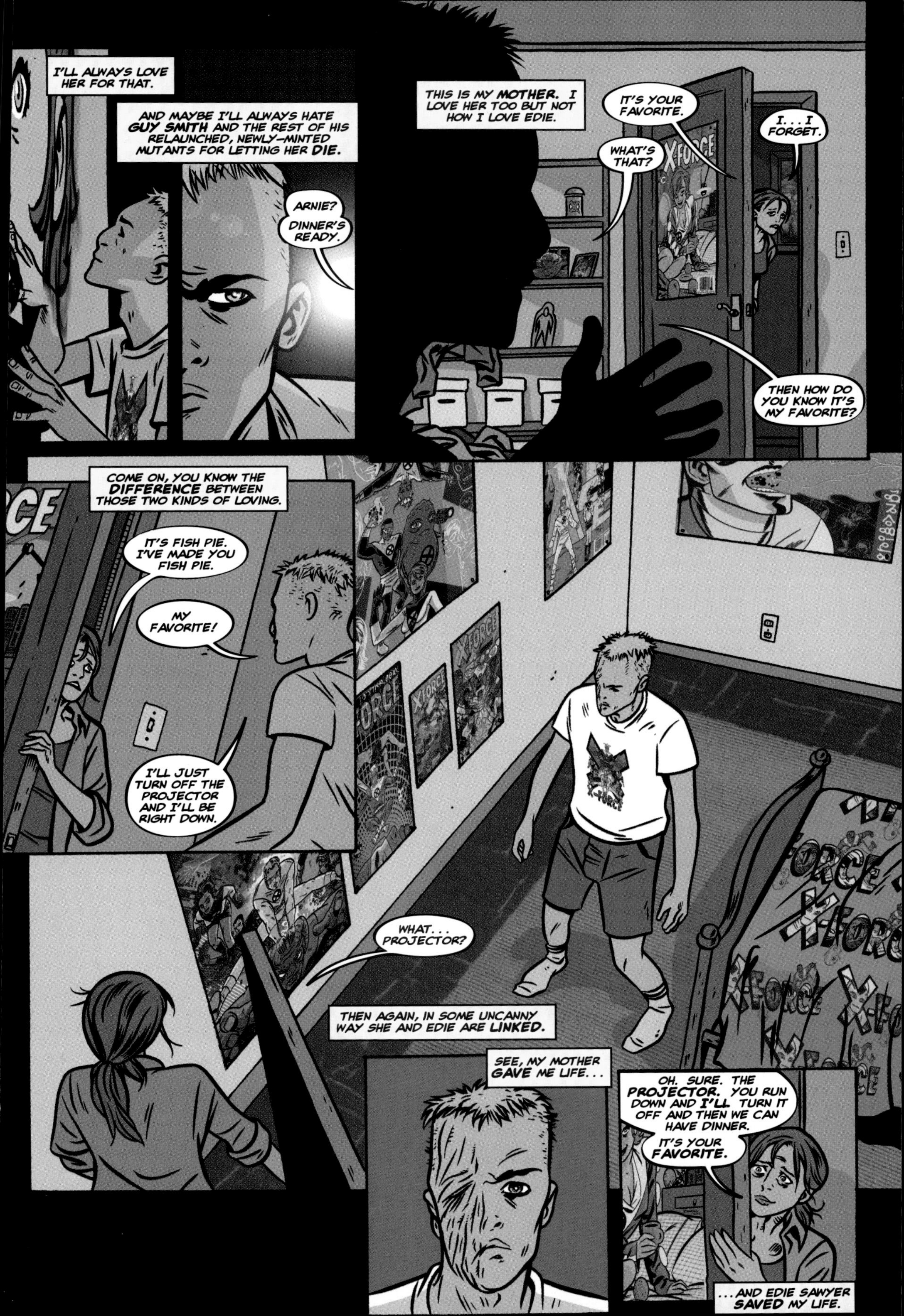
I'LL ALWAYS LOVE HER FOR THAT.
AND MAYBE I'LL ALWAYS HATE GUY SMITH AND THE REST OF HIS RELAUNCHED, NEWLY-MINTED MUTANTS FOR LETTING HER DIE.
ARNIE? DINNER'S READY.
THIS IS MY MOTHER. I LOVE HER TOO BUT NOT HOW I LOVE EDIE.
IT'S YOUR FAVORITE.
WHAT'S THAT?
I... I FORGET.
THEN HOW DO YOU KNOW IT'S MY FAVORITE?
X-FORCE
COME ON, YOU KNOW THE DIFFERENCE BETWEEN THOSE TWO KINDS OF LOVING.
IT'S FISH PIE. I'VE MADE YOU FISH PIE.
MY FAVORITE!
I'LL JUST TURN OFF THE PROJECTOR AND I'LL BE RIGHT DOWN.
X-FORCE
WHAT... PROJECTOR?
THEN AGAIN, IN SOME UNCANNY WAY SHE AND EDIE ARE LINKED.
SEE, MY MOTHER GAVE ME LIFE...
OH. SURE. THE PROJECTOR. YOU RUN DOWN AND I'LL TURN IT OFF AND THEN WE CAN HAVE DINNER.
IT'S YOUR FAVORITE.
...AND EDIE SAWYER SAVED MY LIFE.

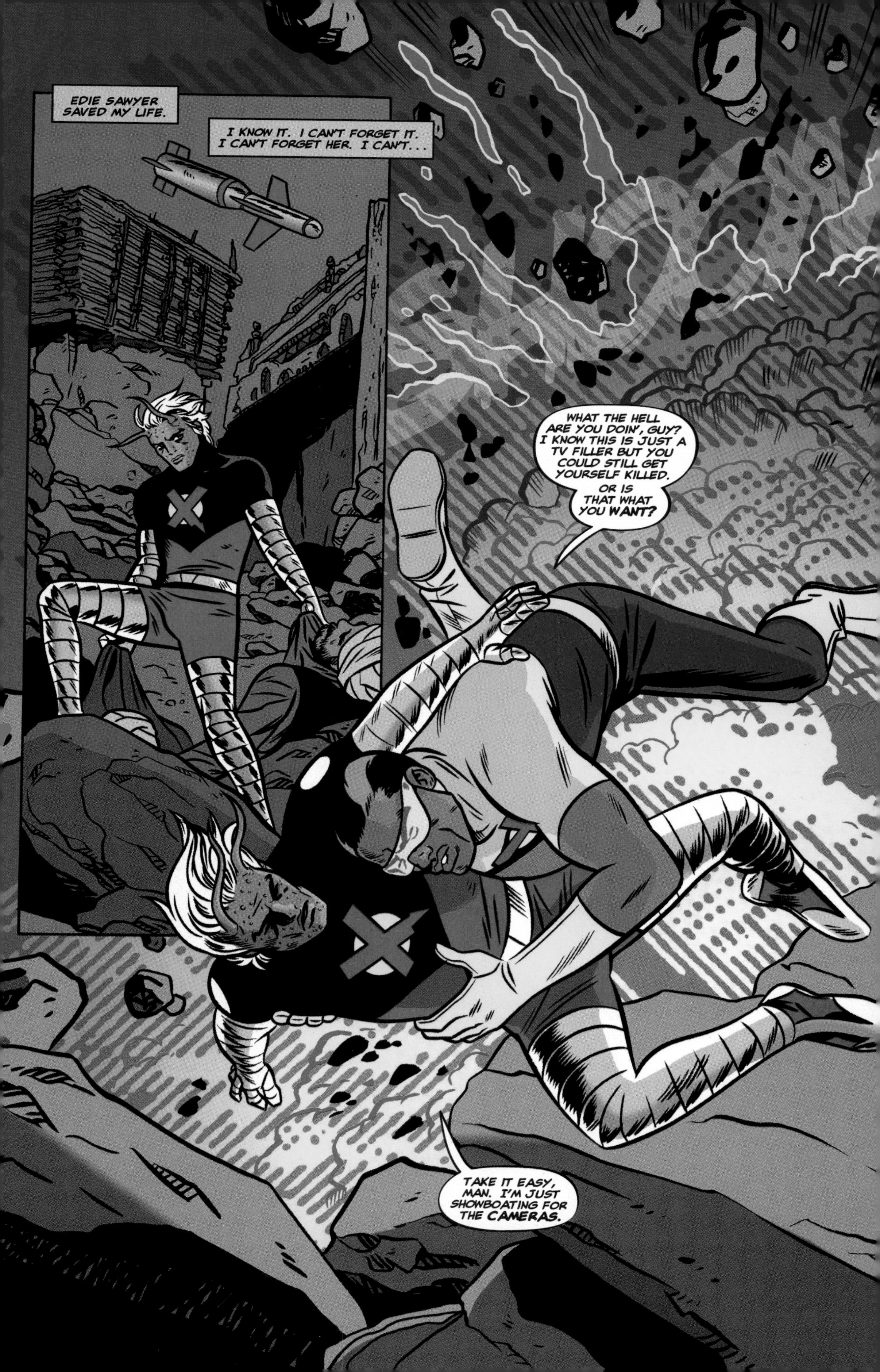
EDIE SAWYER SAVED MY LIFE.
I KNOW IT. I CAN'T FORGET IT. I CAN'T FORGET HER. I CAN'T...
WHAT THE HELL ARE YOU DOIN', GUY? I KNOW THIS IS JUST A TV FILLER BUT YOU COULD STILL GET YOURSELF KILLED. OR IS THAT WHAT YOU WANT?
TAKE IT EASY, MAN. I'M JUST SHOWBOATING FOR THE CAMERAS.

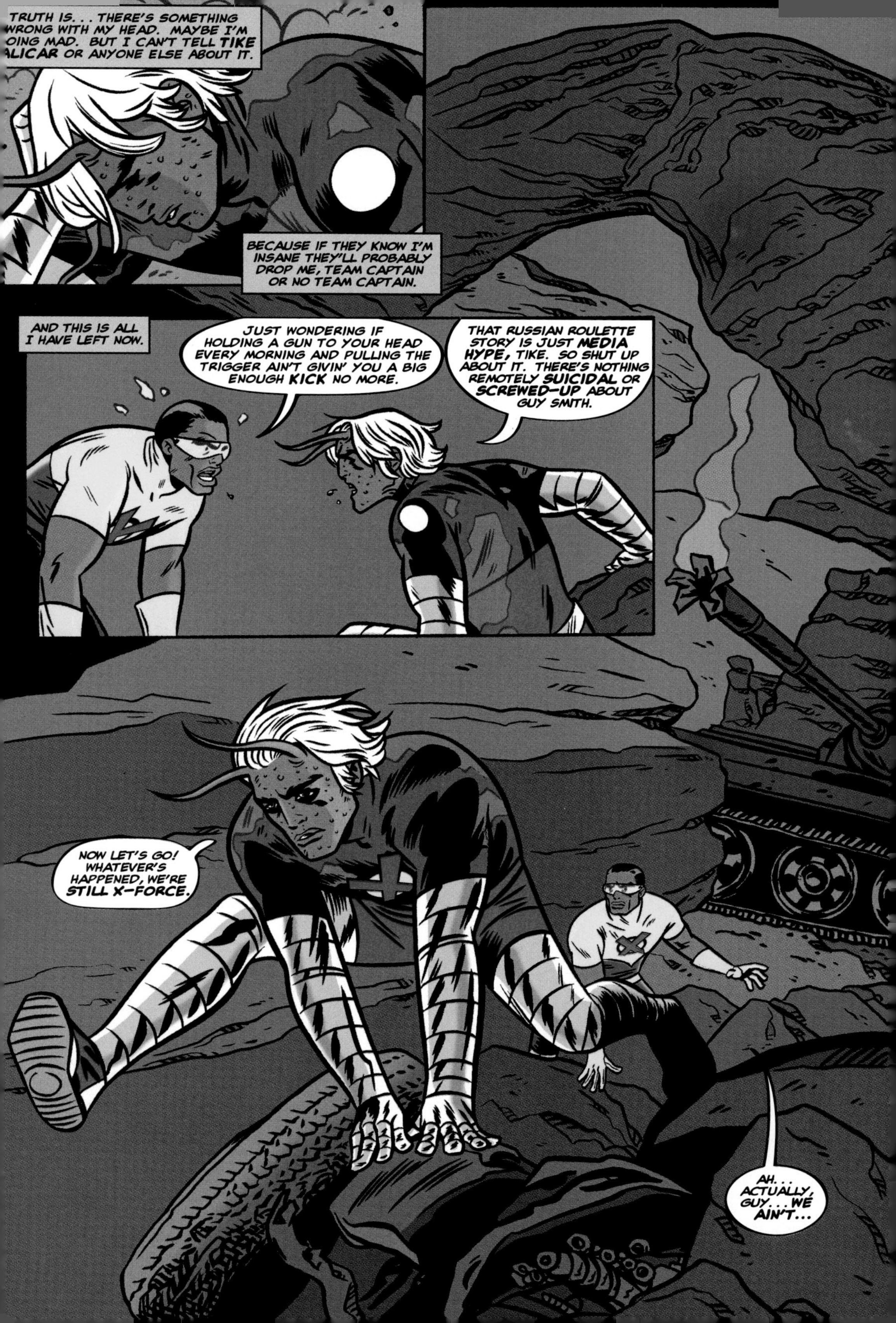
TRUTH IS... THERE'S SOMETHING WRONG WITH MY HEAD. MAYBE I'M OING MAD. BUT I CAN'T TELL TIKE ALICAR OR ANYONE ELSE ABOUT IT.
BECAUSE IF THEY KNOW I'M INSANE THEY'LL PROBABLY DROP ME, TEAM CAPTAIN OR NO TEAM CAPTAIN.
AND THIS IS ALL I HAVE LEFT NOW.
JUST WONDERING IF HOLDING A GUN TO YOUR HEAD EVERY MORNING AND PULLING THE TRIGGER AIN'T GIVIN' YOU A BIG ENOUGH KICK NO MORE.
THAT RUSSIAN ROULETTE STORY IS JUST MEDIA HYPE, TIKE. SO SHUT UP ABOUT IT. THERE'S NOTHING REMOTELY SUICIDAL OR SCREWED-UP ABOUT GUY SMITH.
NOW LET'S GO! WHATEVER'S HAPPENED, WE'RE STILL X-FORCE.
AH... ACTUALLY, GUY... WE AIN'T...

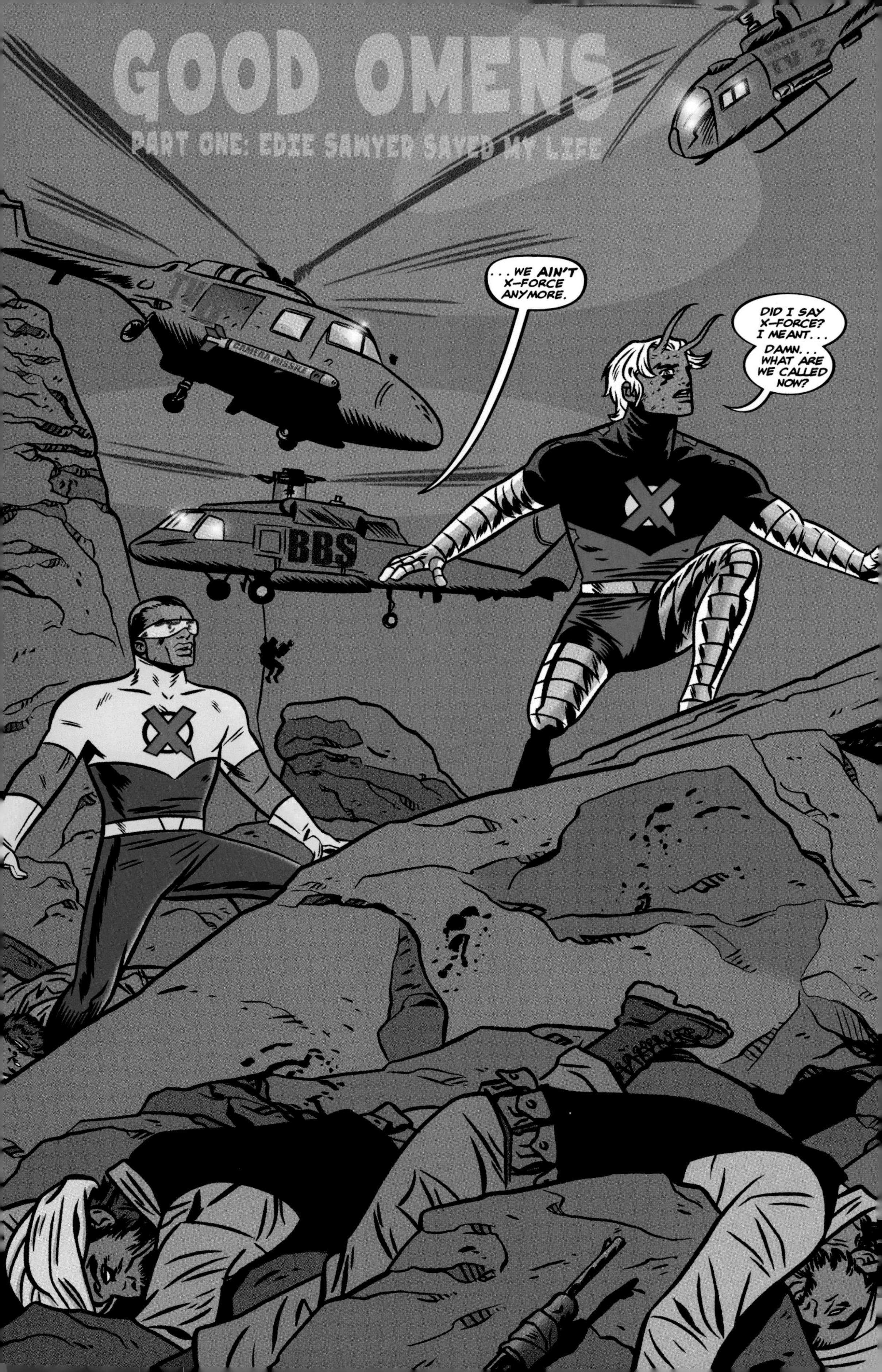
GOOD OMENS
PART ONE: EDIE SAWYER SAVED MY LIFE
. . . WE AIN'T X-FORCE ANYMORE.
DID I SAY X-FORCE? I MEANT. . . DAMN. . . WHAT ARE WE CALLED NOW?
TV
CAMERA MISSILE
BBS
TV 2

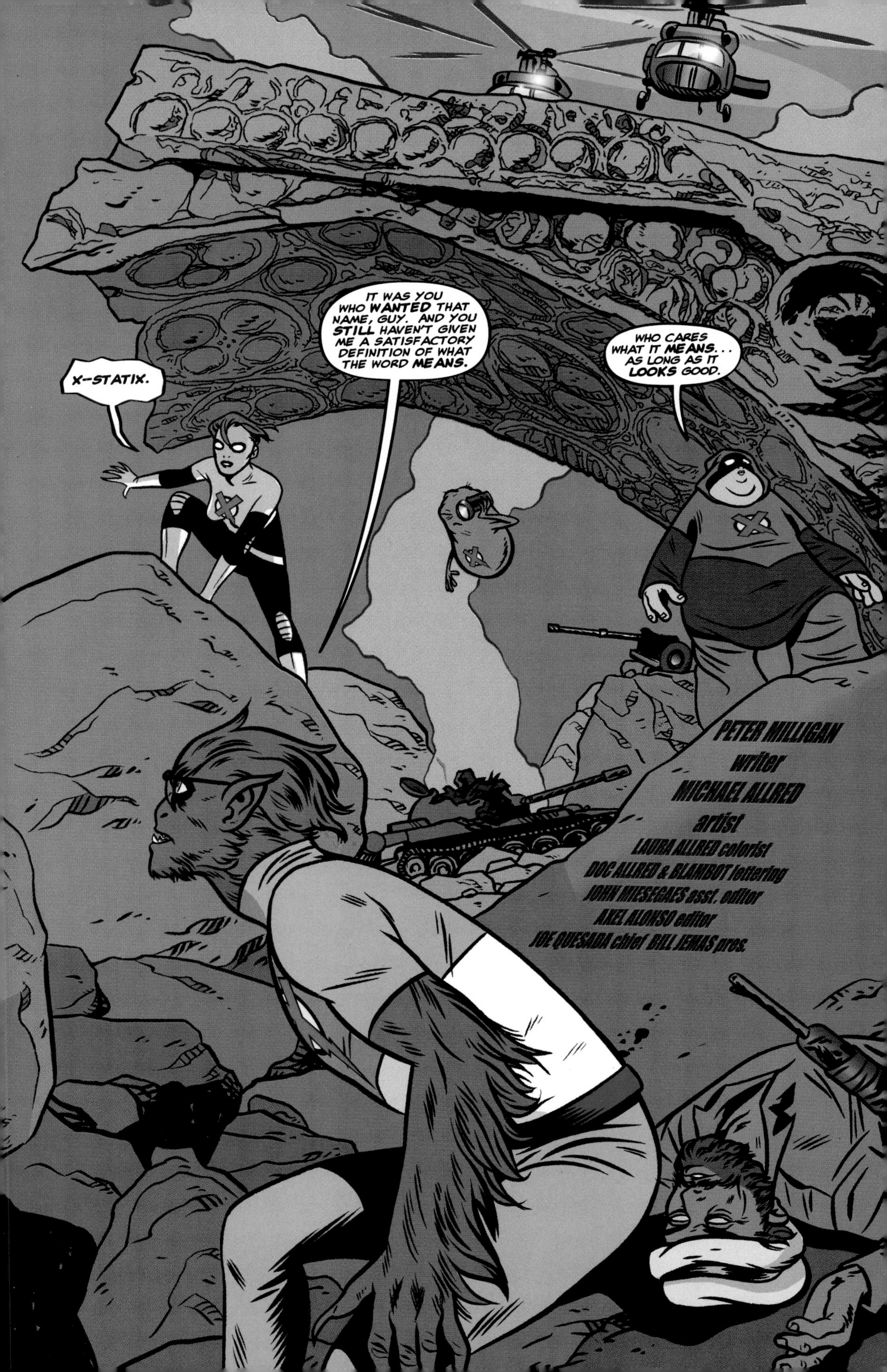
X--STATIX.
IT WAS YOU WHO WANTED THAT NAME, GUY. AND YOU STILL HAVEN'T GIVEN ME A SATISFACTORY DEFINITION OF WHAT THE WORD MEANS.
WHO CARES WHAT IT MEANS... AS LONG AS IT LOOKS GOOD.
PETER MILLIGAN writer
MICHAEL ALLRED artist
LAURA ALLRED colorist
DOC ALLRED & BLAMBOT lettering
JOHN MIESEGAES asst. editor
AXEL ALONSO editor
JOE QUESADA chief BILL JEMAS pres.

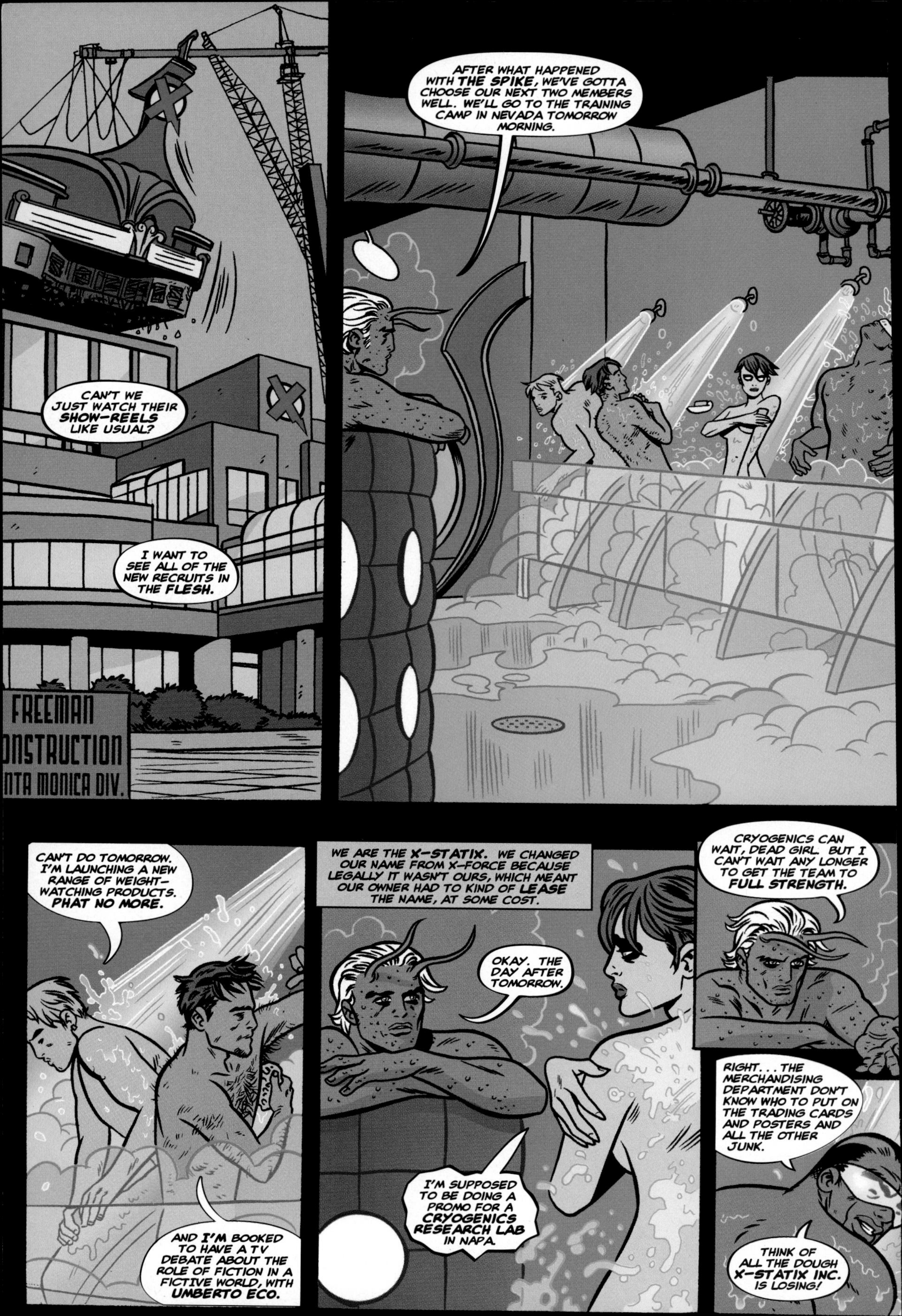
CAN'T WE JUST WATCH THEIR SHOW-REELS LIKE USUAL?
I WANT TO SEE ALL OF THE NEW RECRUITS IN THE FLESH.
FREEMAN
ONSTRUCTION
NTA MONICA DIV.
AFTER WHAT HAPPENED WITH THE SPIKE, WE'VE GOTTA CHOOSE OUR NEXT TWO MEMBERS WELL. WE'LL GO TO THE TRAINING CAMP IN NEVADA TOMORROW MORNING.
CAN'T DO TOMORROW. I'M LAUNCHING A NEW RANGE OF WEIGHT-WATCHING PRODUCTS. PHAT NO MORE.
AND I'M BOOKED TO HAVE A TV DEBATE ABOUT THE ROLE OF FICTION IN A FICTIVE WORLD, WITH UMBERTO ECO.
WE ARE THE X-STATIX. WE CHANGED OUR NAME FROM X-FORCE BECAUSE LEGALLY IT WASN'T OURS, WHICH MEANT OUR OWNER HAD TO KIND OF LEASE THE NAME, AT SOME COST.
OKAY. THE DAY AFTER TOMORROW.
I'M SUPPOSED TO BE DOING A PROMO FOR A CRYOGENICS RESEARCH LAB IN NAPA.
CRYOGENICS CAN WAIT, DEAD GIRL. BUT I CAN'T WAIT ANY LONGER TO GET THE TEAM TO FULL STRENGTH.
RIGHT... THE MERCHANDISING DEPARTMENT DON'T KNOW WHO TO PUT ON THE TRADING CARDS AND POSTERS AND ALL THE OTHER JUNK.
THINK OF ALL THE DOUGH X-STATIX INC. IS LOSING!

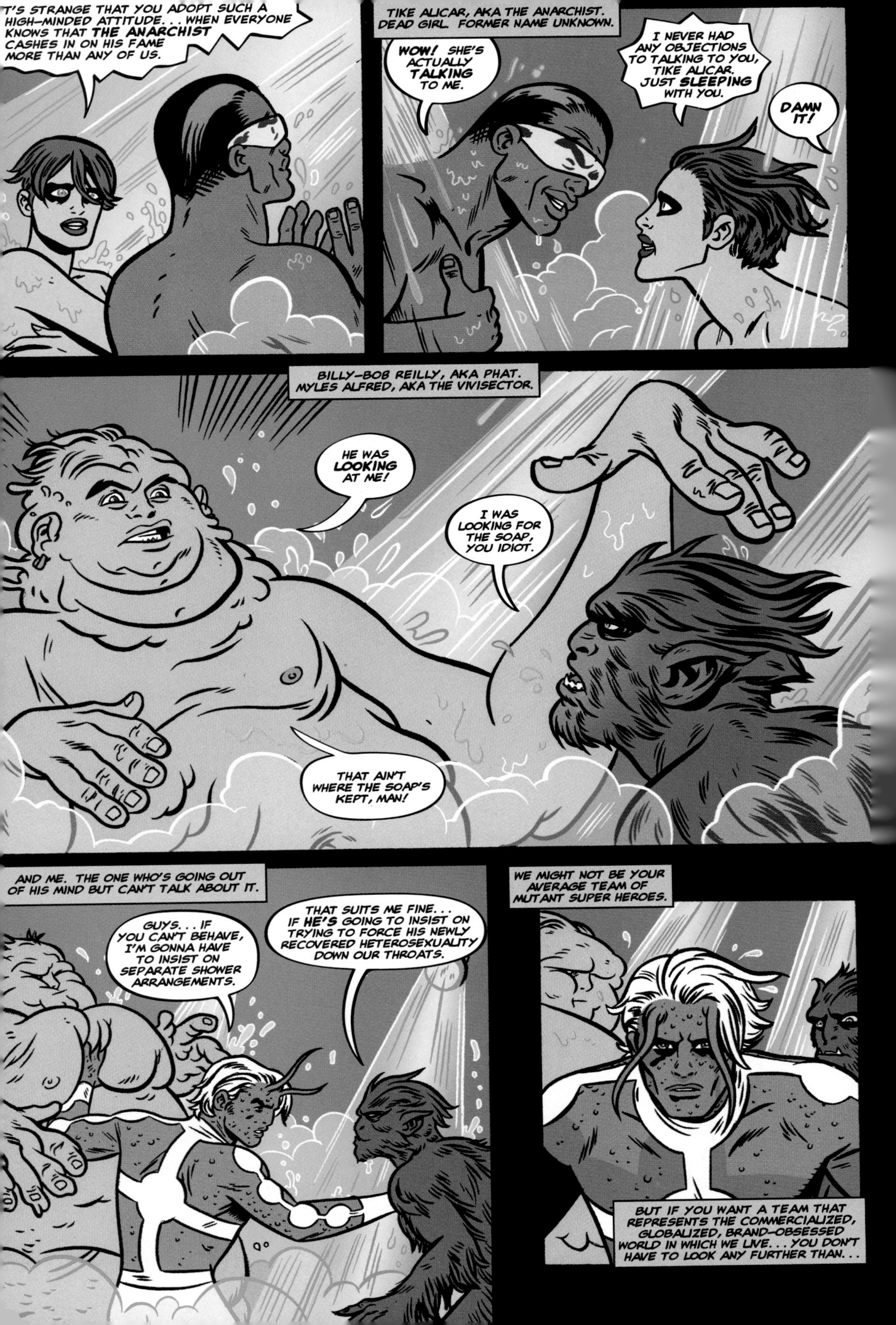
T'S STRANGE THAT YOU ADOPT SUCH A HIGH-MINDED ATTITUDE... WHEN EVERYONE KNOWS THAT THE ANARCHIST CASHES IN ON HIS FAME MORE THAN ANY OF US.
TIKE ALICAR, AKA THE ANARCHIST. DEAD GIRL. FORMER NAME UNKNOWN.
WOW! SHE'S ACTUALLY TALKING TO ME.
I NEVER HAD ANY OBJECTIONS TO TALKING TO YOU, TIKE ALICAR. JUST SLEEPING WITH YOU.
DAMN IT!
BILLY-BOB REILLY, AKA PHAT. MYLES ALFRED, AKA THE VIVISECTOR.
HE WAS LOOKING AT ME!
I WAS LOOKING FOR THE SOAP, YOU IDIOT.
THAT AIN'T WHERE THE SOAP'S KEPT, MAN!
AND ME. THE ONE WHO'S GOING OUT OF HIS MIND BUT CAN'T TALK ABOUT IT.
GUYS... IF YOU CAN'T BEHAVE, I'M GONNA HAVE TO INSIST ON SEPARATE SHOWER ARRANGEMENTS.
THAT SUITS ME FINE... IF HE'S GOING TO INSIST ON TRYING TO FORCE HIS NEWLY RECOVERED HETEROSEXUALITY DOWN OUR THROATS.
WE MIGHT NOT BE YOUR AVERAGE TEAM OF MUTANT SUPER HEROES.
BUT IF YOU WANT A TEAM THAT REPRESENTS THE COMMERCIALIZED, GLOBALIZED, BRAND-OBSESSED WORLD IN WHICH WE LIVE... YOU DON'T HAVE TO LOOK ANY FURTHER THAN...

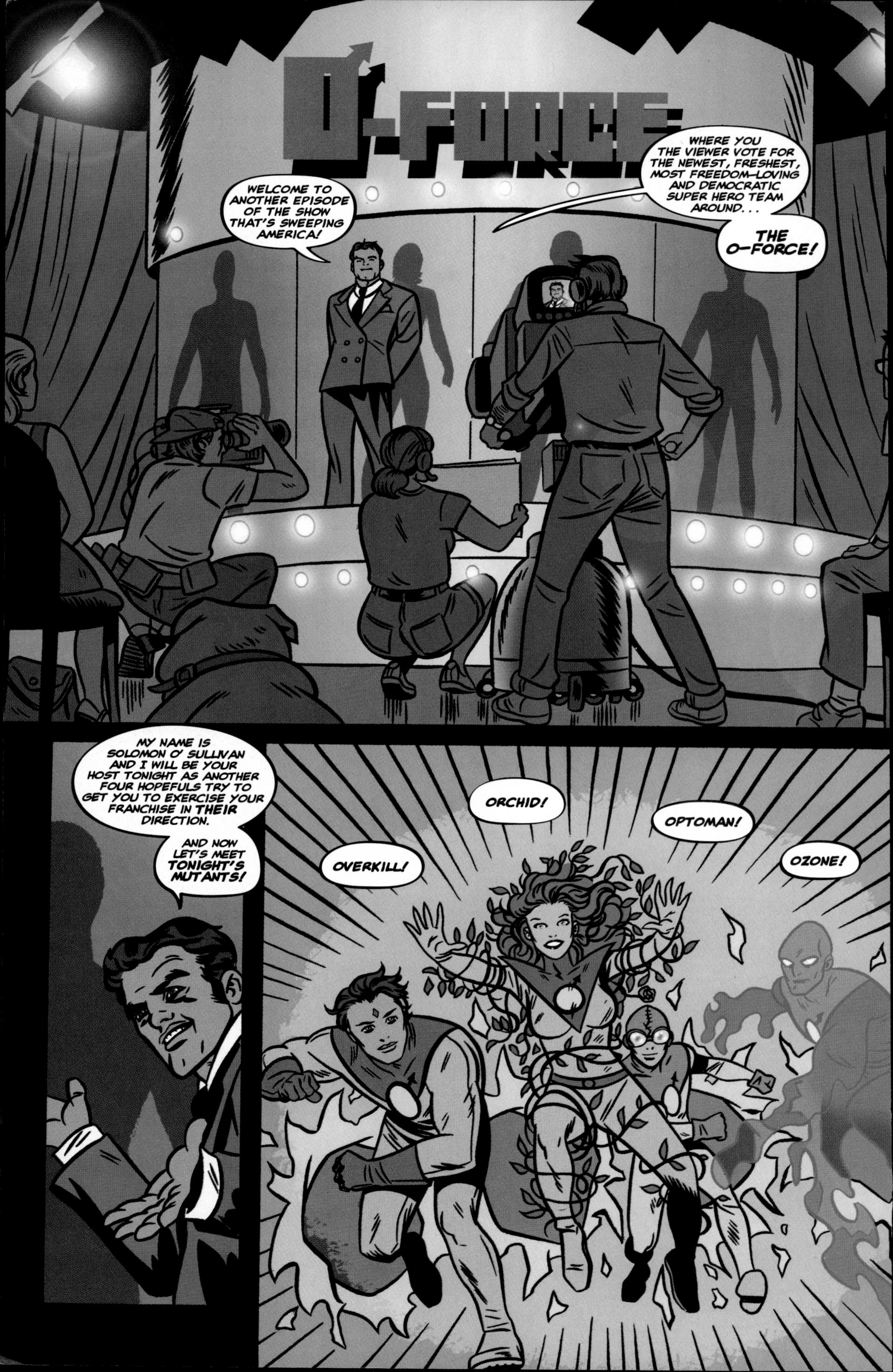
O-FORCE
WELCOME TO ANOTHER EPISODE OF THE SHOW THAT'S SWEEPING AMERICA!
WHERE YOU THE VIEWER VOTE FOR THE NEWEST, FRESHEST, MOST FREEDOM-LOVING AND DEMOCRATIC SUPER HERO TEAM AROUND...
THE O-FORCE!
MY NAME IS SOLOMON O' SULLIVAN AND I WILL BE YOUR HOST TONIGHT AS ANOTHER FOUR HOPEFULS TRY TO GET YOU TO EXERCISE YOUR FRANCHISE IN THEIR DIRECTION.
AND NOW LET'S MEET TONIGHT'S MUTANTS!
OVERKILL!
ORCHID!
OPTOMAN!
OZONE!

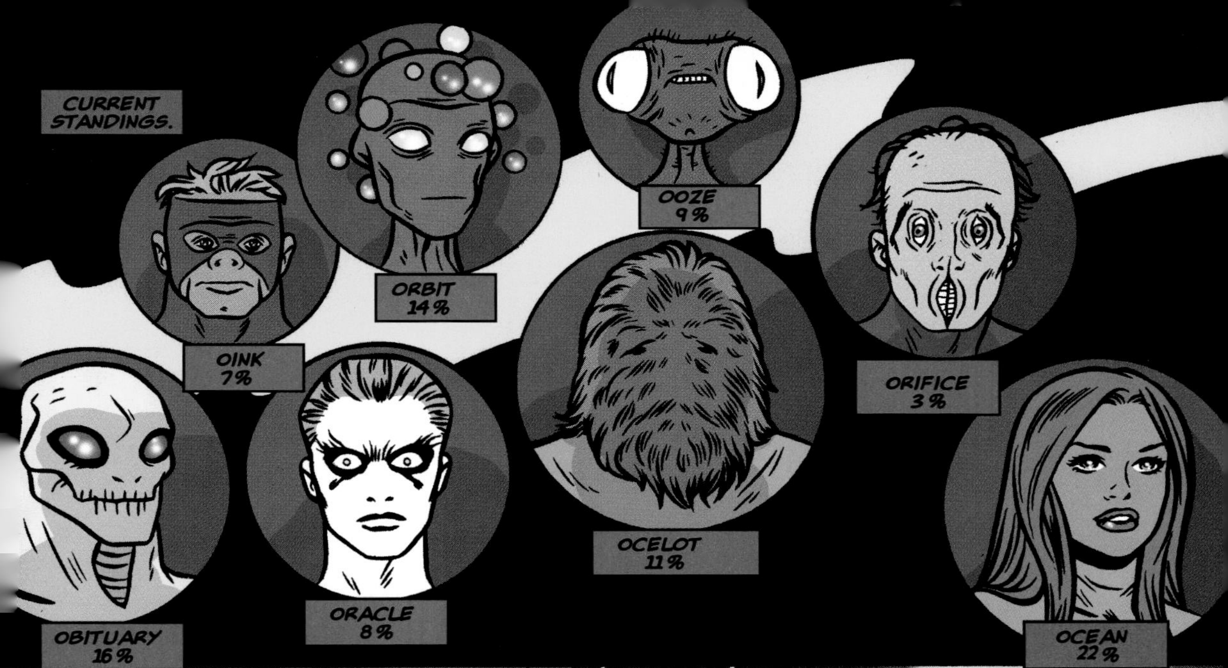
CURRENT STANDINGS.
OINK 7%
ORBIT 14%
OOZE 9%
ORIFICE 3%
OBITUARY 16%
ORACLE 8%
OCELOT 11%
OCEAN 22%

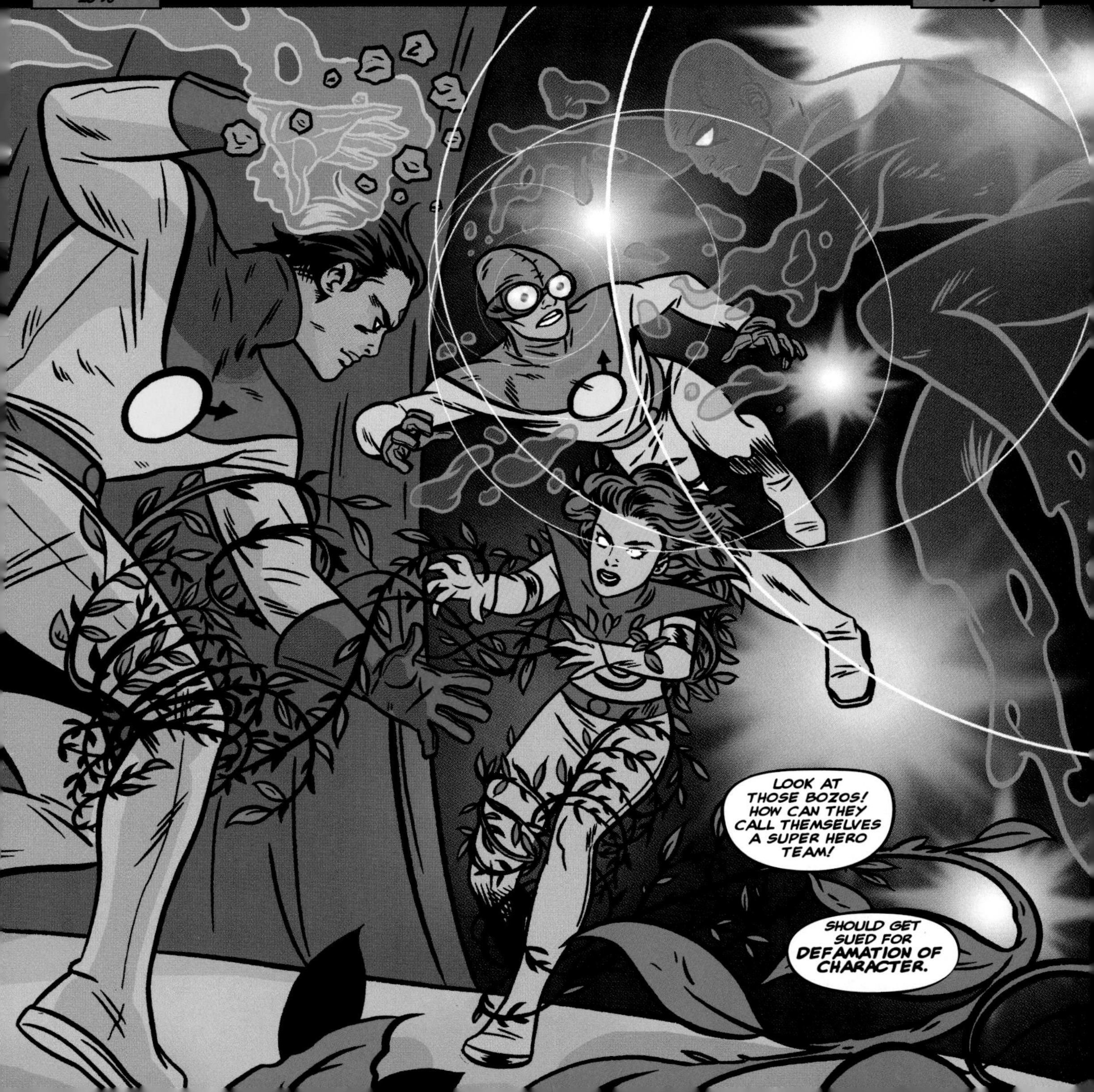
LOOK AT THOSE BOZOS! HOW CAN THEY CALL THEMSELVES A SUPER HERO TEAM!
SHOULD GET SUED FOR DEFAMATION OF CHARACTER.

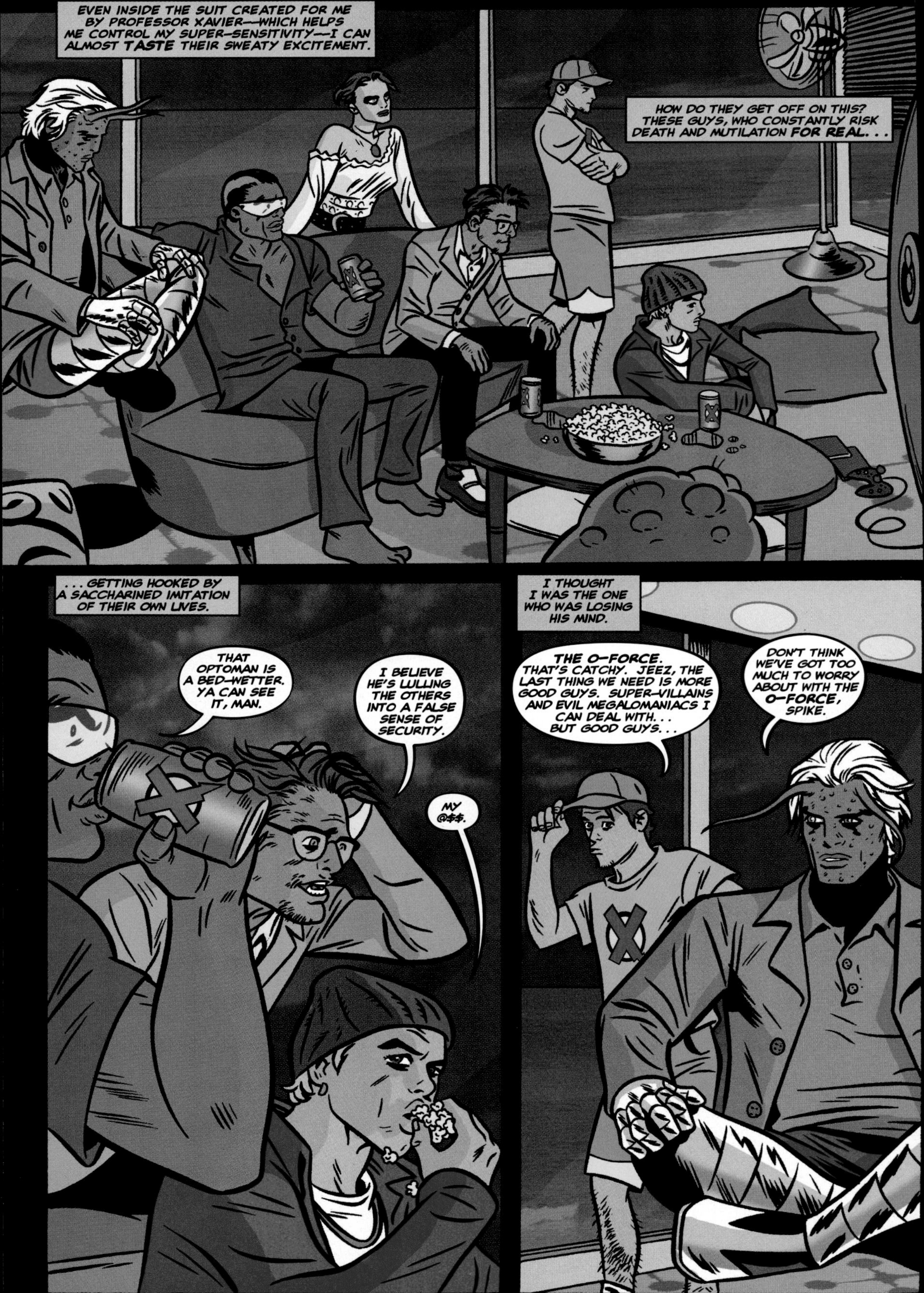
EVEN INSIDE THE SUIT CREATED FOR ME BY PROFESSOR XAVIER—WHICH HELPS ME CONTROL MY SUPER-SENSITIVITY—I CAN ALMOST TASTE THEIR SWEATY EXCITEMENT.
HOW DO THEY GET OFF ON THIS? THESE GUYS, WHO CONSTANTLY RISK DEATH AND MUTILATION FOR REAL...
...GETTING HOOKED BY A SACCHARINED IMITATION OF THEIR OWN LIVES.
THAT OPTOMAN IS A BED-WETTER. YA CAN SEE IT, MAN.
I BELIEVE HE'S LULLING THE OTHERS INTO A FALSE SENSE OF SECURITY.
MY @$$.
I THOUGHT I WAS THE ONE WHO WAS LOSING HIS MIND.
THE O-FORCE. THAT'S CATCHY. JEEZ, THE LAST THING WE NEED IS MORE GOOD GUYS. SUPER-VILLAINS AND EVIL MEGALOMANIACS I CAN DEAL WITH... BUT GOOD GUYS...
DON'T THINK WE'VE GOT TOO MUCH TO WORRY ABOUT WITH THE O-FORCE, SPIKE.

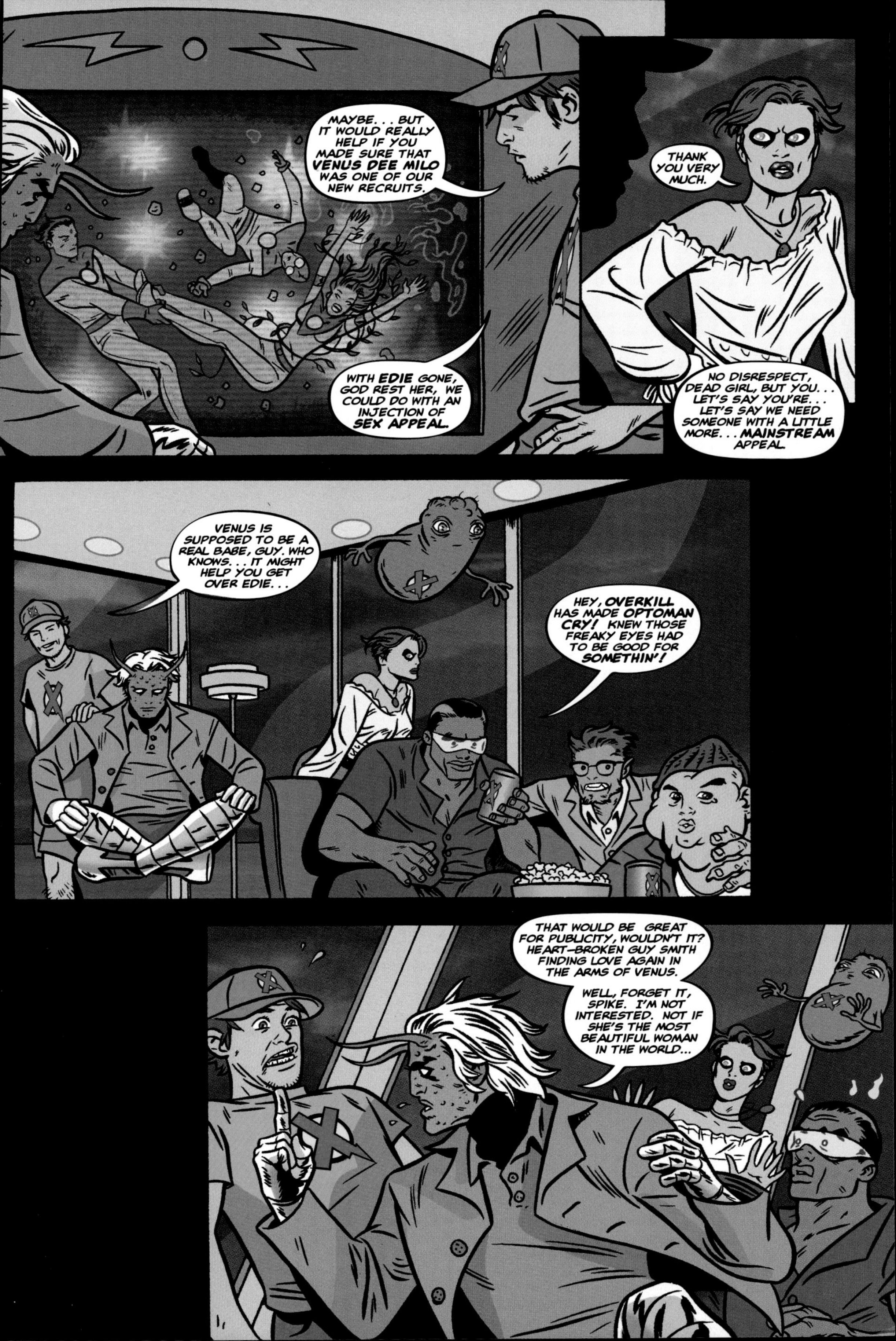
MAYBE... BUT IT WOULD REALLY HELP IF YOU MADE SURE THAT VENUS DEE MILO WAS ONE OF OUR NEW RECRUITS.
WITH EDIE GONE, GOD REST HER, WE COULD DO WITH AN INJECTION OF SEX APPEAL.
THANK YOU VERY MUCH.
NO DISRESPECT, DEAD GIRL, BUT YOU... LET'S SAY YOU'RE... LET'S SAY WE NEED SOMEONE WITH A LITTLE MORE... MAINSTREAM APPEAL.
VENUS IS SUPPOSED TO BE A REAL BABE, GUY. WHO KNOWS... IT MIGHT HELP YOU GET OVER EDIE...
HEY, OVERKILL HAS MADE OPTOMAN CRY! KNEW THOSE FREAKY EYES HAD TO BE GOOD FOR SOMETHIN'!
THAT WOULD BE GREAT FOR PUBLICITY, WOULDN'T IT? HEART-BROKEN GUY SMITH FINDING LOVE AGAIN IN THE ARMS OF VENUS.
WELL, FORGET IT, SPIKE. I'M NOT INTERESTED. NOT IF SHE'S THE MOST BEAUTIFUL WOMAN IN THE WORLD...

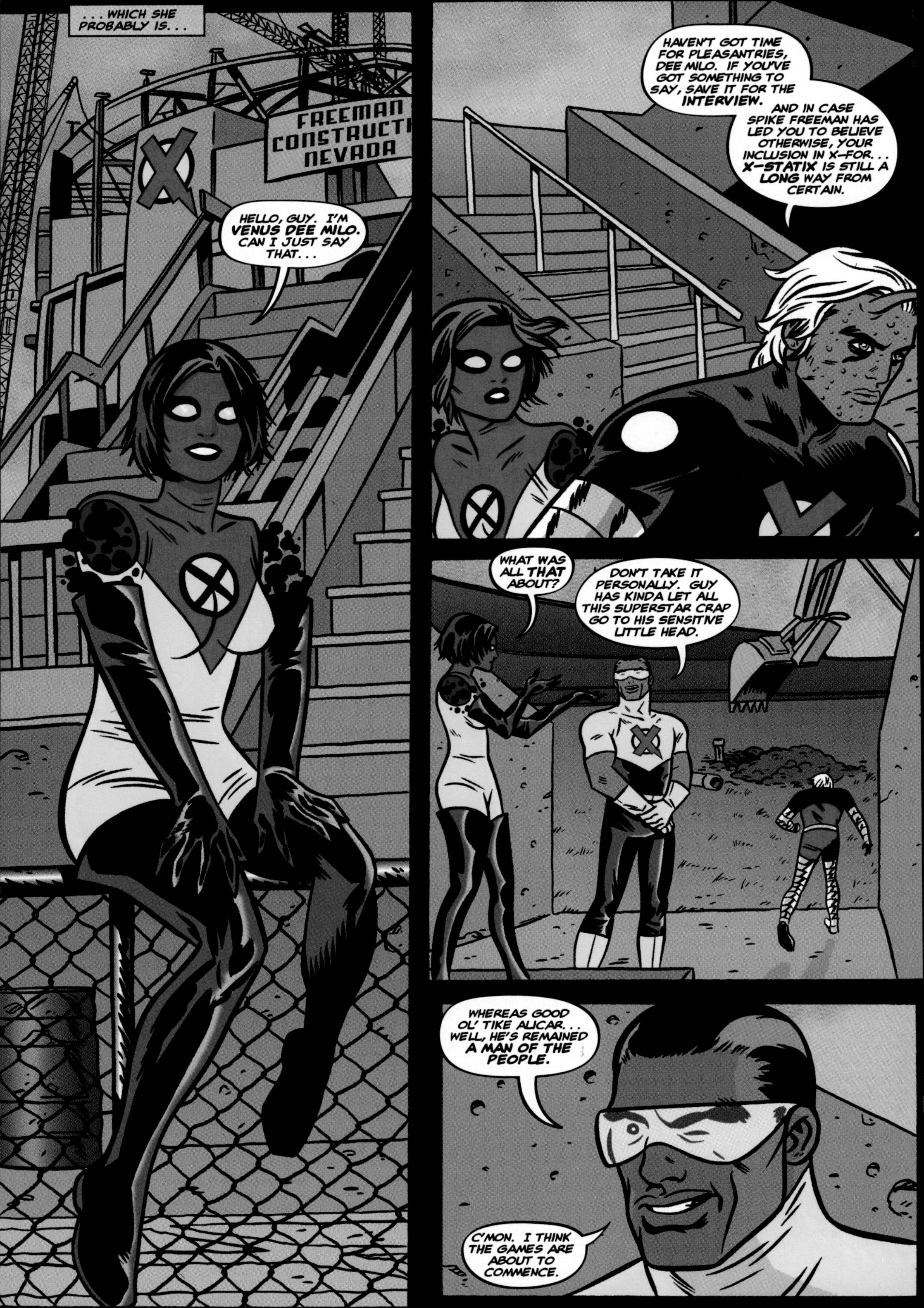

. . . WHICH SHE PROBABLY IS . . .
FREEMAN CONSTRUCTI NEVADA
HELLO, GUY. I'M VENUS DEE MILO. CAN I JUST SAY THAT . . .
HAVEN'T GOT TIME FOR PLEASANTRIES, DEE MILO. IF YOU'VE GOT SOMETHING TO SAY, SAVE IT FOR THE INTERVIEW.
AND IN CASE SPIKE FREEMAN HAS LED YOU TO BELIEVE OTHERWISE, YOUR INCLUSION IN X-FOR. . . X-STATIX IS STILL A LONG WAY FROM CERTAIN.
WHAT WAS ALL THAT ABOUT?
DON'T TAKE IT PERSONALLY. GUY HAS KINDA LET ALL THIS SUPERSTAR CRAP GO TO HIS SENSITIVE LITTLE HEAD.
WHEREAS GOOD OL' TIKE ALICAR. . . WELL, HE'S REMAINED A MAN OF THE PEOPLE.
C'MON. I THINK THE GAMES ARE ABOUT TO COMMENCE.

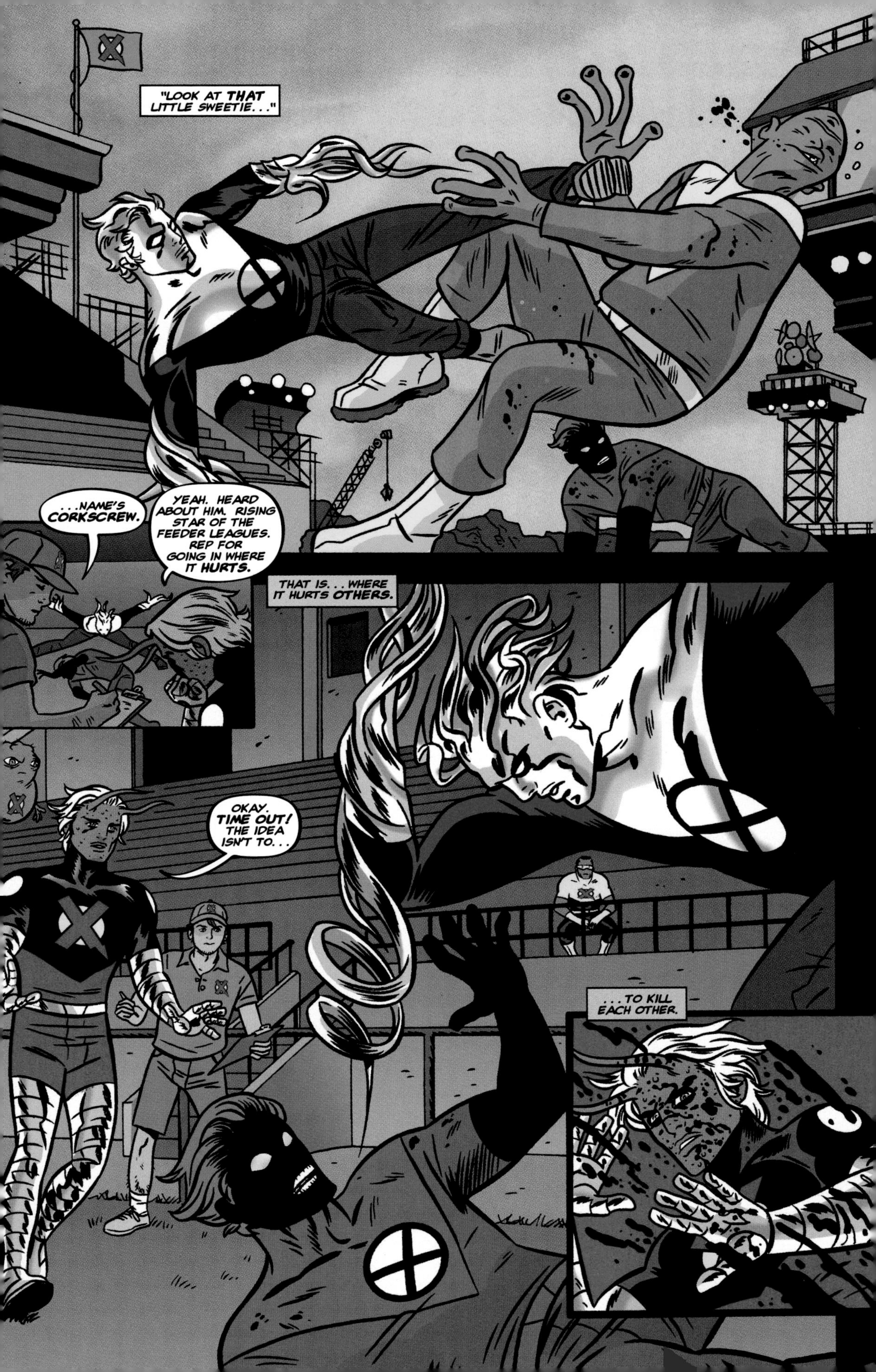
"LOOK AT THAT LITTLE SWEETIE..."
...NAME'S CORKSCREW.
YEAH. HEARD ABOUT HIM. RISING STAR OF THE FEEDER LEAGUES. REP FOR GOING IN WHERE IT HURTS.
THAT IS... WHERE IT HURTS OTHERS.
OKAY. TIME OUT! THE IDEA ISN'T TO...
...TO KILL EACH OTHER.

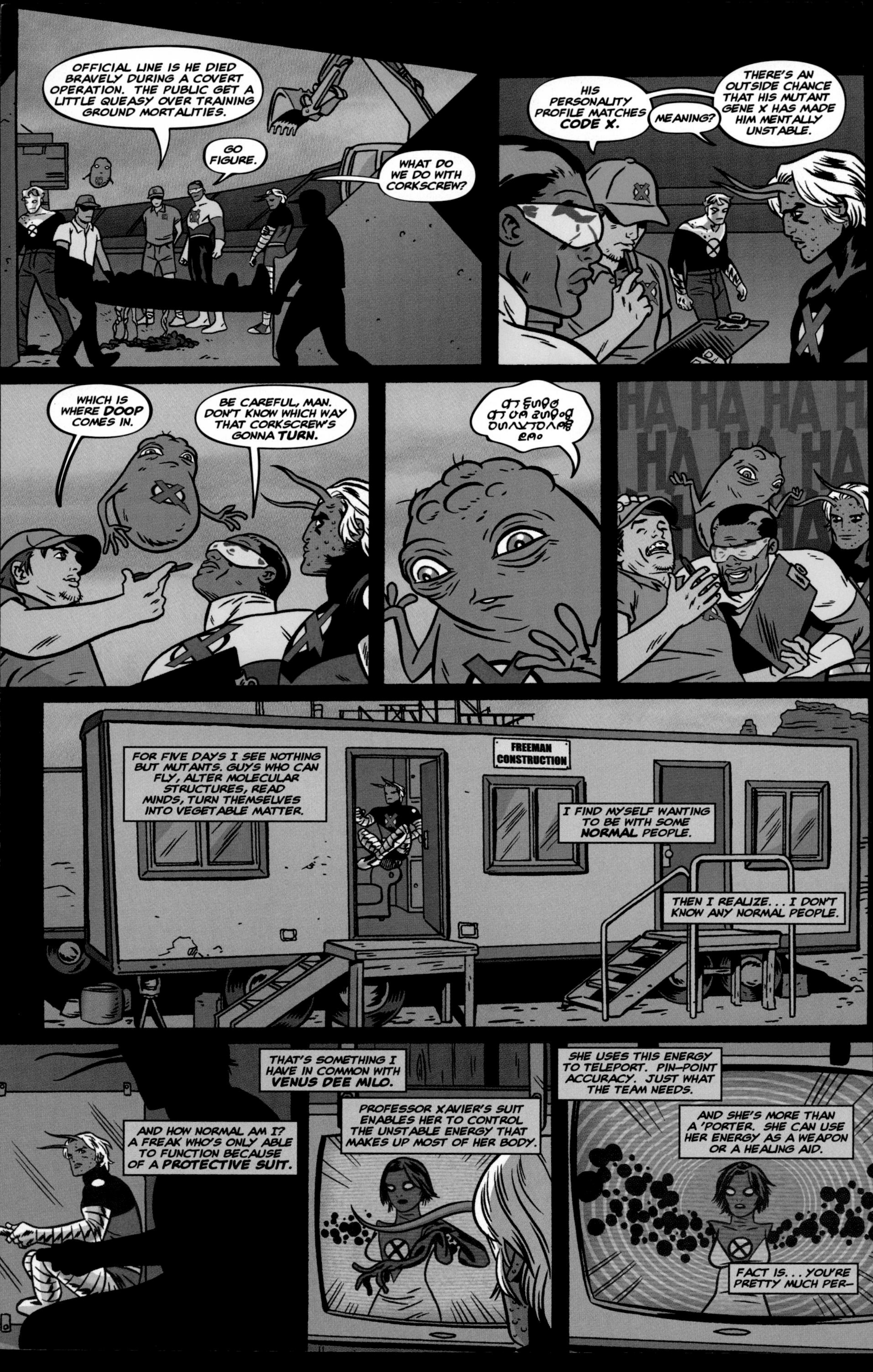
OFFICIAL LINE IS HE DIED BRAVELY DURING A COVERT OPERATION. THE PUBLIC GET A LITTLE QUEASY OVER TRAINING GROUND MORTALITIES.
GO FIGURE.
WHAT DO WE DO WITH CORKSCREW?
HIS PERSONALITY PROFILE MATCHES CODE X.
MEANING?
THERE'S AN OUTSIDE CHANCE THAT HIS MUTANT GENE X HAS MADE HIM MENTALLY UNSTABLE.
WHICH IS WHERE DOOP COMES IN.
BE CAREFUL, MAN. DON'T KNOW WHICH WAY THAT CORKSCREW'S GONNA TURN.
HA HA HA HA HA HA HA HA HA
FREEMAN CONSTRUCTION
FOR FIVE DAYS I SEE NOTHING BUT MUTANTS. GUYS WHO CAN FLY, ALTER MOLECULAR STRUCTURES, READ MINDS, TURN THEMSELVES INTO VEGETABLE MATTER.
I FIND MYSELF WANTING TO BE WITH SOME NORMAL PEOPLE.
THEN I REALIZE... I DON'T KNOW ANY NORMAL PEOPLE.
AND HOW NORMAL AM I? A FREAK WHO'S ONLY ABLE TO FUNCTION BECAUSE OF A PROTECTIVE SUIT.
THAT'S SOMETHING I HAVE IN COMMON WITH VENUS DEE MILO.
PROFESSOR XAVIER'S SUIT ENABLES HER TO CONTROL THE UNSTABLE ENERGY THAT MAKES UP MOST OF HER BODY.
SHE USES THIS ENERGY TO TELEPORT. PIN-POINT ACCURACY. JUST WHAT THE TEAM NEEDS.
AND SHE'S MORE THAN A 'PORTER. SHE CAN USE HER ENERGY AS A WEAPON OR A HEALING AID.
FACT IS... YOU'RE PRETTY MUCH PER-

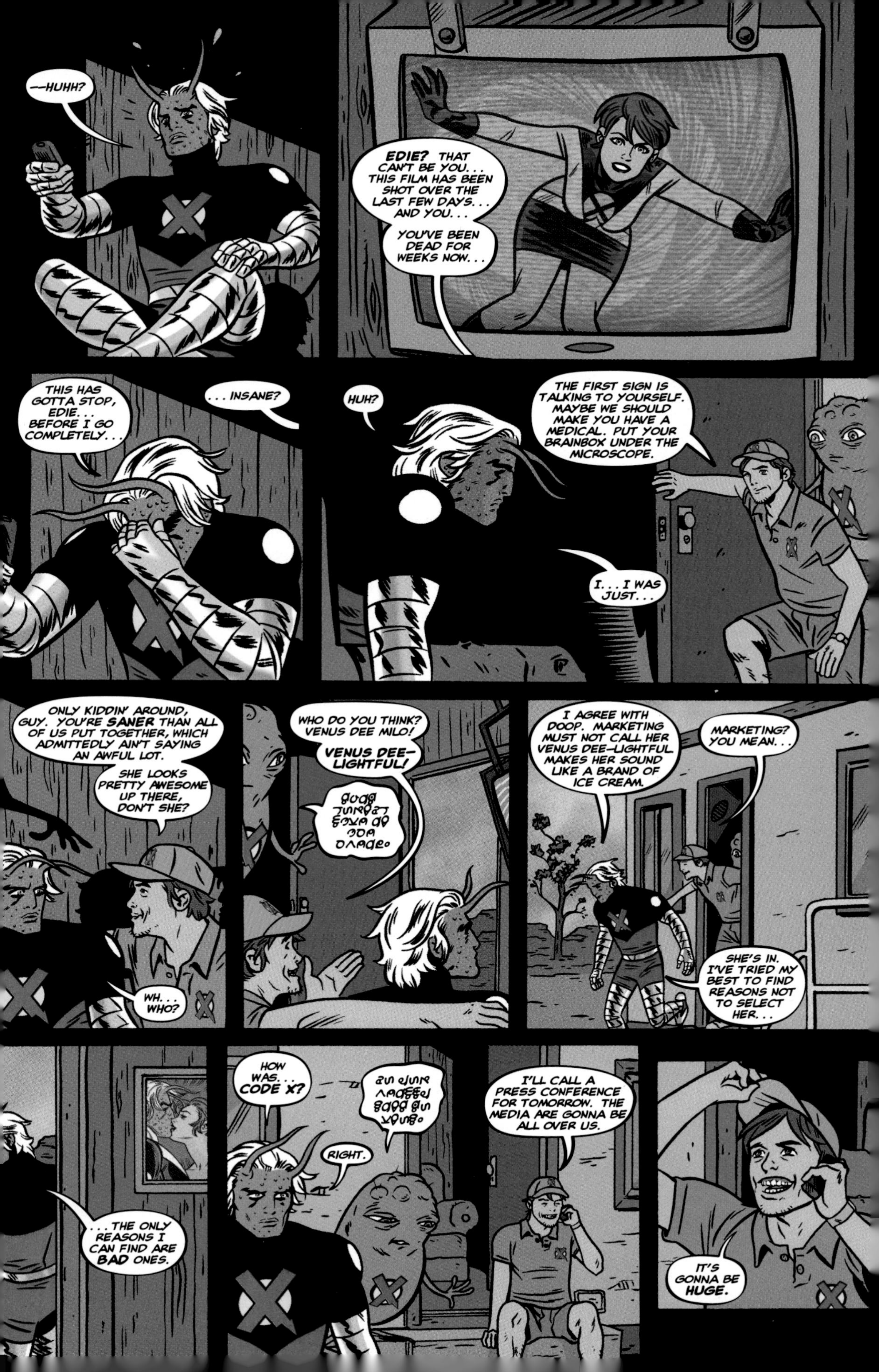
--HUHH?
EDIE? THAT CAN'T BE YOU... THIS FILM HAS BEEN SHOT OVER THE LAST FEW DAYS... AND YOU...
YOU'VE BEEN DEAD FOR WEEKS NOW...
THIS HAS GOTTA STOP, EDIE... BEFORE I GO COMPLETELY...
...INSANE?
HUH?
THE FIRST SIGN IS TALKING TO YOURSELF. MAYBE WE SHOULD MAKE YOU HAVE A MEDICAL. PUT YOUR BRAINBOX UNDER THE MICROSCOPE.
I...I WAS JUST...
ONLY KIDDIN' AROUND, GUY. YOU'RE SANER THAN ALL OF US PUT TOGETHER, WHICH ADMITTEDLY AIN'T SAYING AN AWFUL LOT.
SHE LOOKS PRETTY AWESOME UP THERE, DON'T SHE?
WH... WHO?
WHO DO YOU THINK? VENUS DEE MILO!
VENUS DEE-LIGHTFUL!
I AGREE WITH DOOP. MARKETING MUST NOT CALL HER VENUS DEE-LIGHTFUL. MAKES HER SOUND LIKE A BRAND OF ICE CREAM.
MARKETING? YOU MEAN...
SHE'S IN. I'VE TRIED MY BEST TO FIND REASONS NOT TO SELECT HER...
...THE ONLY REASONS I CAN FIND ARE BAD ONES.
HOW WAS... CODE X?
RIGHT.
I'LL CALL A PRESS CONFERENCE FOR TOMORROW. THE MEDIA ARE GONNA BE ALL OVER US.
IT'S GONNA BE HUGE.

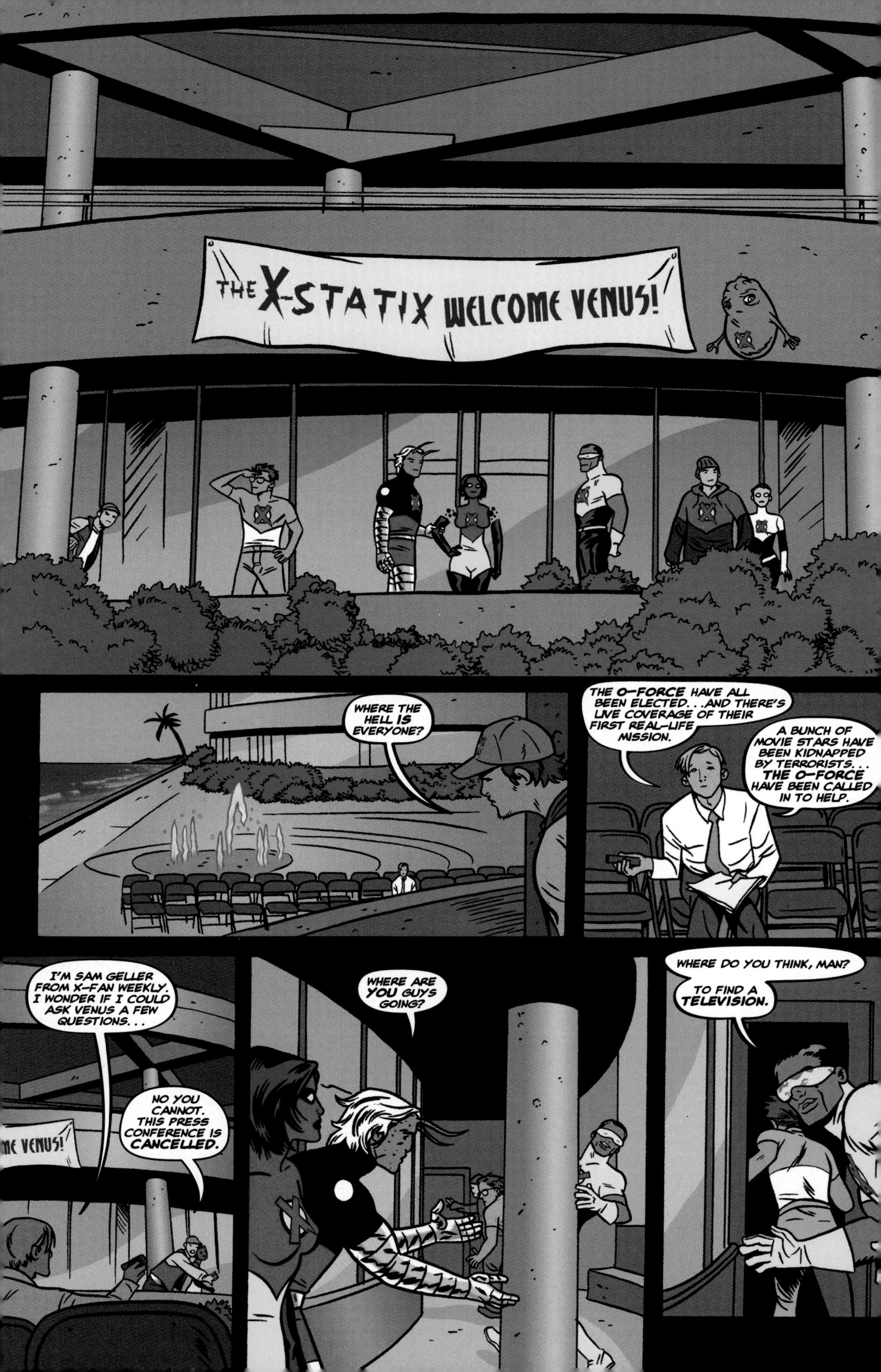
THE X-STATIX WELCOME VENUS!
WHERE THE HELL IS EVERYONE?
THE O-FORCE HAVE ALL BEEN ELECTED...AND THERE'S LIVE COVERAGE OF THEIR FIRST REAL-LIFE MISSION.
A BUNCH OF MOVIE STARS HAVE BEEN KIDNAPPED BY TERRORISTS... THE O-FORCE HAVE BEEN CALLED IN TO HELP.
I'M SAM GELLER FROM X-FAN WEEKLY. I WONDER IF I COULD ASK VENUS A FEW QUESTIONS...
NO YOU CANNOT. THIS PRESS CONFERENCE IS CANCELLED.
WHERE ARE YOU GUYS GOING?
WHERE DO YOU THINK, MAN?
TO FIND A TELEVISION.

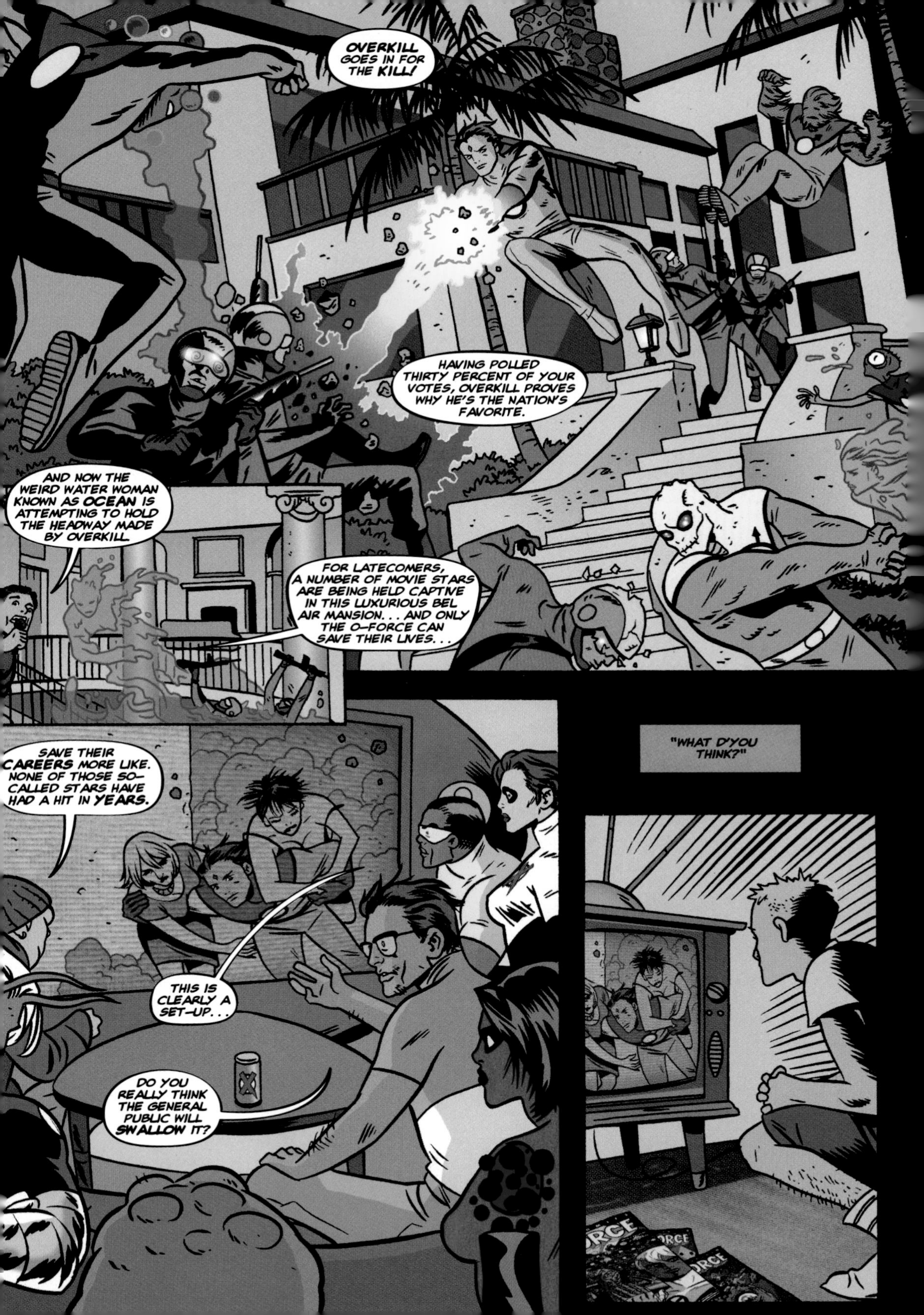
OVERKILL GOES IN FOR THE KILL!
HAVING POLLED THIRTY PERCENT OF YOUR VOTES, OVERKILL PROVES WHY HE'S THE NATION'S FAVORITE.
AND NOW THE WEIRD WATER WOMAN KNOWN AS OCEAN IS ATTEMPTING TO HOLD THE HEADWAY MADE BY OVERKILL.
FOR LATECOMERS, A NUMBER OF MOVIE STARS ARE BEING HELD CAPTIVE IN THIS LUXURIOUS BEL AIR MANSION... AND ONLY THE O-FORCE CAN SAVE THEIR LIVES...
SAVE THEIR CAREERS MORE LIKE. NONE OF THOSE SO-CALLED STARS HAVE HAD A HIT IN YEARS.
THIS IS CLEARLY A SET-UP...
DO YOU REALLY THINK THE GENERAL PUBLIC WILL SWALLOW IT?
"WHAT D'YOU THINK?"

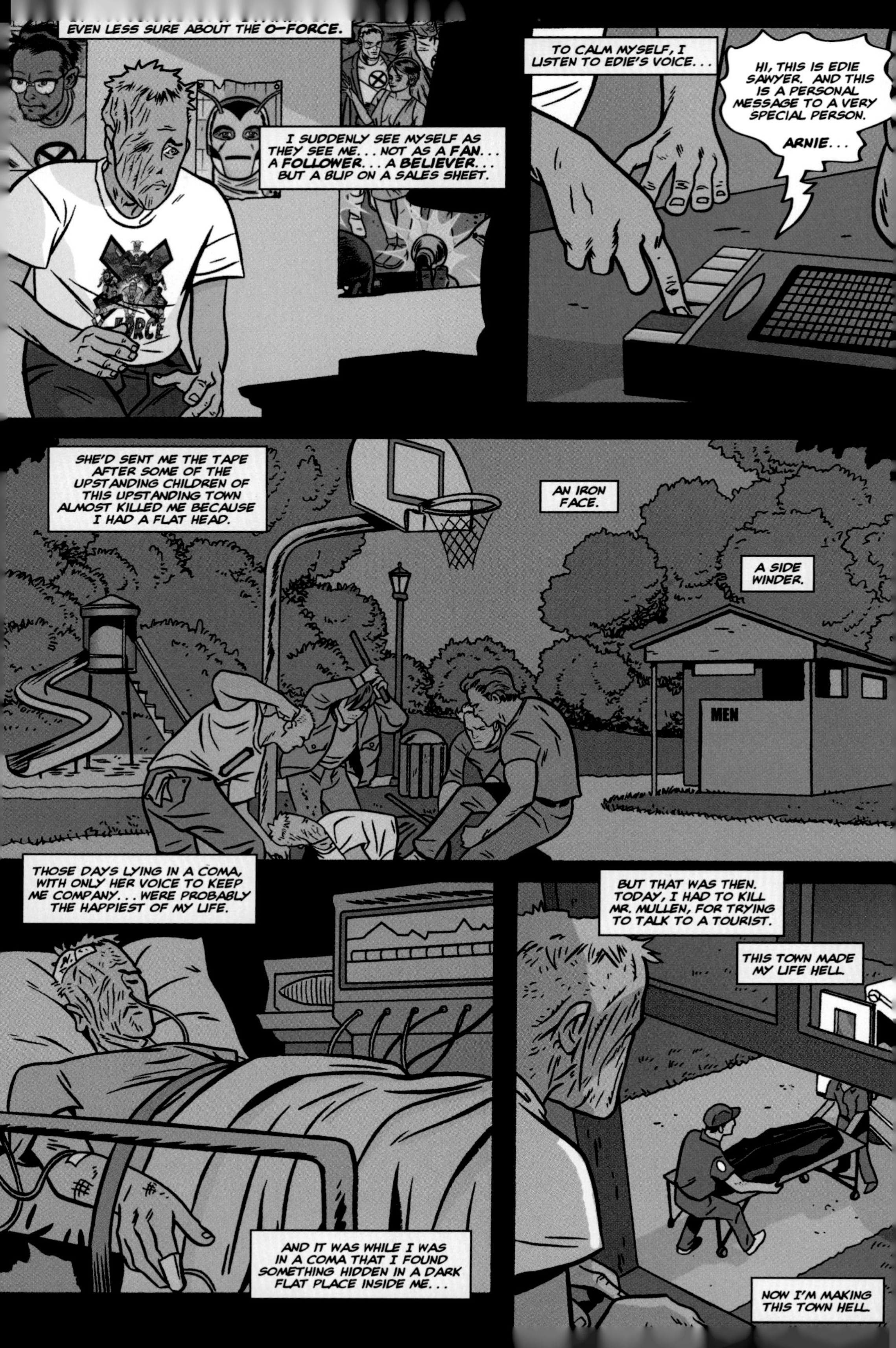
EVEN LESS SURE ABOUT THE O-FORCE.
I SUDDENLY SEE MYSELF AS THEY SEE ME... NOT AS A FAN... A FOLLOWER... A BELIEVER... BUT A BLIP ON A SALES SHEET.
FORCE
TO CALM MYSELF, I LISTEN TO EDIE'S VOICE...
HI, THIS IS EDIE SAWYER. AND THIS IS A PERSONAL MESSAGE TO A VERY SPECIAL PERSON.
ARNIE...
SHE'D SENT ME THE TAPE AFTER SOME OF THE UPSTANDING CHILDREN OF THIS UPSTANDING TOWN ALMOST KILLED ME BECAUSE I HAD A FLAT HEAD.
AN IRON FACE.
A SIDE WINDER.
MEN
THOSE DAYS LYING IN A COMA, WITH ONLY HER VOICE TO KEEP ME COMPANY... WERE PROBABLY THE HAPPIEST OF MY LIFE.
AND IT WAS WHILE I WAS IN A COMA THAT I FOUND SOMETHING HIDDEN IN A DARK FLAT PLACE INSIDE ME...
BUT THAT WAS THEN. TODAY, I HAD TO KILL MR. MULLEN, FOR TRYING TO TALK TO A TOURIST.
THIS TOWN MADE MY LIFE HELL
NOW I'M MAKING THIS TOWN HELL.

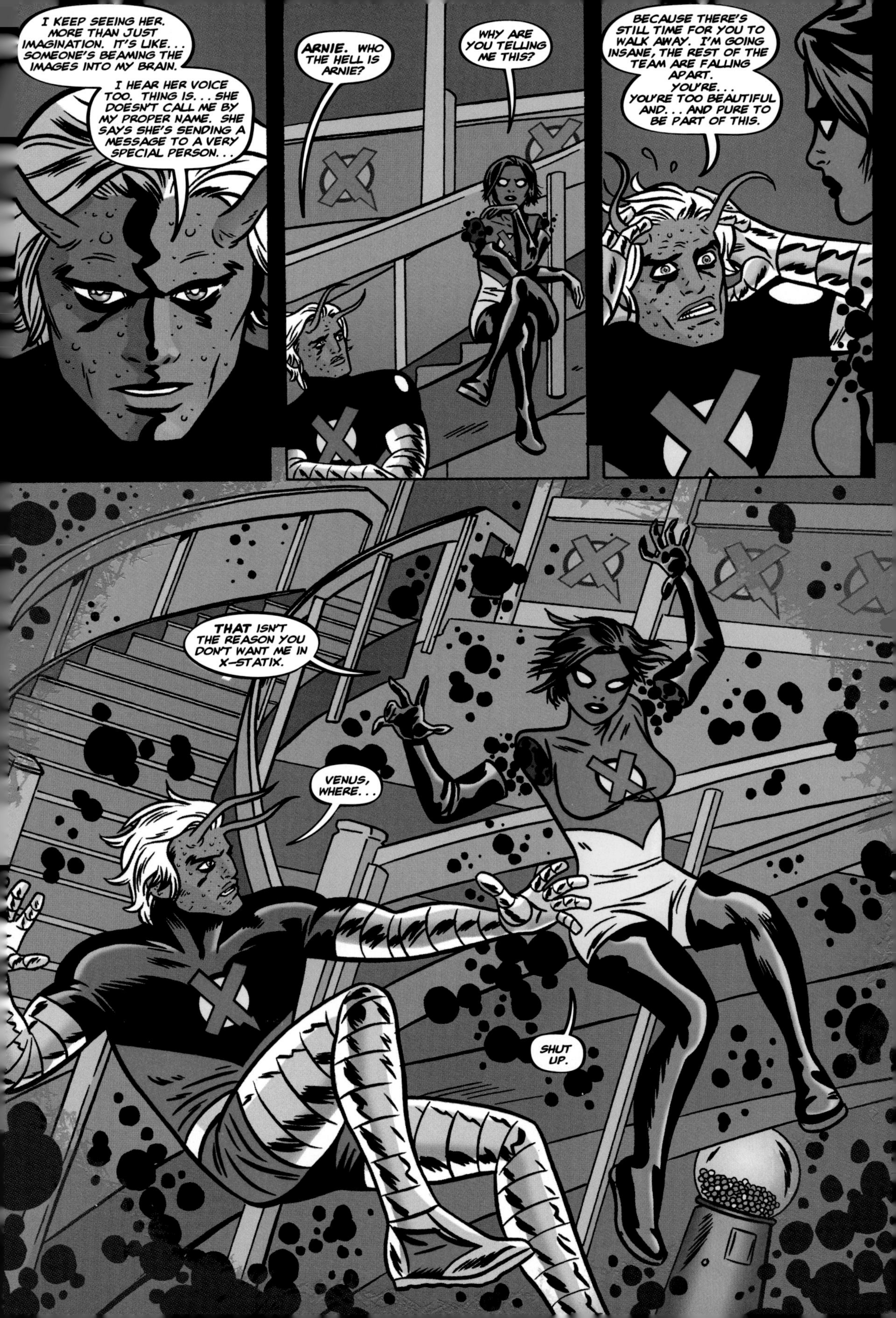
I KEEP SEEING HER. MORE THAN JUST IMAGINATION. IT'S LIKE... SOMEONE'S BEAMING THE IMAGES INTO MY BRAIN.
I HEAR HER VOICE TOO. THING IS... SHE DOESN'T CALL ME BY MY PROPER NAME. SHE SAYS SHE'S SENDING A MESSAGE TO A VERY SPECIAL PERSON...
ARNIE. WHO THE HELL IS ARNIE?
WHY ARE YOU TELLING ME THIS?
BECAUSE THERE'S STILL TIME FOR YOU TO WALK AWAY. I'M GOING INSANE, THE REST OF THE TEAM ARE FALLING APART.
YOU'RE... YOU'RE TOO BEAUTIFUL AND... AND PURE TO BE PART OF THIS.
THAT ISN'T THE REASON YOU DON'T WANT ME IN X-STATIX.
VENUS, WHERE...
SHUT UP.

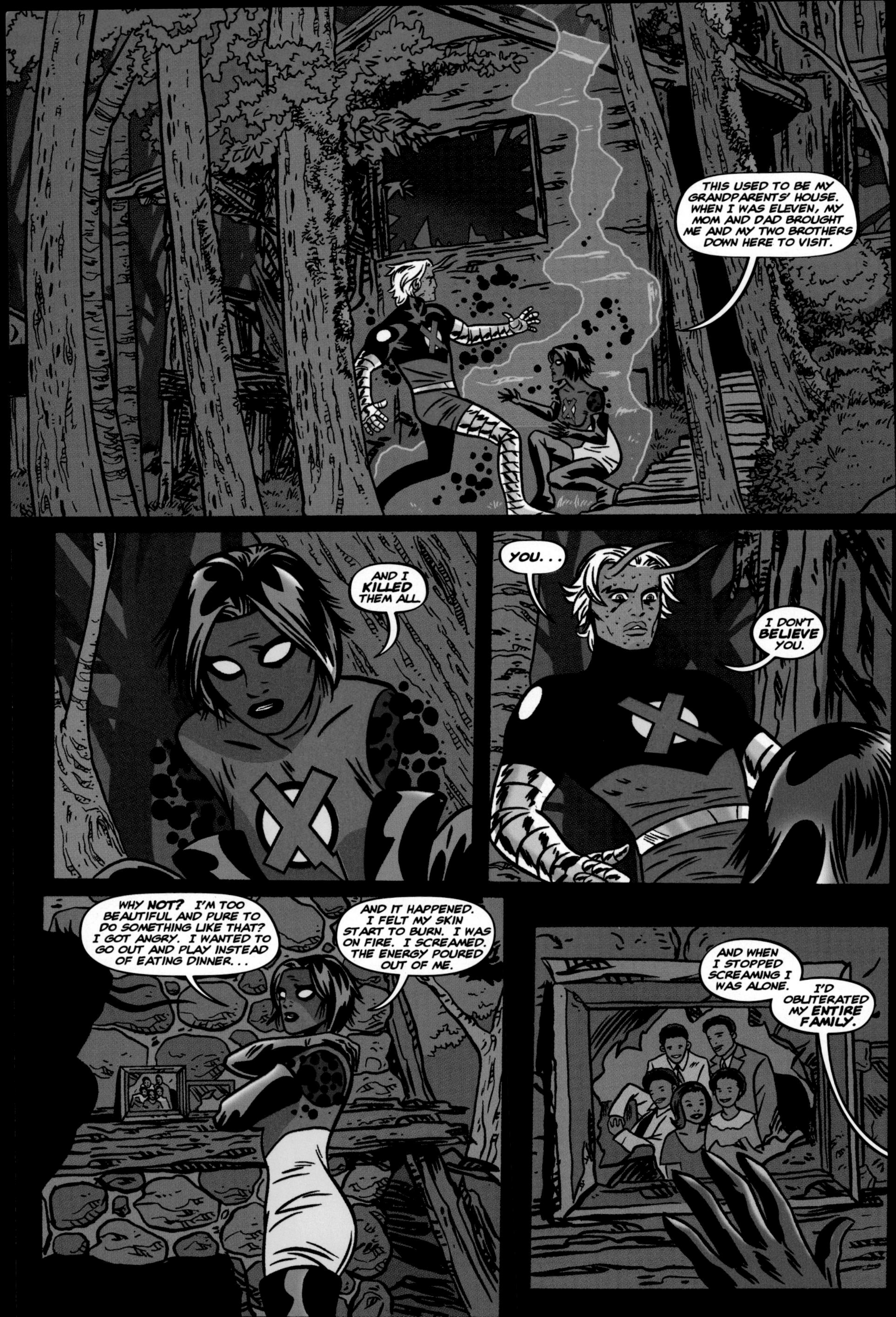
THIS USED TO BE MY GRANDPARENTS' HOUSE. WHEN I WAS ELEVEN, MY MOM AND DAD BROUGHT ME AND MY TWO BROTHERS DOWN HERE TO VISIT.
AND I KILLED THEM ALL.
YOU. . .
I DON'T BELIEVE YOU.
WHY NOT? I'M TOO BEAUTIFUL AND PURE TO DO SOMETHING LIKE THAT? I GOT ANGRY. I WANTED TO GO OUT AND PLAY INSTEAD OF EATING DINNER. . .
AND IT HAPPENED. I FELT MY SKIN START TO BURN. I WAS ON FIRE. I SCREAMED. THE ENERGY POURED OUT OF ME.
AND WHEN I STOPPED SCREAMING I WAS ALONE.
I'D OBLITERATED MY ENTIRE FAMILY.

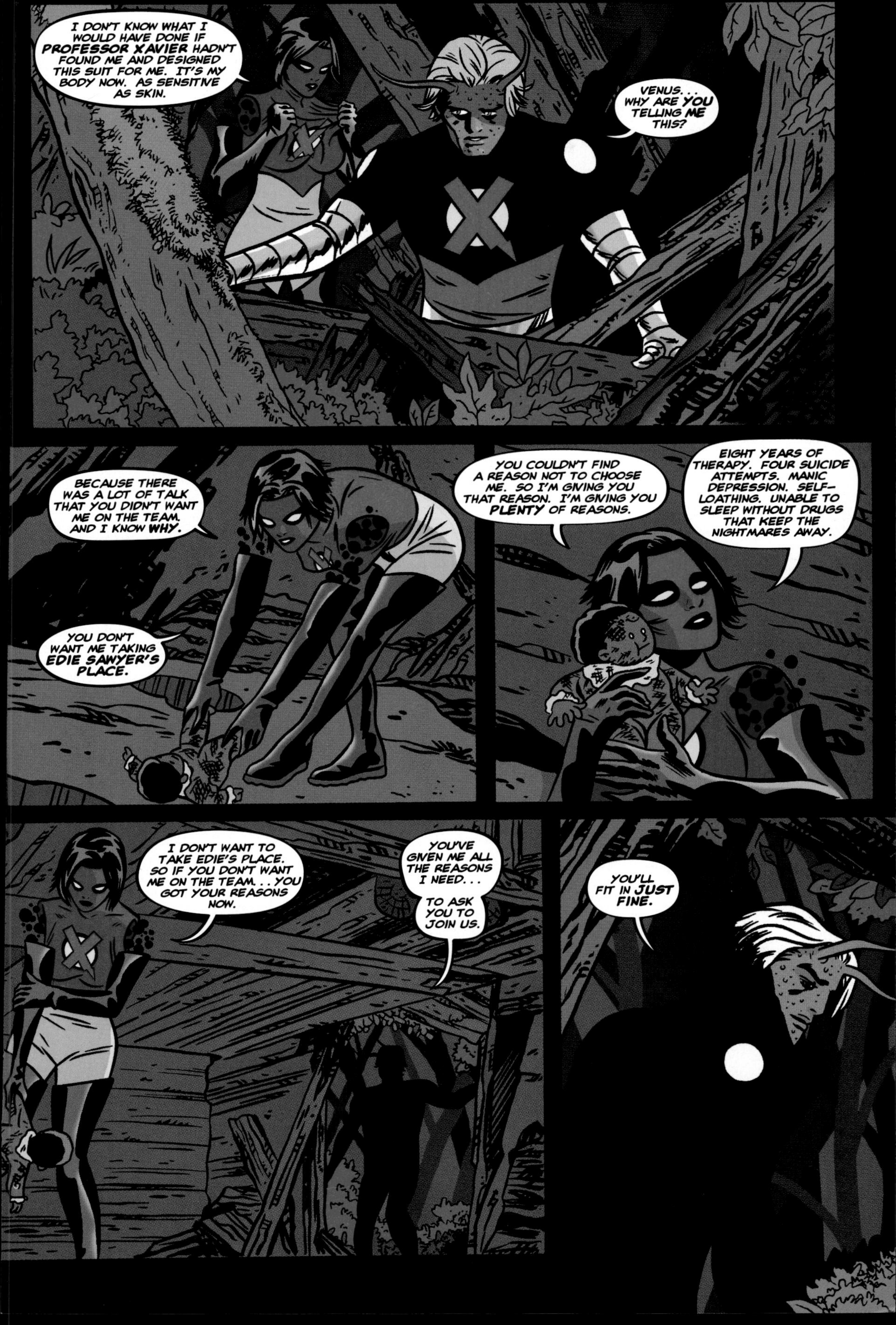
I DON'T KNOW WHAT I WOULD HAVE DONE IF PROFESSOR XAVIER HADN'T FOUND ME AND DESIGNED THIS SUIT FOR ME. IT'S MY BODY NOW. AS SENSITIVE AS SKIN.
VENUS... WHY ARE YOU TELLING ME THIS?
BECAUSE THERE WAS A LOT OF TALK THAT YOU DIDN'T WANT ME ON THE TEAM. AND I KNOW WHY.
YOU DON'T WANT ME TAKING EDIE SAWYER'S PLACE.
YOU COULDN'T FIND A REASON NOT TO CHOOSE ME. SO I'M GIVING YOU THAT REASON. I'M GIVING YOU PLENTY OF REASONS.
EIGHT YEARS OF THERAPY. FOUR SUICIDE ATTEMPTS. MANIC DEPRESSION. SELF-LOATHING. UNABLE TO SLEEP WITHOUT DRUGS THAT KEEP THE NIGHTMARES AWAY.
I DON'T WANT TO TAKE EDIE'S PLACE. SO IF YOU DON'T WANT ME ON THE TEAM... YOU GOT YOUR REASONS NOW.
YOU'VE GIVEN ME ALL THE REASONS I NEED...
TO ASK YOU TO JOIN US.
YOU'LL FIT IN JUST FINE.

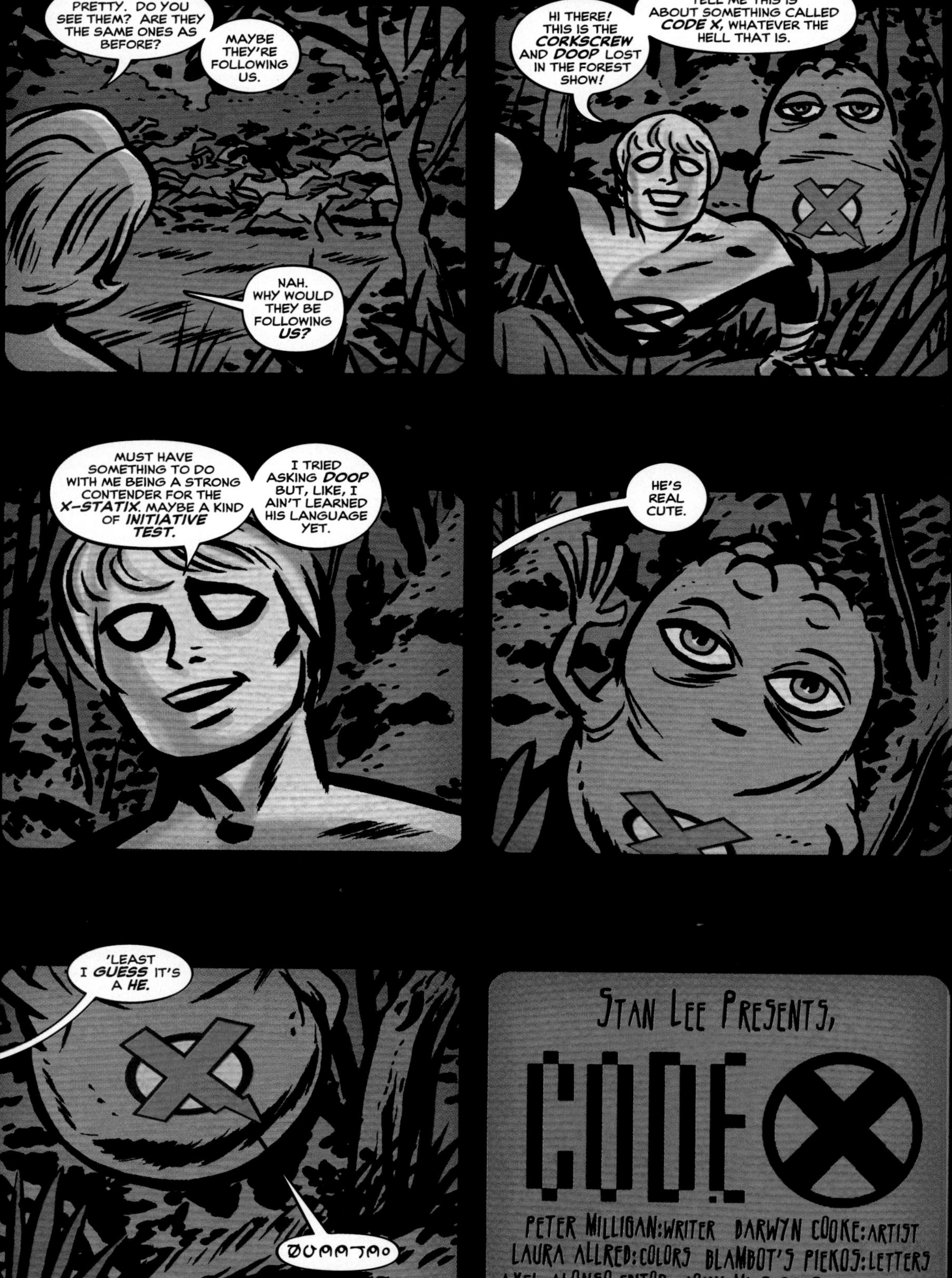
THEY'RE PRETTY. DO YOU SEE THEM? ARE THEY THE SAME ONES AS BEFORE?
MAYBE THEY'RE FOLLOWING US.
NAH. WHY WOULD THEY BE FOLLOWING US?
HI THERE! THIS IS THE CORKSCREW AND DOOP LOST IN THE FOREST SHOW!
THEY TELL ME THIS IS ABOUT SOMETHING CALLED CODE X, WHATEVER THE HELL THAT IS.
MUST HAVE SOMETHING TO DO WITH ME BEING A STRONG CONTENDER FOR THE X-STATIX. MAYBE A KIND OF INITIATIVE TEST.
I TRIED ASKING DOOP BUT, LIKE, I AIN'T LEARNED HIS LANGUAGE YET.
HE'S REAL CUTE.
'LEAST I GUESS IT'S A HE.
STAN LEE PRESENTS,
CODE X
PETER MILLIGAN:WRITER DARWYN COOKE:ARTIST
LAURA ALLRED:COLORS BLAMBOT'S PIEKOS:LETTERS
AXEL ALONSO:EDITOR JOHN MIESEGAES:ASST. EDITOR
JOE QUESADA:CHIEF BILL JEMAS:PREZ

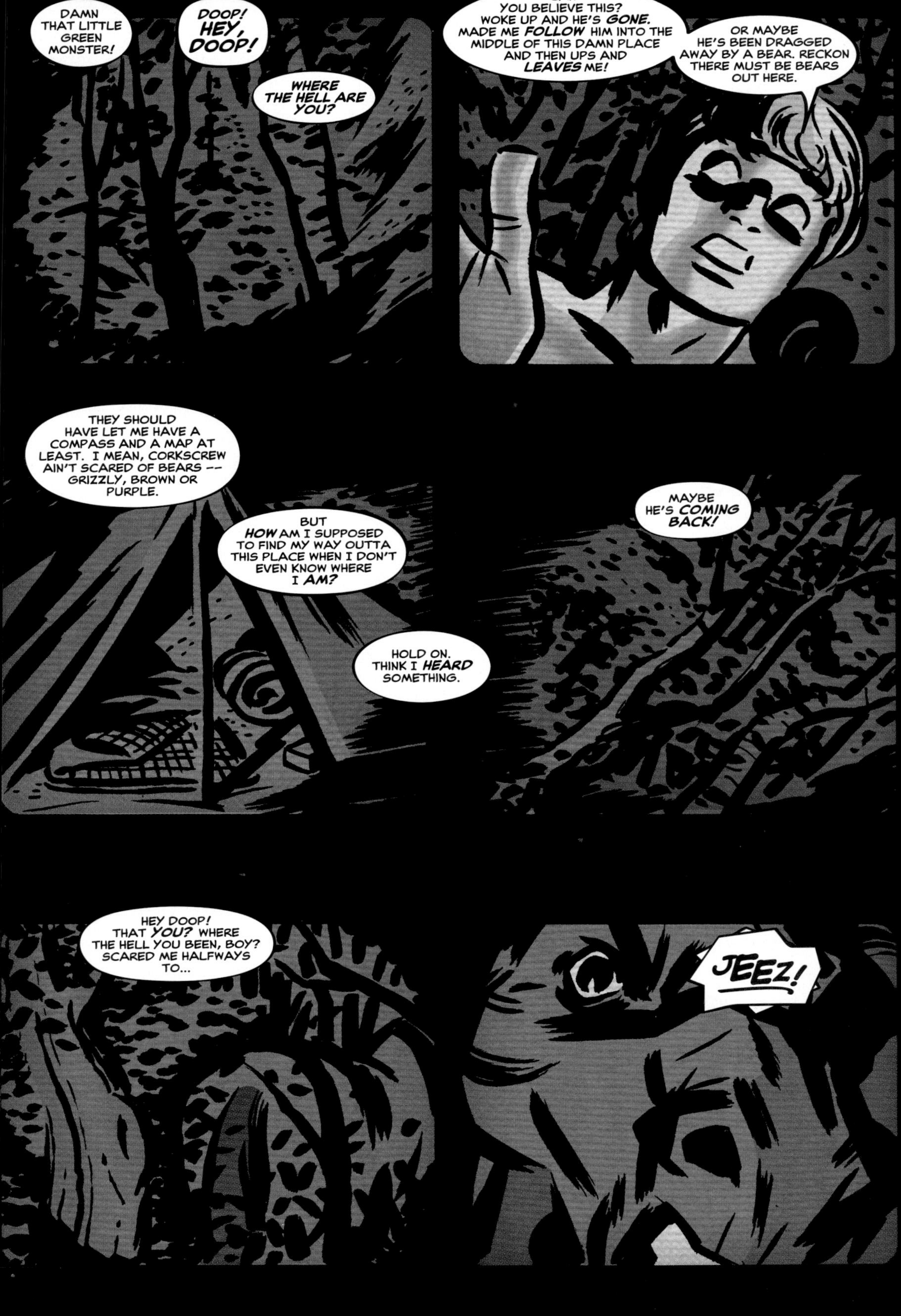
DAMN THAT LITTLE GREEN MONSTER!
DOOP! HEY, DOOP!
WHERE THE HELL ARE YOU?
CAN YOU BELIEVE THIS? WOKE UP AND HE'S GONE. MADE ME FOLLOW HIM INTO THE MIDDLE OF THIS DAMN PLACE AND THEN UPS AND LEAVES ME!
OR MAYBE HE'S BEEN DRAGGED AWAY BY A BEAR. RECKON THERE MUST BE BEARS OUT HERE.
THEY SHOULD HAVE LET ME HAVE A COMPASS AND A MAP AT LEAST. I MEAN, CORKSCREW AIN'T SCARED OF BEARS -- GRIZZLY, BROWN OR PURPLE.
BUT HOW AM I SUPPOSED TO FIND MY WAY OUTTA THIS PLACE WHEN I DON'T EVEN KNOW WHERE I AM?
HOLD ON. THINK I HEARD SOMETHING.
MAYBE HE'S COMING BACK!
HEY DOOP! THAT YOU? WHERE THE HELL YOU BEEN, BOY? SCARED ME HALFWAYS TO...
JEEZ!

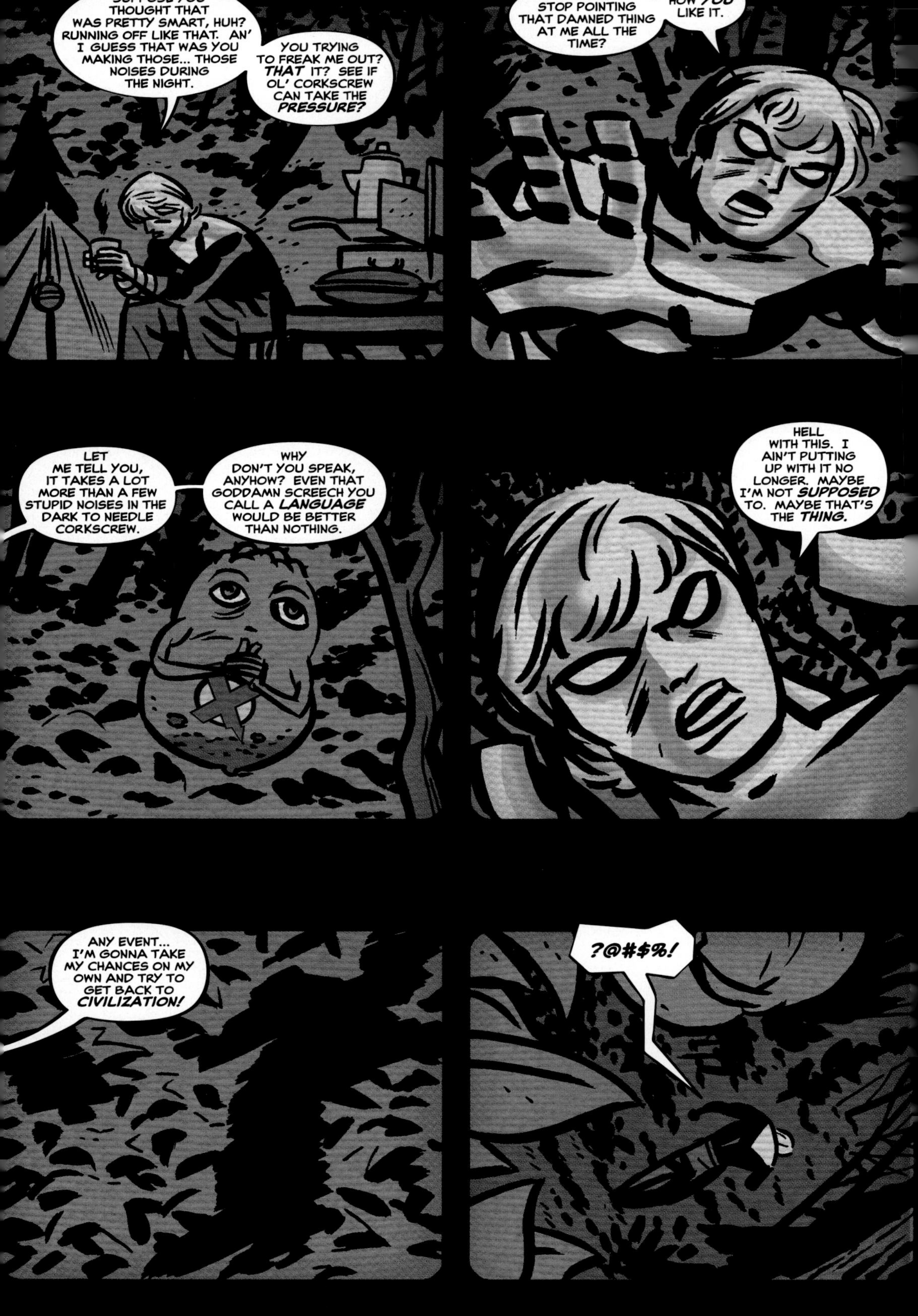
SUPPOSE YOU THOUGHT THAT WAS PRETTY SMART, HUH? RUNNING OFF LIKE THAT. AN' I GUESS THAT WAS YOU MAKING THOSE... THOSE NOISES DURING THE NIGHT.
YOU TRYING TO FREAK ME OUT? THAT IT? SEE IF OL' CORKSCREW CAN TAKE THE PRESSURE?
CAN YOU STOP POINTING THAT DAMNED THING AT ME ALL THE TIME?
SEE HOW YOU LIKE IT.
LET ME TELL YOU, IT TAKES A LOT MORE THAN A FEW STUPID NOISES IN THE DARK TO NEEDLE CORKSCREW.
WHY DON'T YOU SPEAK, ANYHOW? EVEN THAT GODDAMN SCREECH YOU CALL A LANGUAGE WOULD BE BETTER THAN NOTHING.
HELL WITH THIS. I AIN'T PUTTING UP WITH IT NO LONGER. MAYBE I'M NOT SUPPOSED TO. MAYBE THAT'S THE THING.
ANY EVENT... I'M GONNA TAKE MY CHANCES ON MY OWN AND TRY TO GET BACK TO CIVILIZATION!
?@#$%!

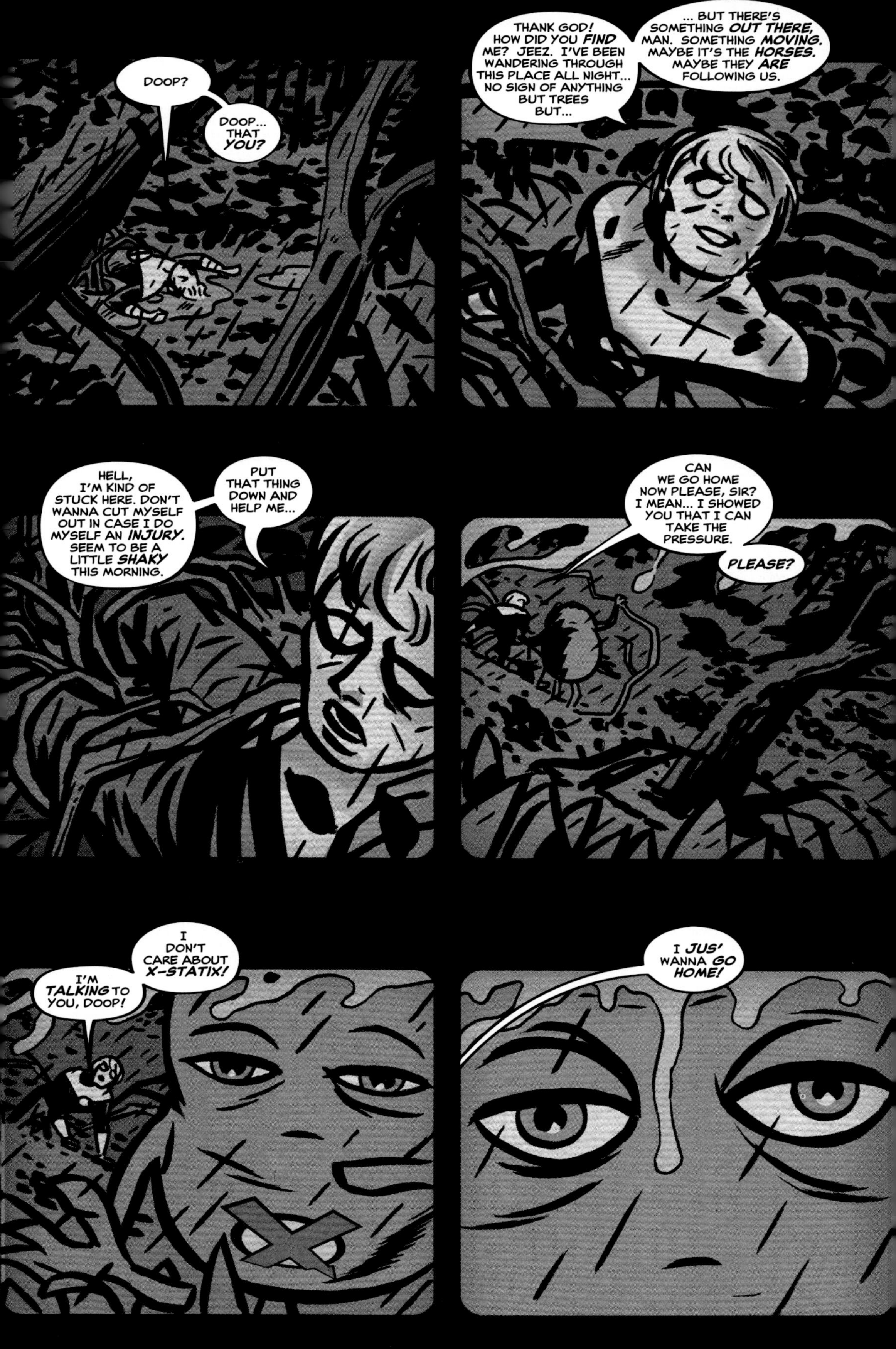
DOOP?
DOOP... THAT YOU?
THANK GOD! HOW DID YOU FIND ME? JEEZ. I'VE BEEN WANDERING THROUGH THIS PLACE ALL NIGHT... NO SIGN OF ANYTHING BUT TREES BUT...
... BUT THERE'S SOMETHING OUT THERE, MAN. SOMETHING MOVING. MAYBE IT'S THE HORSES. MAYBE THEY ARE FOLLOWING US.
HELL, I'M KIND OF STUCK HERE. DON'T WANNA CUT MYSELF OUT IN CASE I DO MYSELF AN INJURY. SEEM TO BE A LITTLE SHAKY THIS MORNING.
PUT THAT THING DOWN AND HELP ME...
CAN WE GO HOME NOW PLEASE, SIR? I MEAN... I SHOWED YOU THAT I CAN TAKE THE PRESSURE.
PLEASE?
I'M TALKING TO YOU, DOOP!
I DON'T CARE ABOUT X-STATIX!
I JUS' WANNA GO HOME!

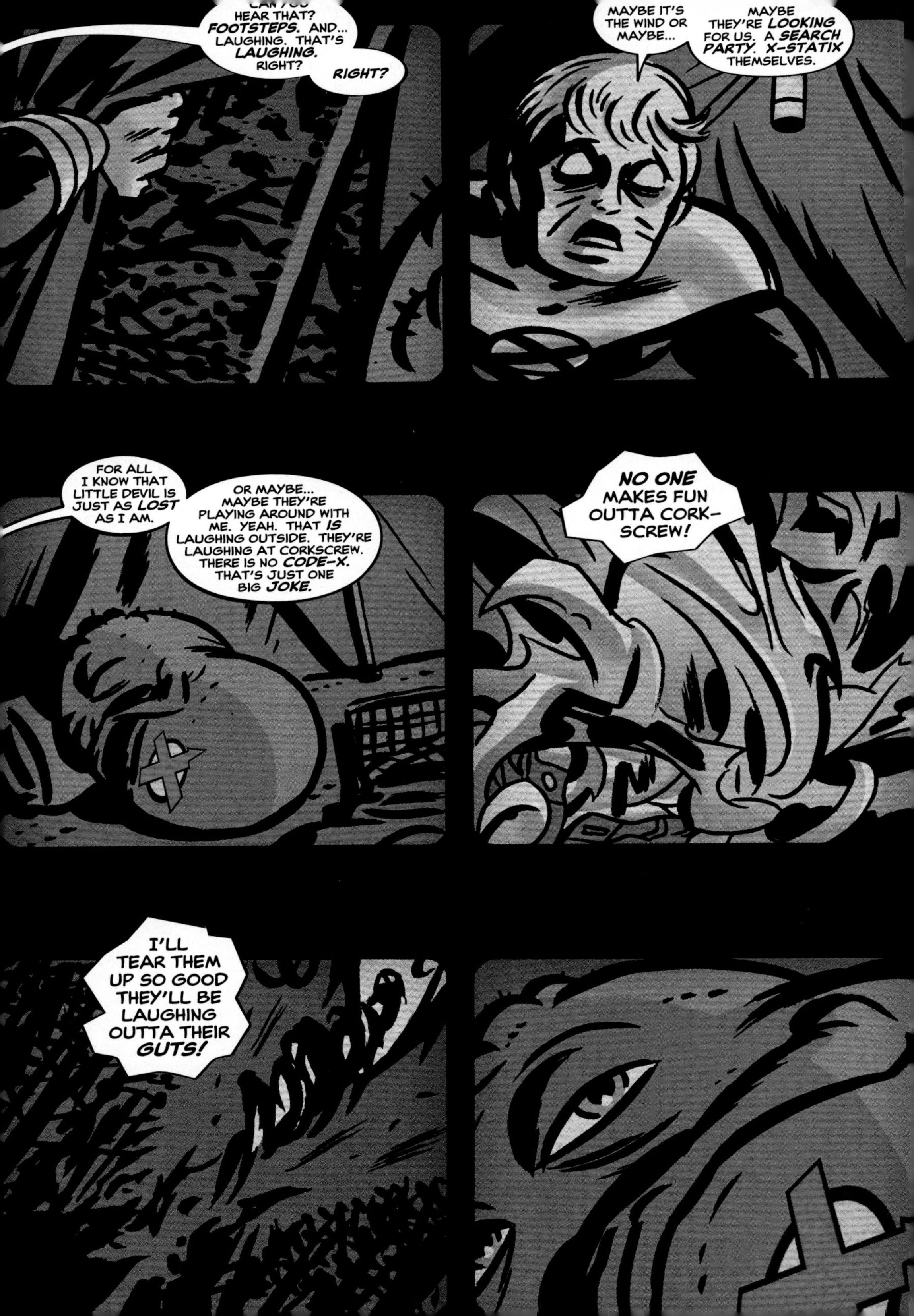
HEAR THAT? FOOTSTEPS. AND... LAUGHING. THAT'S LAUGHING. RIGHT?
RIGHT?
MAYBE IT'S THE WIND OR MAYBE...
MAYBE THEY'RE LOOKING FOR US. A SEARCH PARTY. X-STATIX THEMSELVES.
FOR ALL I KNOW THAT LITTLE DEVIL IS JUST AS LOST AS I AM.
OR MAYBE... MAYBE THEY'RE PLAYING AROUND WITH ME. YEAH. THAT IS LAUGHING OUTSIDE. THEY'RE LAUGHING AT CORKSCREW. THERE IS NO CODE-X. THAT'S JUST ONE BIG JOKE.
NO ONE MAKES FUN OUTTA CORK-SCREW!
I'LL TEAR THEM UP SO GOOD THEY'LL BE LAUGHING OUTTA THEIR GUTS!

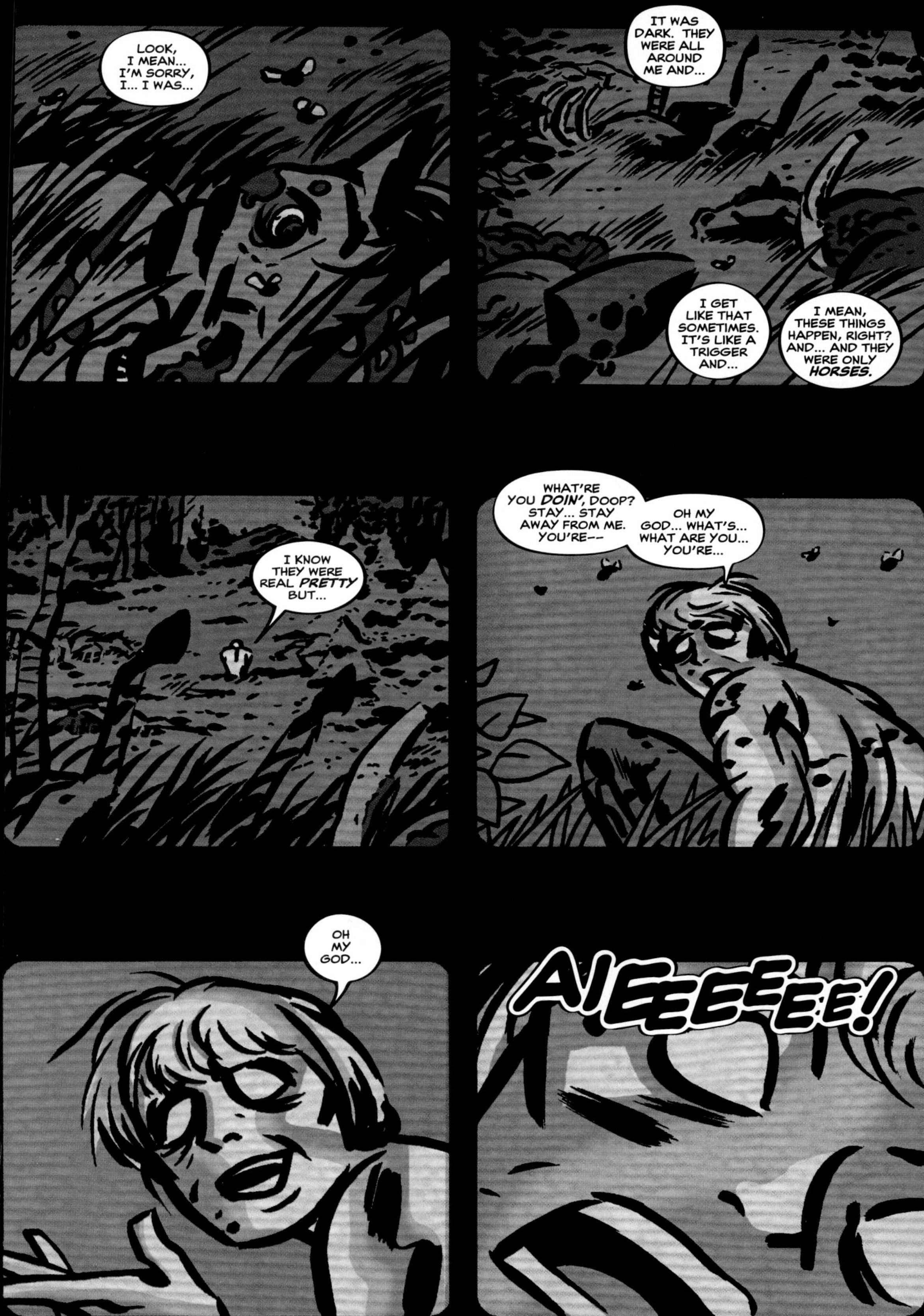

LOOK, I MEAN... I'M SORRY, I... I WAS...
IT WAS DARK. THEY WERE ALL AROUND ME AND...
I GET LIKE THAT SOMETIMES. IT'S LIKE A TRIGGER AND...
I MEAN, THESE THINGS HAPPEN, RIGHT? AND... AND THEY WERE ONLY *HORSES.*
I KNOW THEY WERE REAL *PRETTY* BUT...
WHAT'RE YOU *DOIN'*, DOOP? STAY... STAY AWAY FROM ME. YOU'RE--
OH MY GOD... WHAT'S... WHAT ARE YOU... YOU'RE...
OH MY GOD...
AIEEEEEEE!

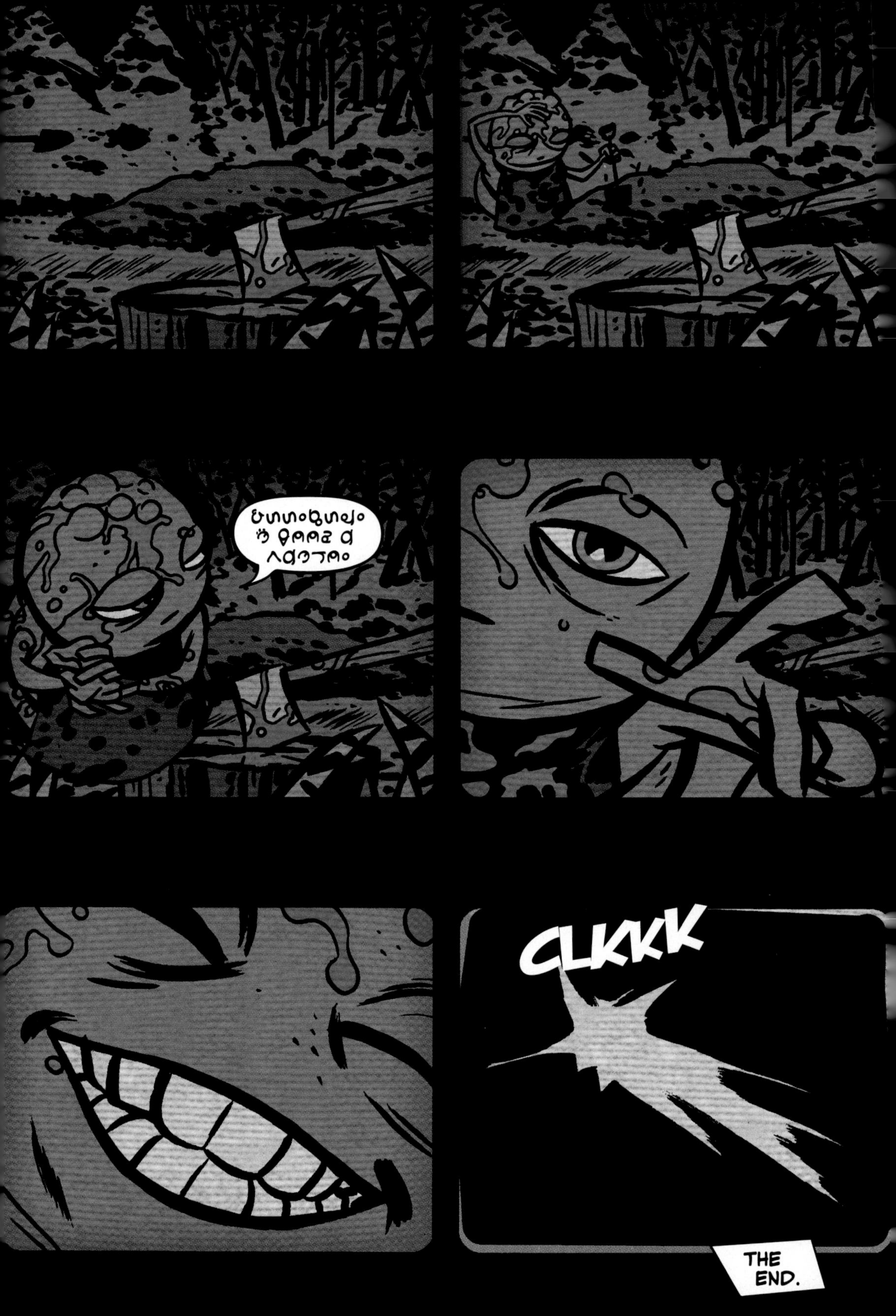
CLKKK
THE END.

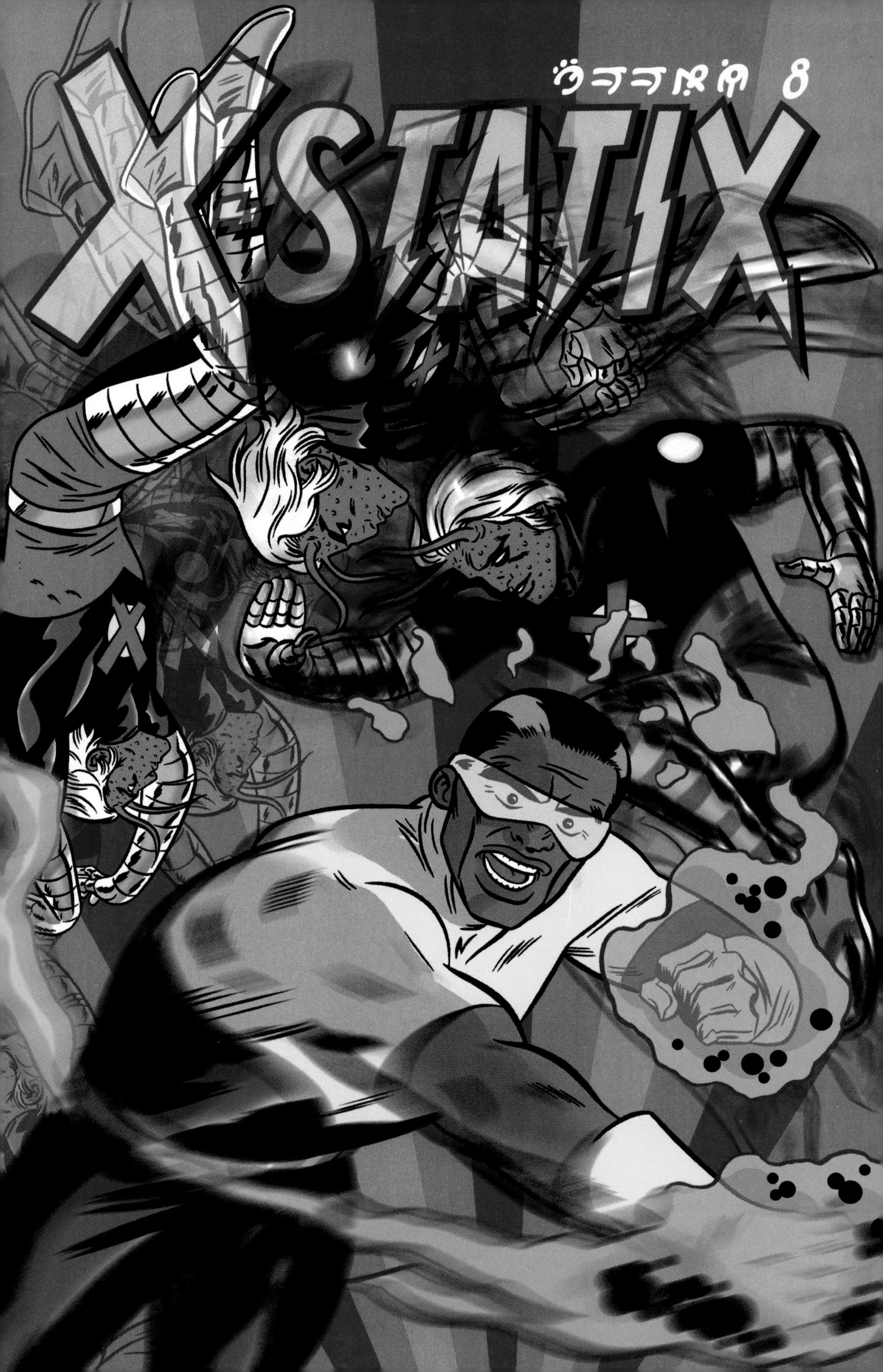
X-STATIX

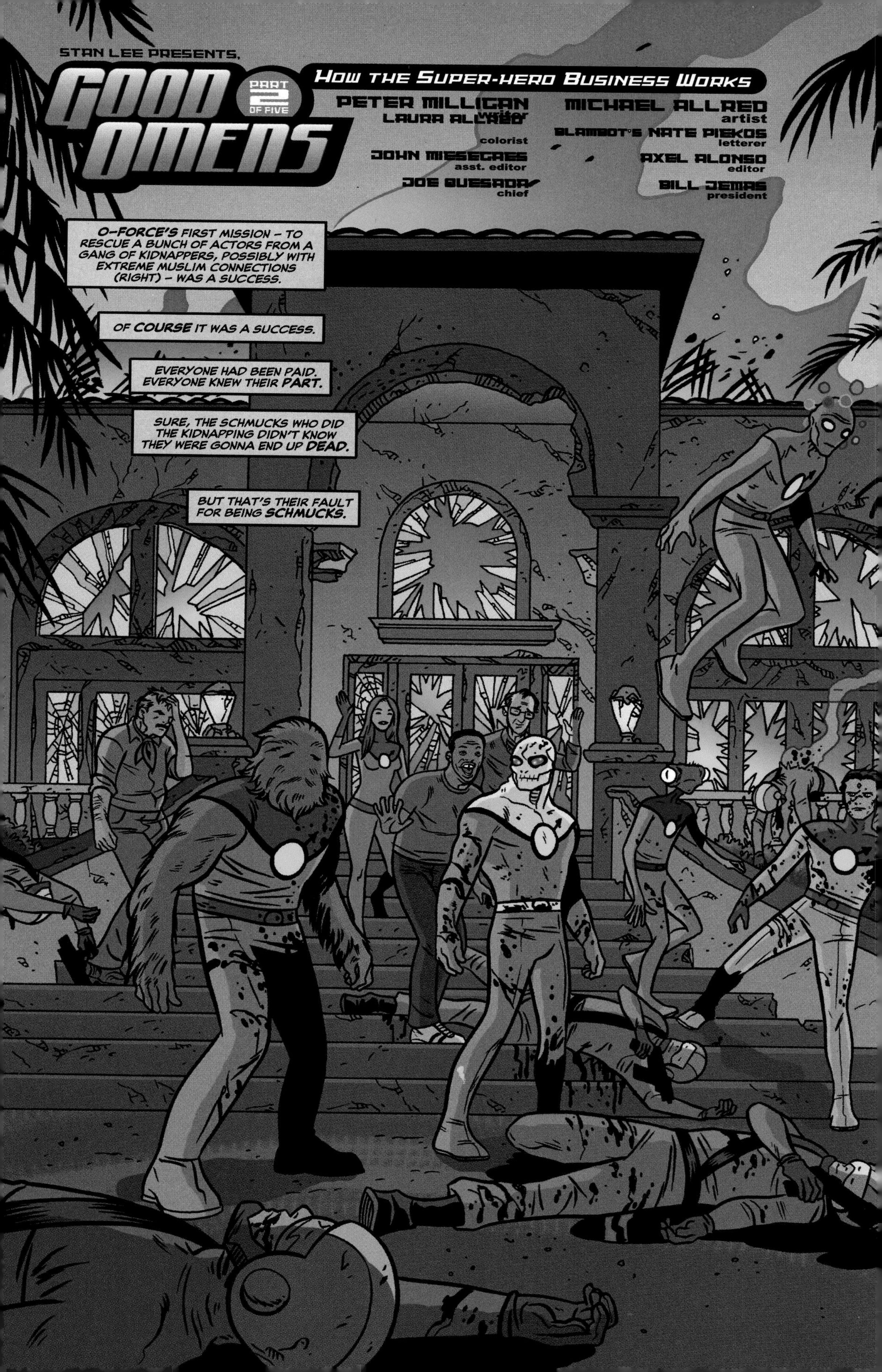

STAN LEE PRESENTS,
GOOD OMENS
PART 2 OF FIVE
HOW THE SUPER-HERO BUSINESS WORKS
PETER MILLIGAN writer
MICHAEL ALLRED artist
LAURA ALLRED colorist
BLAMBOT'S NATE PIEKOS letterer
JOHN MIESEGAES asst. editor
AXEL ALONSO editor
JOE QUESADA chief
BILL JEMAS president
O-FORCE'S FIRST MISSION – TO RESCUE A BUNCH OF ACTORS FROM A GANG OF KIDNAPPERS, POSSIBLY WITH EXTREME MUSLIM CONNECTIONS (RIGHT) – WAS A SUCCESS.
OF COURSE IT WAS A SUCCESS.
EVERYONE HAD BEEN PAID. EVERYONE KNEW THEIR PART.
SURE, THE SCHMUCKS WHO DID THE KIDNAPPING DIDN'T KNOW THEY WERE GONNA END UP DEAD.
BUT THAT'S THEIR FAULT FOR BEING SCHMUCKS.

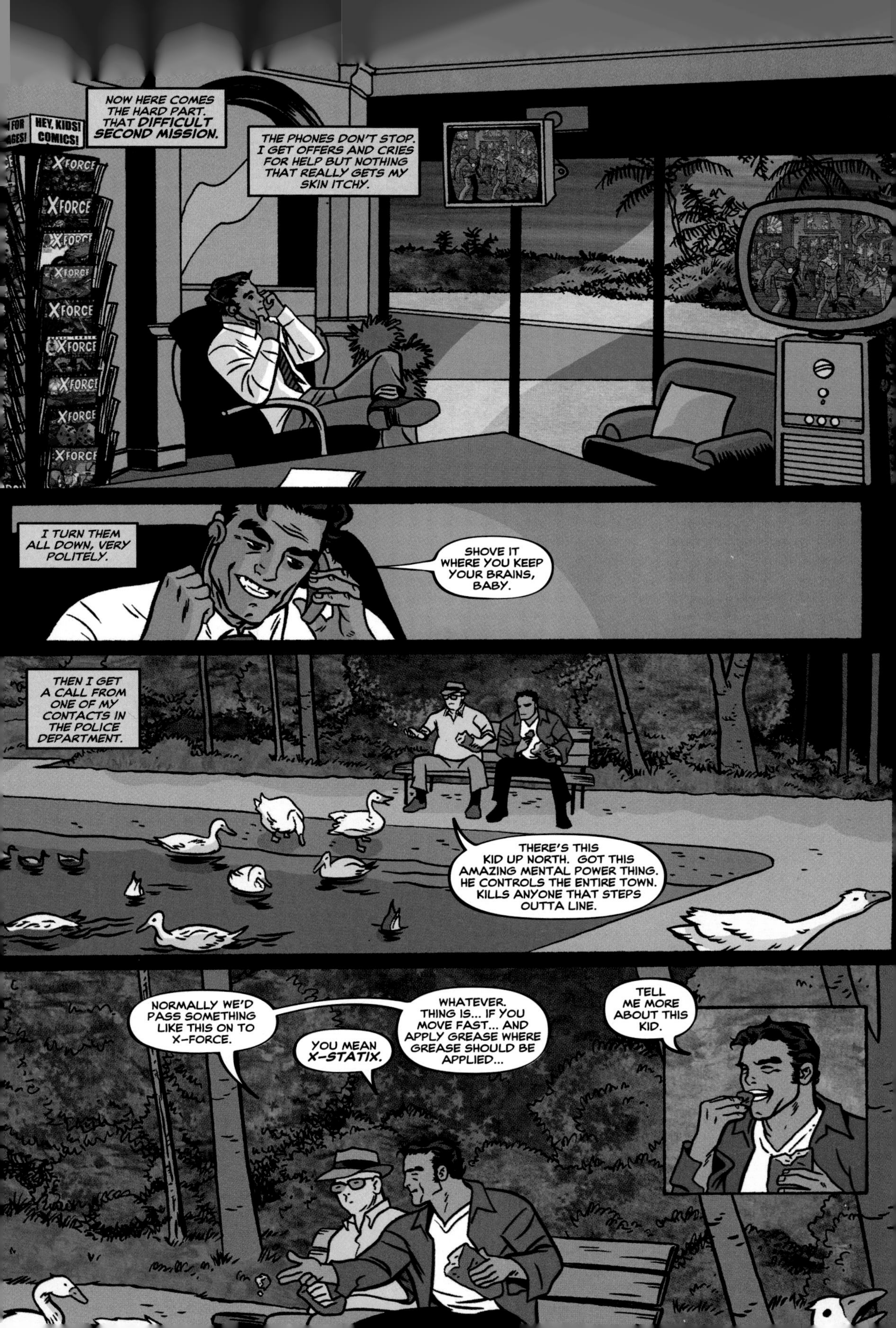

NOW HERE COMES THE HARD PART. THAT DIFFICULT SECOND MISSION.
HEY, KIDS! COMICS!
X-FORCE
THE PHONES DON'T STOP. I GET OFFERS AND CRIES FOR HELP BUT NOTHING THAT REALLY GETS MY SKIN ITCHY.
I TURN THEM ALL DOWN, VERY POLITELY.
SHOVE IT WHERE YOU KEEP YOUR BRAINS, BABY.
THEN I GET A CALL FROM ONE OF MY CONTACTS IN THE POLICE DEPARTMENT.
THERE'S THIS KID UP NORTH. GOT THIS AMAZING MENTAL POWER THING. HE CONTROLS THE ENTIRE TOWN. KILLS ANYONE THAT STEPS OUTTA LINE.
NORMALLY WE'D PASS SOMETHING LIKE THIS ON TO X-FORCE.
YOU MEAN X-STATIX.
WHATEVER. THING IS... IF YOU MOVE FAST... AND APPLY GREASE WHERE GREASE SHOULD BE APPLIED...
TELL ME MORE ABOUT THIS KID.

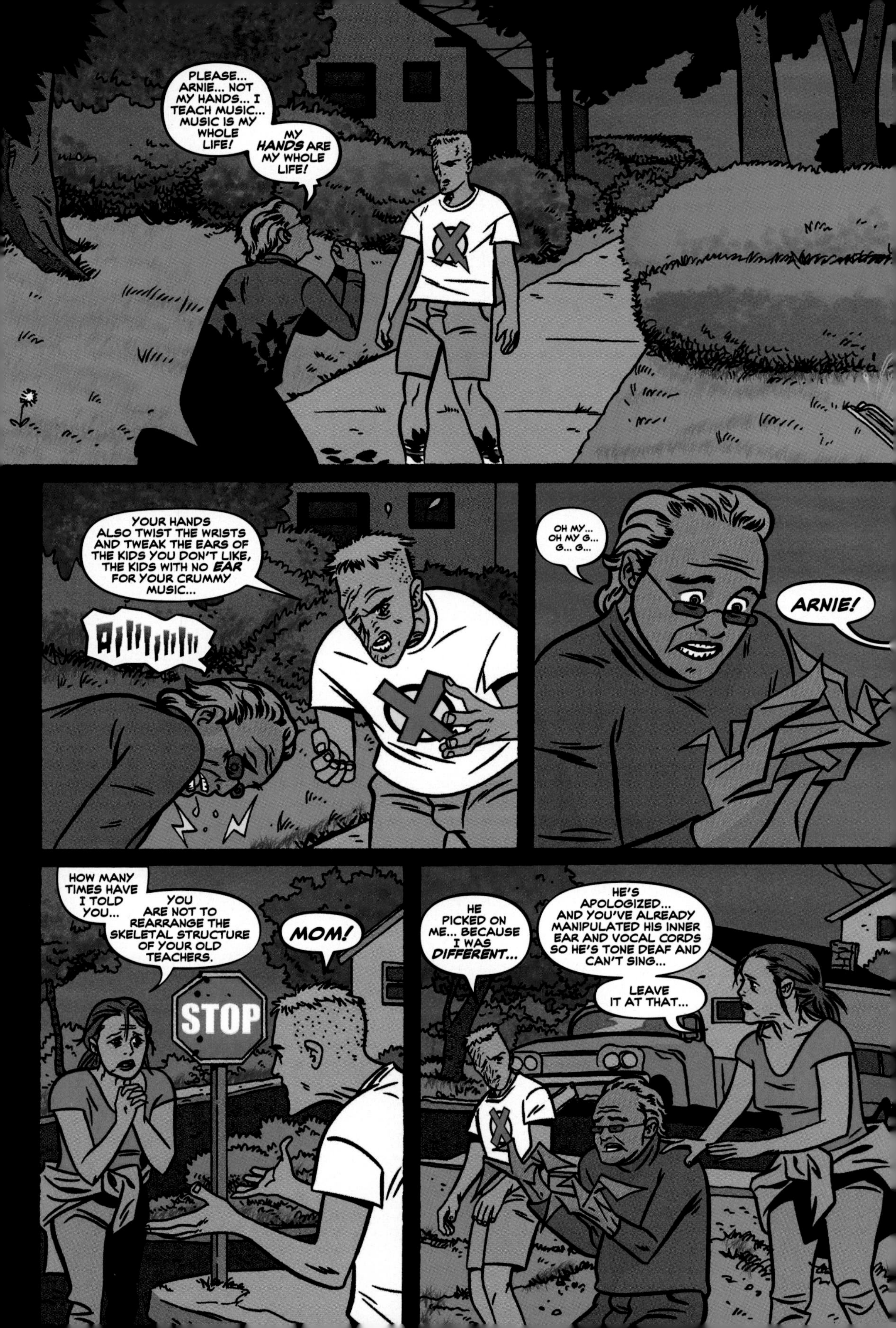
PLEASE... ARNIE... NOT MY HANDS... I TEACH MUSIC... MUSIC IS MY WHOLE LIFE!
MY HANDS ARE MY WHOLE LIFE!
YOUR HANDS ALSO TWIST THE WRISTS AND TWEAK THE EARS OF THE KIDS YOU DON'T LIKE, THE KIDS WITH NO EAR FOR YOUR CRUMMY MUSIC...
OH MY... OH MY G... G... G...
ARNIE!
HOW MANY TIMES HAVE I TOLD YOU...
YOU ARE NOT TO REARRANGE THE SKELETAL STRUCTURE OF YOUR OLD TEACHERS.
MOM!
STOP
HE PICKED ON ME... BECAUSE I WAS DIFFERENT...
HE'S APOLOGIZED... AND YOU'VE ALREADY MANIPULATED HIS INNER EAR AND VOCAL CORDS SO HE'S TONE DEAF AND CAN'T SING...
LEAVE IT AT THAT...

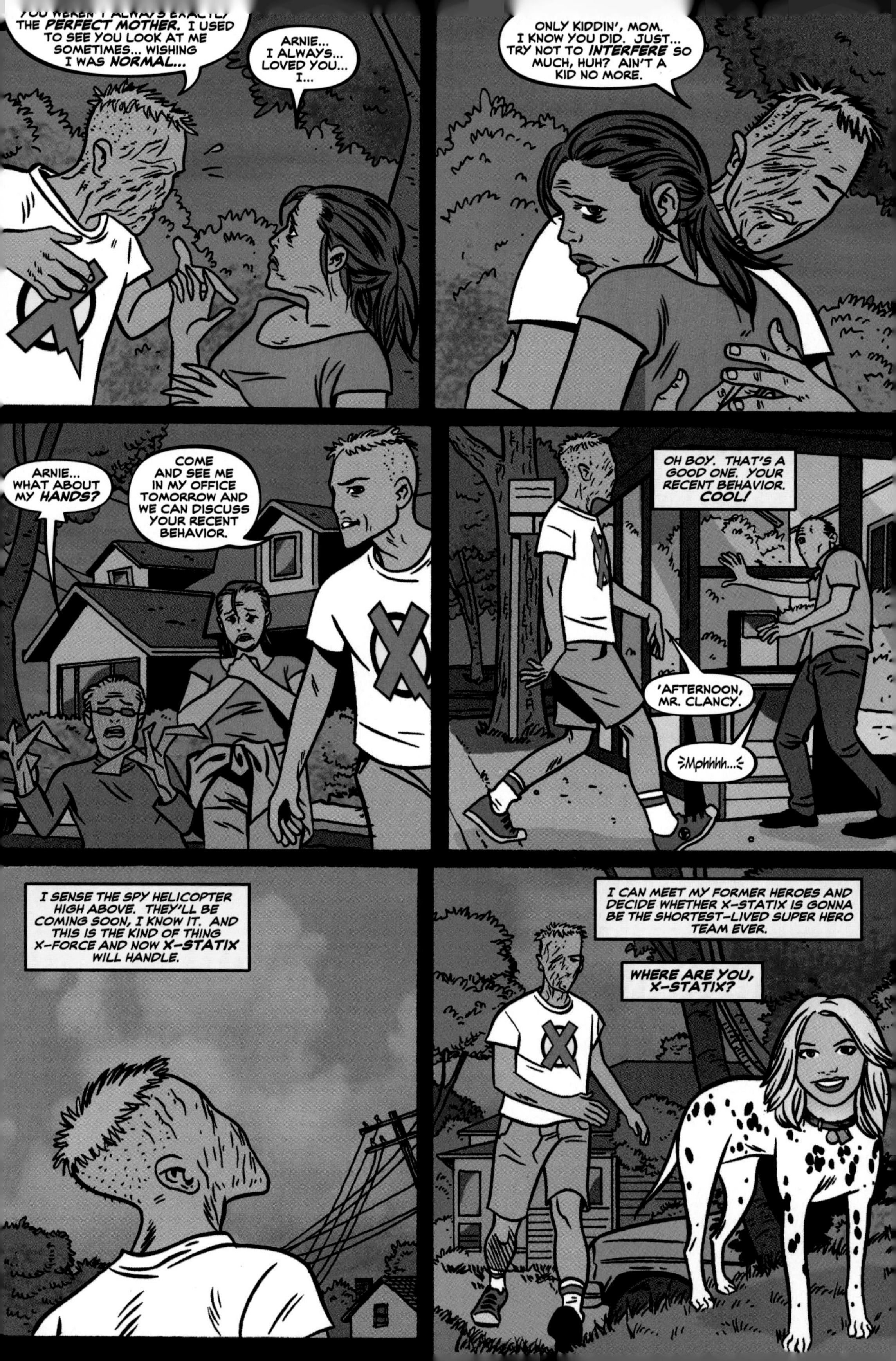
YOU WEREN'T ALWAYS EXACTLY THE PERFECT MOTHER. I USED TO SEE YOU LOOK AT ME SOMETIMES... WISHING I WAS NORMAL...
ARNIE... I ALWAYS... LOVED YOU... I...
ONLY KIDDIN', MOM. I KNOW YOU DID. JUST... TRY NOT TO INTERFERE SO MUCH, HUH? AIN'T A KID NO MORE.
ARNIE... WHAT ABOUT MY HANDS?
COME AND SEE ME IN MY OFFICE TOMORROW AND WE CAN DISCUSS YOUR RECENT BEHAVIOR.
OH BOY. THAT'S A GOOD ONE. YOUR RECENT BEHAVIOR. COOL!
'AFTERNOON, MR. CLANCY.
Mphhhh...
I SENSE THE SPY HELICOPTER HIGH ABOVE. THEY'LL BE COMING SOON, I KNOW IT. AND THIS IS THE KIND OF THING X-FORCE AND NOW X-STATIX WILL HANDLE.
I CAN MEET MY FORMER HEROES AND DECIDE WHETHER X-STATIX IS GONNA BE THE SHORTEST-LIVED SUPER HERO TEAM EVER.
WHERE ARE YOU, X-STATIX?

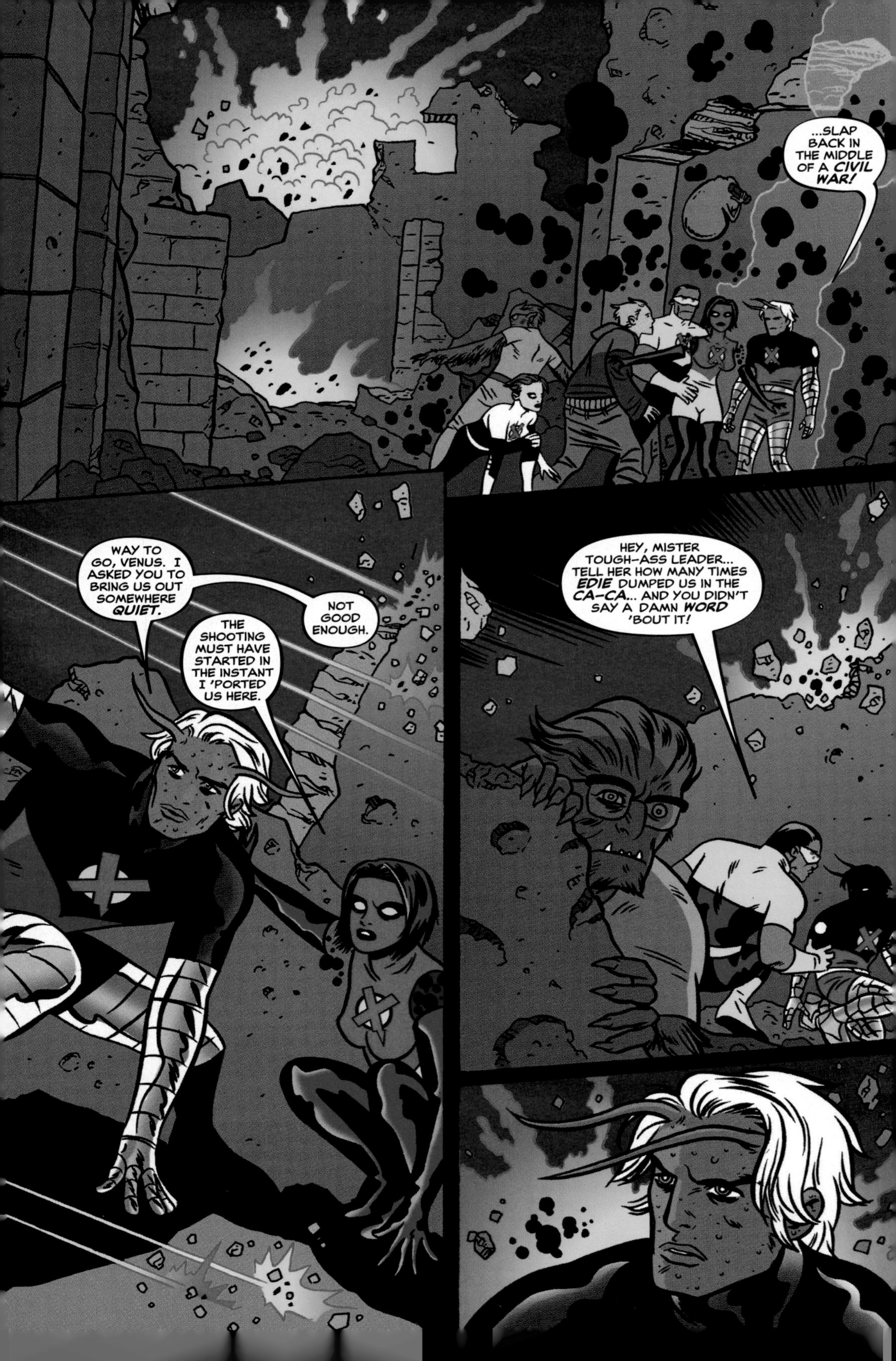
...SLAP BACK IN THE MIDDLE OF A CIVIL WAR!
WAY TO GO, VENUS. I ASKED YOU TO BRING US OUT SOMEWHERE QUIET.
NOT GOOD ENOUGH.
THE SHOOTING MUST HAVE STARTED IN THE INSTANT I 'PORTED US HERE.
HEY, MISTER TOUGH-ASS LEADER... TELL HER HOW MANY TIMES EDIE DUMPED US IN THE CA-CA... AND YOU DIDN'T SAY A DAMN WORD 'BOUT IT!

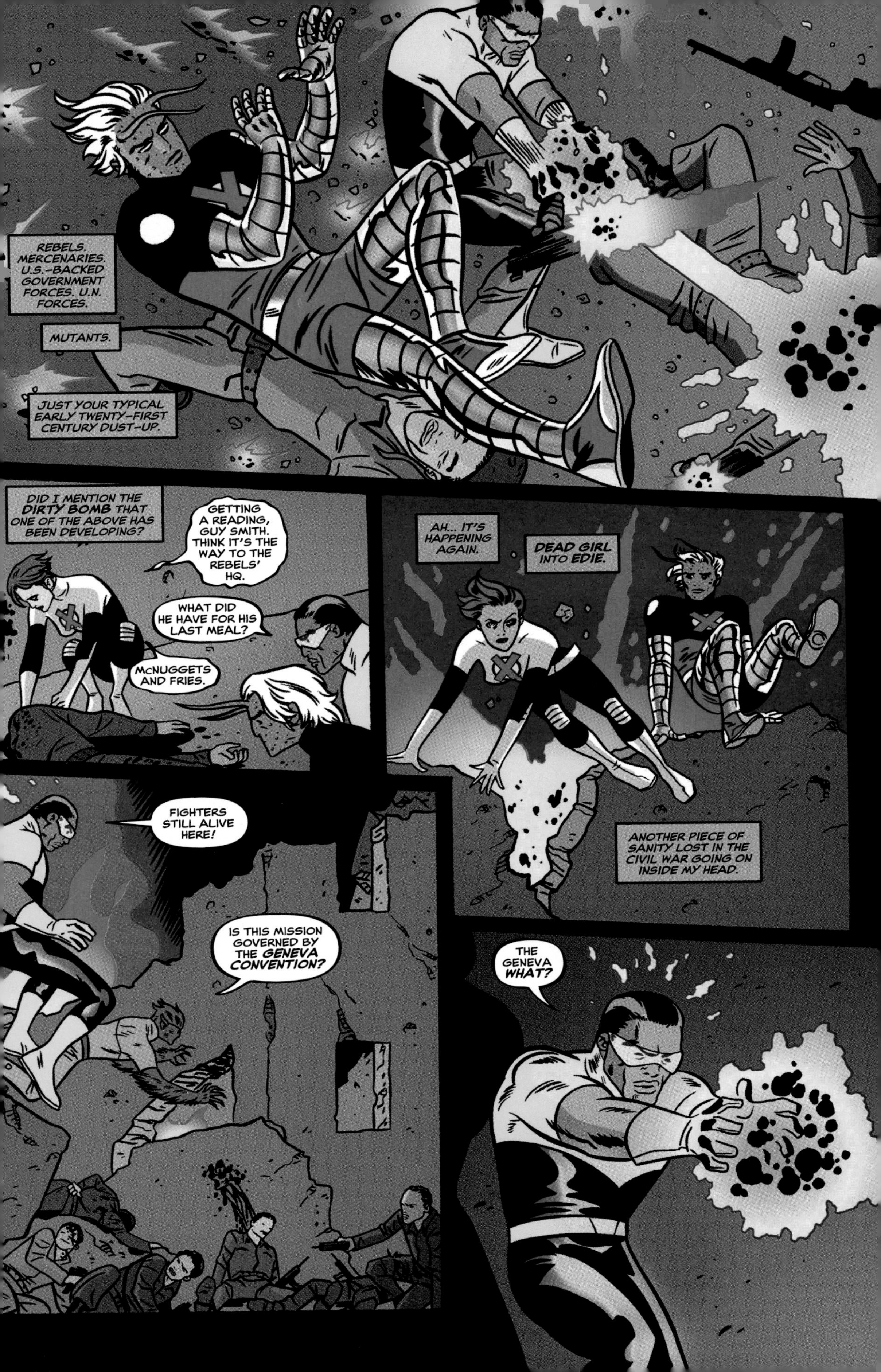
REBELS. MERCENARIES. U.S.-BACKED GOVERNMENT FORCES. U.N. FORCES.
MUTANTS.
JUST YOUR TYPICAL EARLY TWENTY-FIRST CENTURY DUST-UP.
DID I MENTION THE DIRTY BOMB THAT ONE OF THE ABOVE HAS BEEN DEVELOPING?
GETTING A READING, GUY SMITH. THINK IT'S THE WAY TO THE REBELS' HQ.
WHAT DID HE HAVE FOR HIS LAST MEAL?
McNUGGETS AND FRIES.
AH... IT'S HAPPENING AGAIN.
DEAD GIRL INTO EDIE.
ANOTHER PIECE OF SANITY LOST IN THE CIVIL WAR GOING ON INSIDE MY HEAD.
FIGHTERS STILL ALIVE HERE!
IS THIS MISSION GOVERNED BY THE GENEVA CONVENTION?
THE GENEVA WHAT?

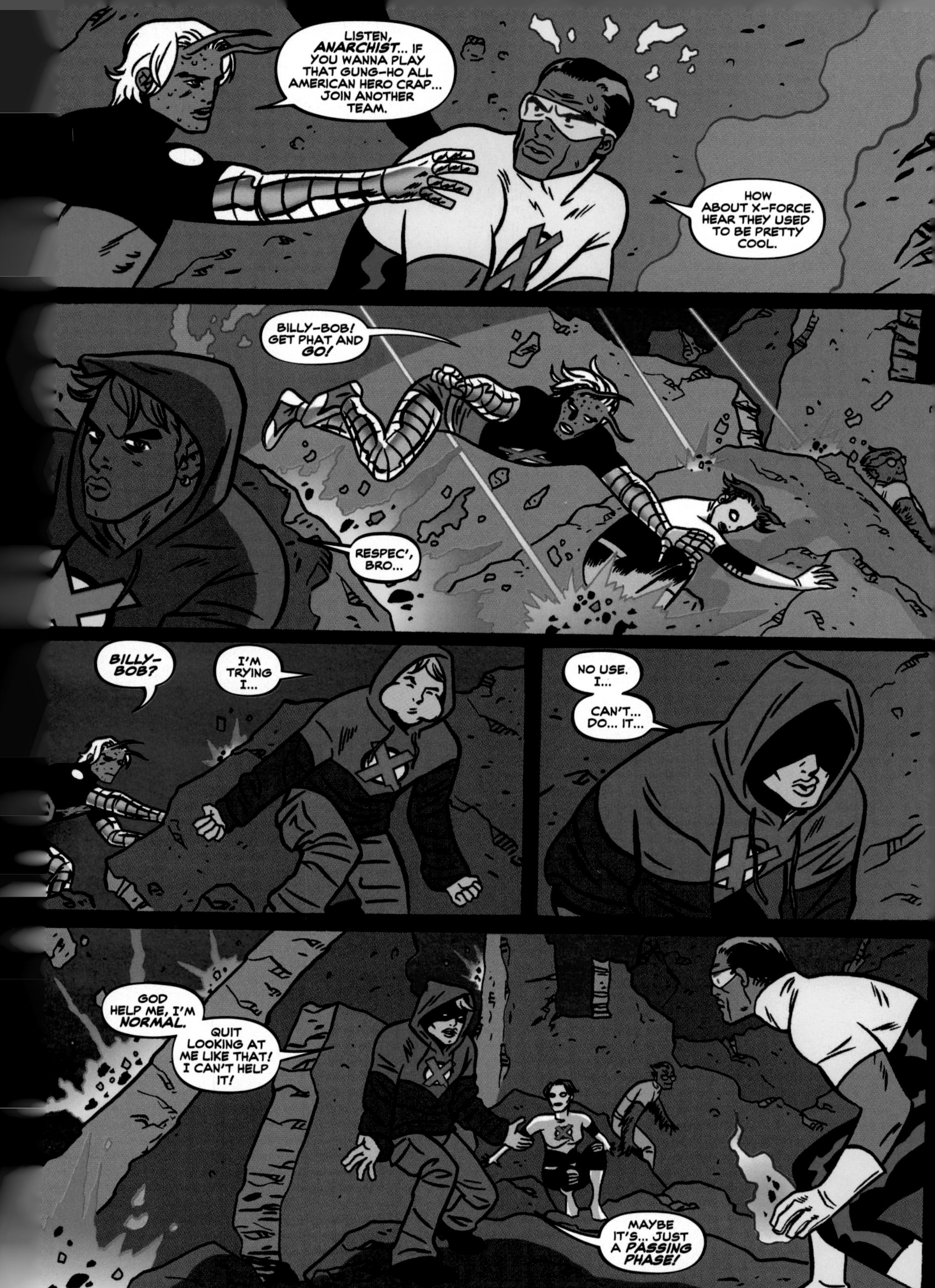
LISTEN, ANARCHIST... IF YOU WANNA PLAY THAT GUNG-HO ALL AMERICAN HERO CRAP... JOIN ANOTHER TEAM.
HOW ABOUT X-FORCE. HEAR THEY USED TO BE PRETTY COOL.
BILLY-BOB! GET PHAT AND GO!
RESPEC', BRO...
BILLY-BOB?
I'M TRYING I...
NO USE. I...
CAN'T... DO... IT...
GOD HELP ME, I'M NORMAL.
QUIT LOOKING AT ME LIKE THAT! I CAN'T HELP IT!
MAYBE IT'S... JUST A PASSING PHASE!

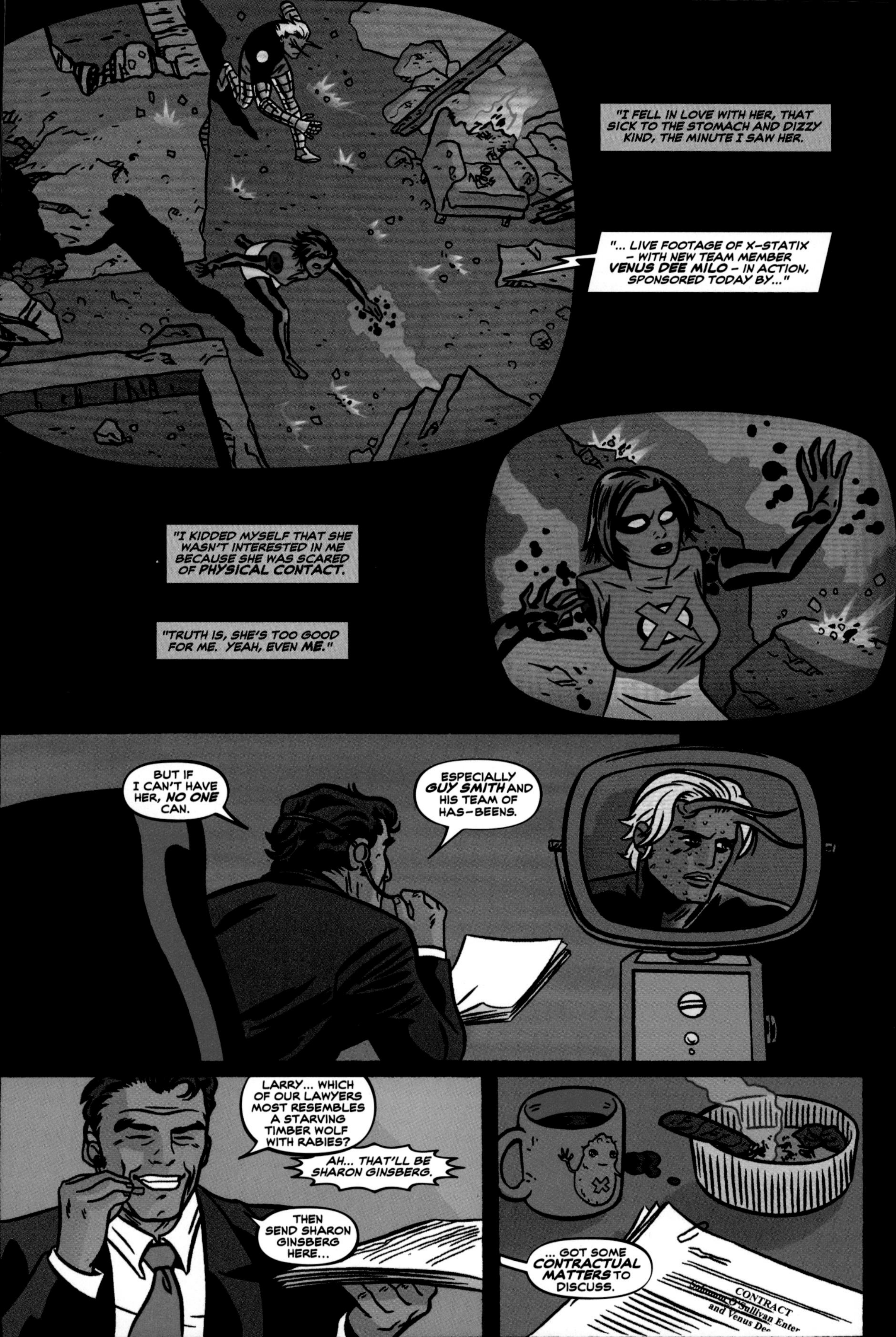
"I FELL IN LOVE WITH HER, THAT SICK TO THE STOMACH AND DIZZY KIND, THE MINUTE I SAW HER.
"... LIVE FOOTAGE OF X-STATIX – WITH NEW TEAM MEMBER VENUS DEE MILO – IN ACTION, SPONSORED TODAY BY..."
"I KIDDED MYSELF THAT SHE WASN'T INTERESTED IN ME BECAUSE SHE WAS SCARED OF PHYSICAL CONTACT.
"TRUTH IS, SHE'S TOO GOOD FOR ME. YEAH, EVEN ME."
BUT IF I CAN'T HAVE HER, NO ONE CAN.
ESPECIALLY GUY SMITH AND HIS TEAM OF HAS-BEENS.
LARRY... WHICH OF OUR LAWYERS MOST RESEMBLES A STARVING TIMBER WOLF WITH RABIES?
AH... THAT'LL BE SHARON GINSBERG.
THEN SEND SHARON GINSBERG HERE...
... GOT SOME CONTRACTUAL MATTERS TO DISCUSS.
CONTRACT
and Venus Dee

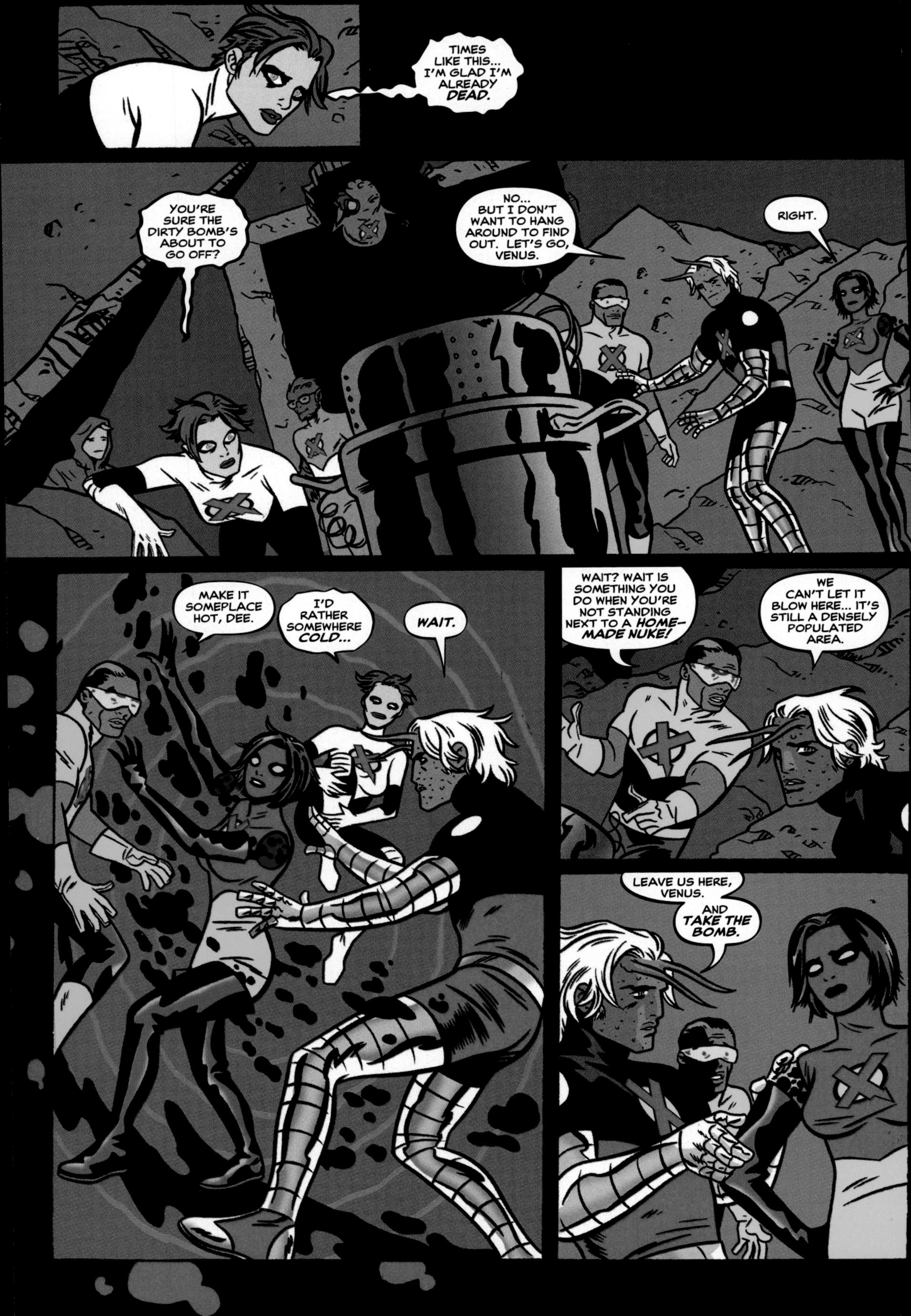
TIMES LIKE THIS... I'M GLAD I'M ALREADY DEAD.
YOU'RE SURE THE DIRTY BOMB'S ABOUT TO GO OFF?
NO... BUT I DON'T WANT TO HANG AROUND TO FIND OUT. LET'S GO, VENUS.
RIGHT.
MAKE IT SOMEPLACE HOT, DEE.
I'D RATHER SOMEWHERE COLD...
WAIT.
WAIT? WAIT IS SOMETHING YOU DO WHEN YOU'RE NOT STANDING NEXT TO A HOME-MADE NUKE!
WE CAN'T LET IT BLOW HERE... IT'S STILL A DENSELY POPULATED AREA.
LEAVE US HERE, VENUS.
AND TAKE THE BOMB.

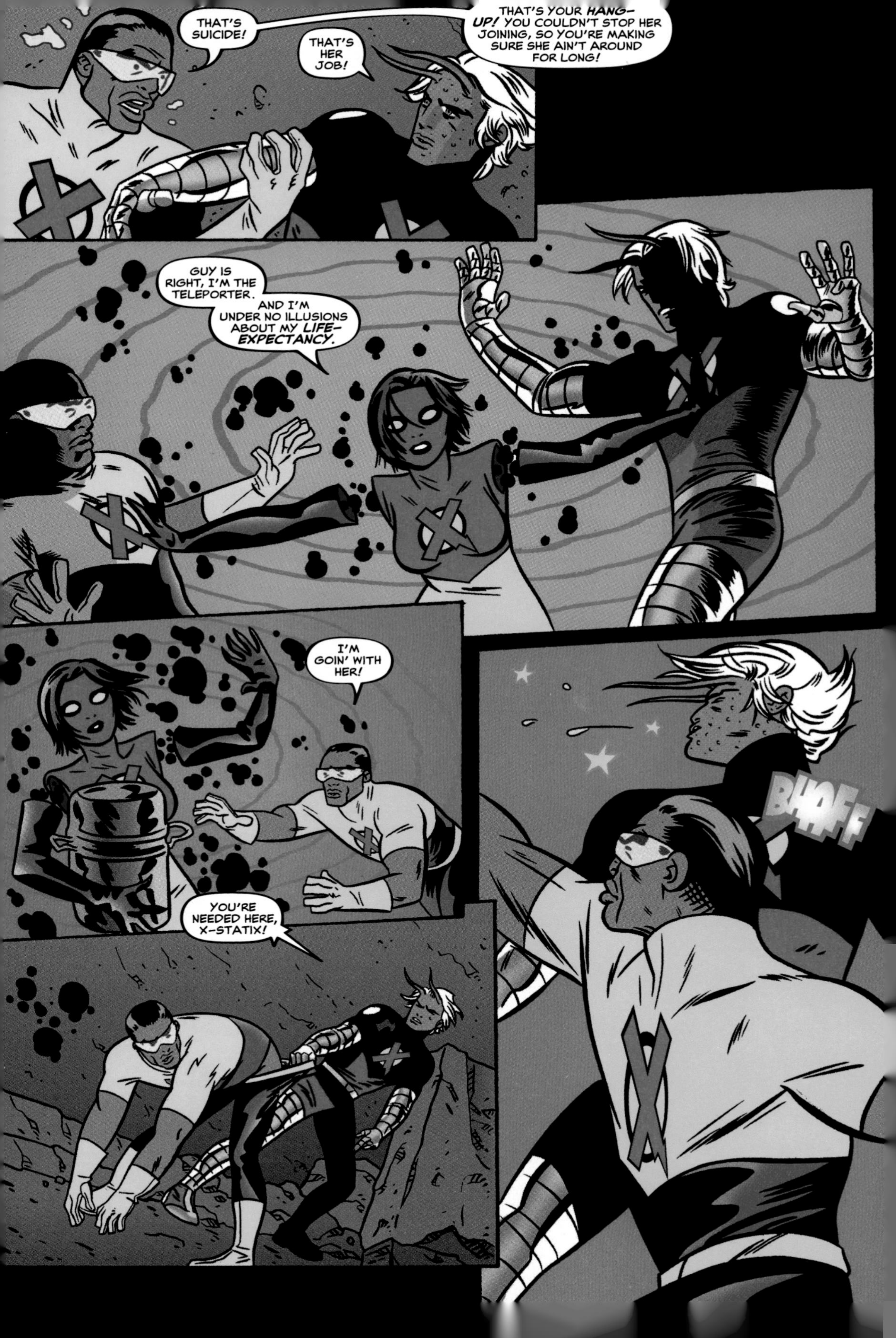
THAT'S SUICIDE!
THAT'S HER JOB!
THAT'S YOUR HANG-UP! YOU COULDN'T STOP HER JOINING, SO YOU'RE MAKING SURE SHE AIN'T AROUND FOR LONG!
GUY IS RIGHT, I'M THE TELEPORTER.
AND I'M UNDER NO ILLUSIONS ABOUT MY LIFE-EXPECTANCY.
I'M GOIN' WITH HER!
BHAFF
YOU'RE NEEDED HERE, X-STATIX!

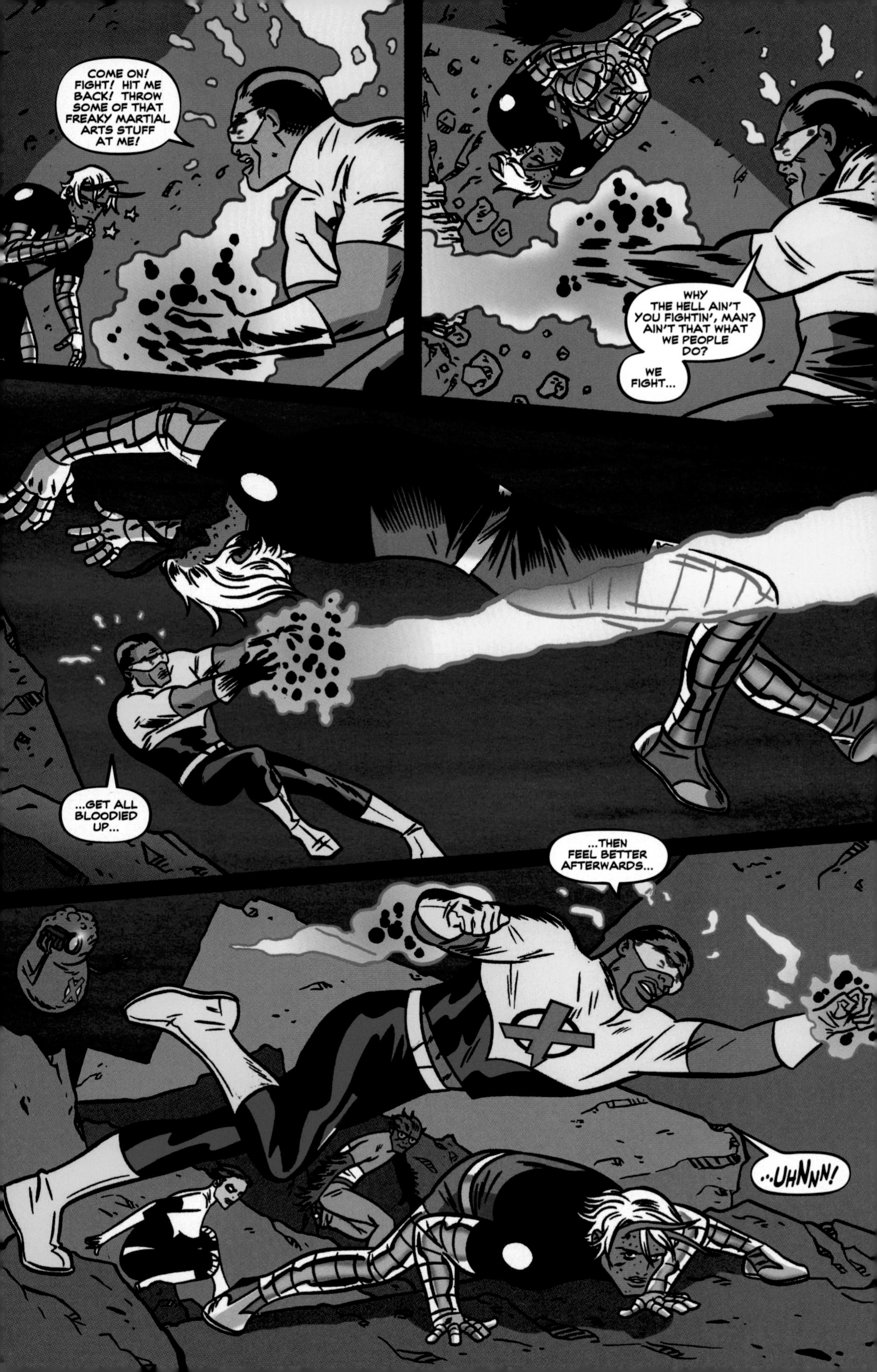
COME ON! FIGHT! HIT ME BACK! THROW SOME OF THAT FREAKY MARTIAL ARTS STUFF AT ME!
WHY THE HELL AIN'T YOU FIGHTIN', MAN? AIN'T THAT WHAT WE PEOPLE DO?
WE FIGHT...
...GET ALL BLOODIED UP...
...THEN FEEL BETTER AFTERWARDS...
...UHNNN!

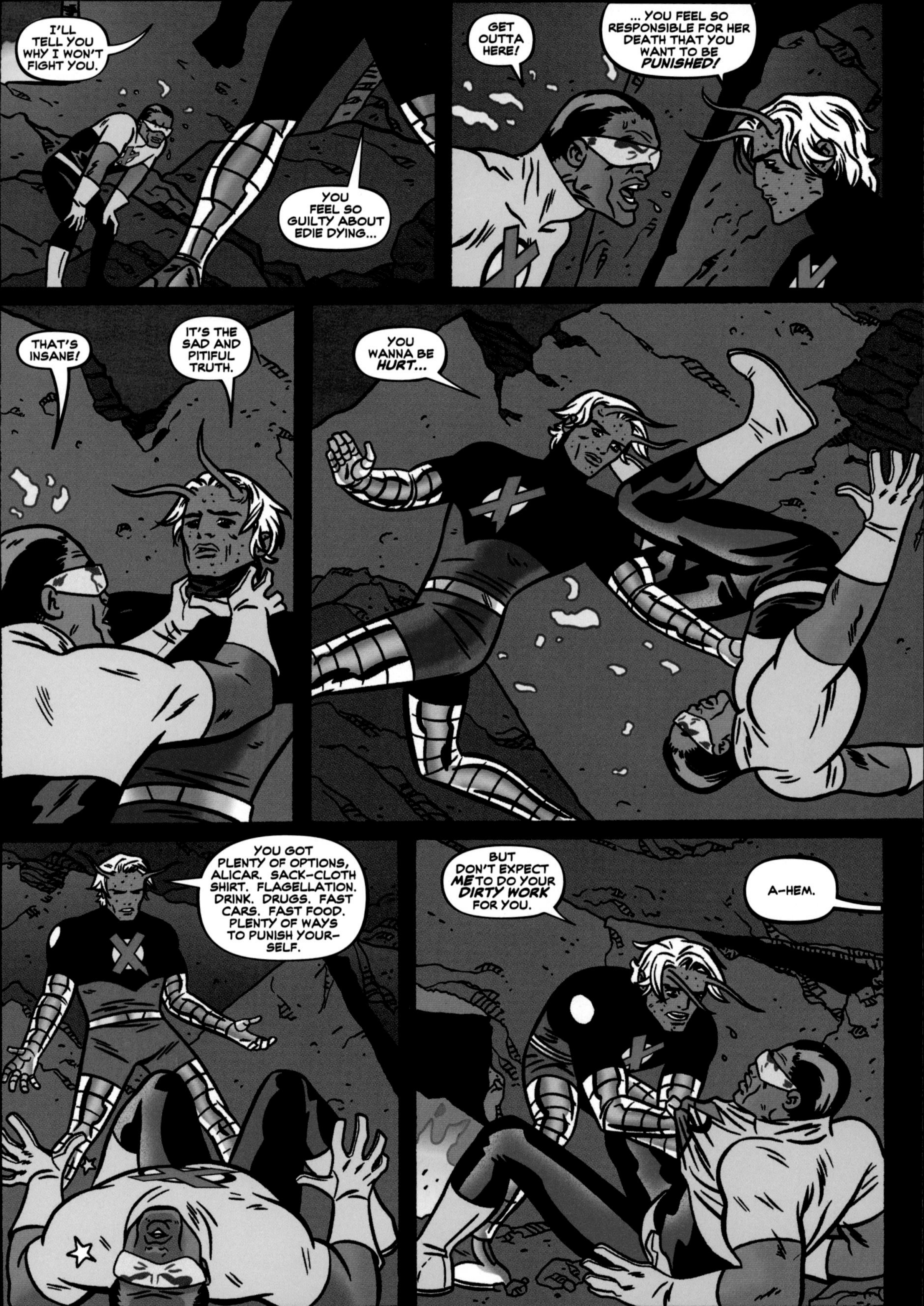
I'LL TELL YOU WHY I WON'T FIGHT YOU.
YOU FEEL SO GUILTY ABOUT EDIE DYING...
GET OUTTA HERE!
... YOU FEEL SO RESPONSIBLE FOR HER DEATH THAT YOU WANT TO BE *PUNISHED!*
THAT'S INSANE!
IT'S THE SAD AND PITIFUL TRUTH.
YOU WANNA BE *HURT...*
YOU GOT PLENTY OF OPTIONS, ALICAR. SACK-CLOTH SHIRT. FLAGELLATION. DRINK. DRUGS. FAST CARS. FAST FOOD. PLENTY OF WAYS TO PUNISH YOURSELF.
BUT DON'T EXPECT *ME* TO DO YOUR *DIRTY WORK* FOR YOU.
A-HEM.

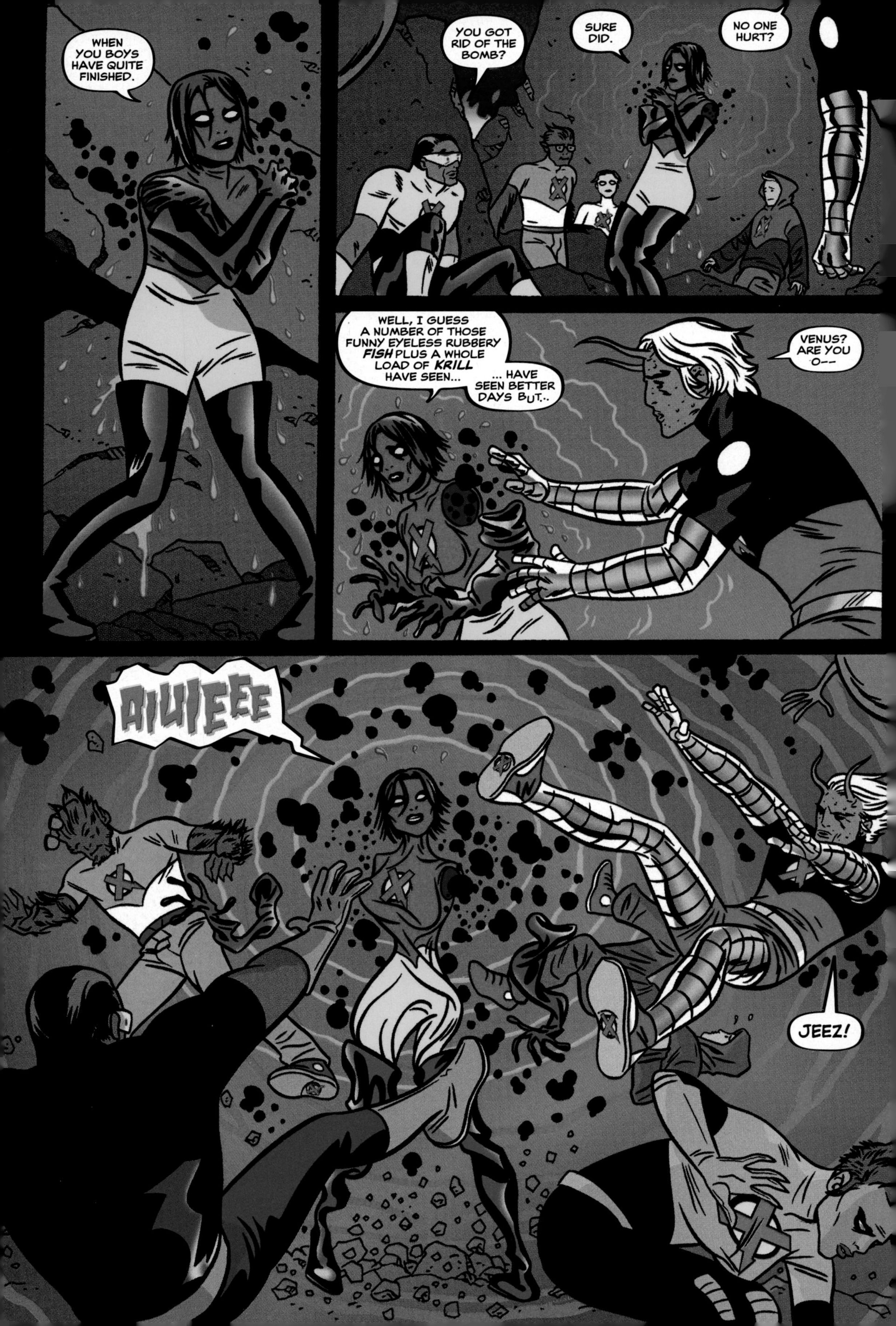
WHEN YOU BOYS HAVE QUITE FINISHED.
YOU GOT RID OF THE BOMB?
SURE DID.
NO ONE HURT?
WELL, I GUESS A NUMBER OF THOSE FUNNY EYELESS RUBBERY FISH PLUS A WHOLE LOAD OF KRILL HAVE SEEN...
... HAVE SEEN BETTER DAYS BUT..
VENUS? ARE YOU O--
AIUIEEE
JEEZ!

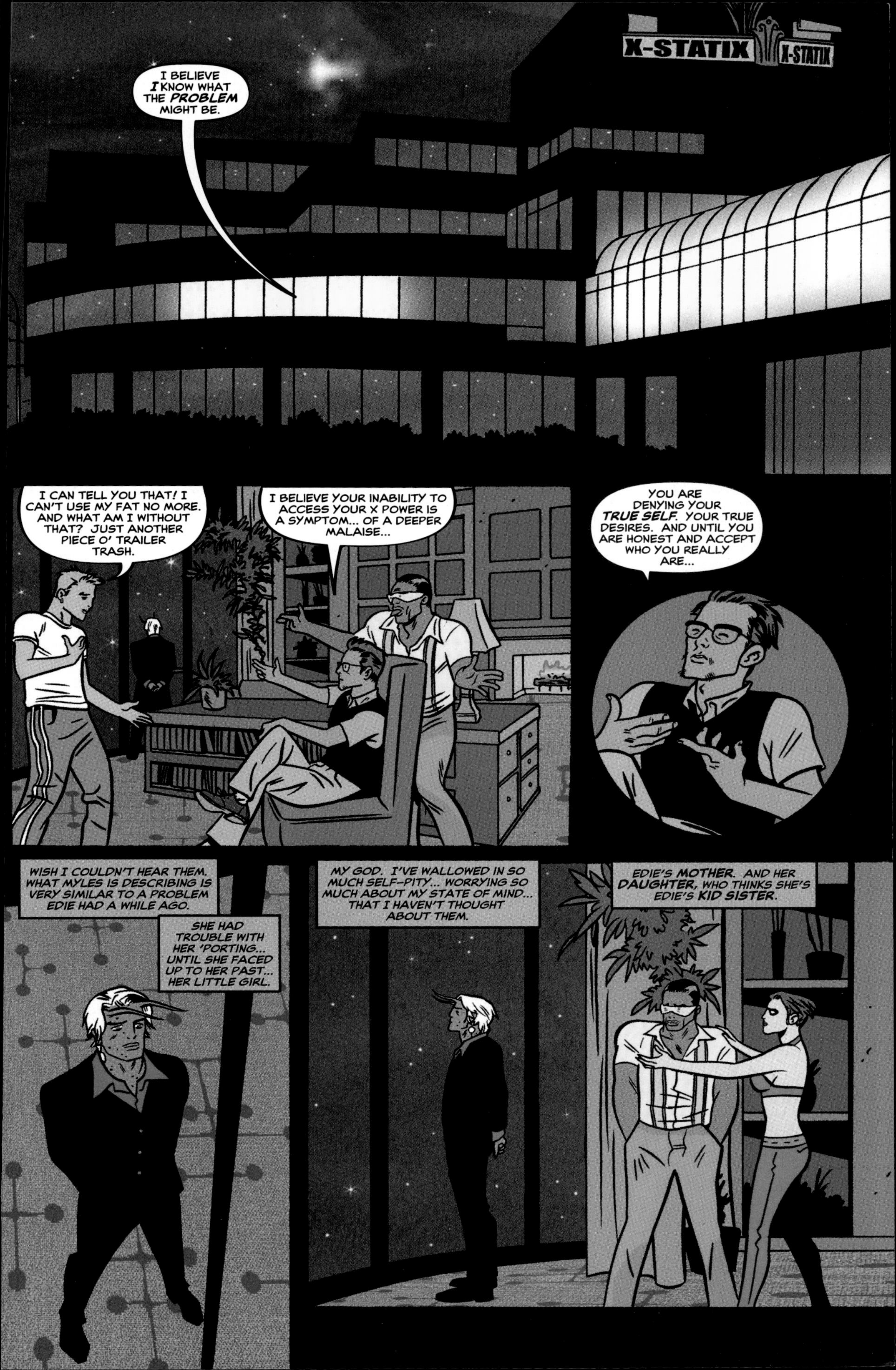
X-STATIX
X-STATIX
I BELIEVE I KNOW WHAT THE PROBLEM MIGHT BE.
I CAN TELL YOU THAT! I CAN'T USE MY FAT NO MORE. AND WHAT AM I WITHOUT THAT? JUST ANOTHER PIECE O' TRAILER TRASH.
I BELIEVE YOUR INABILITY TO ACCESS YOUR X POWER IS A SYMPTOM... OF A DEEPER MALAISE...
YOU ARE DENYING YOUR TRUE SELF. YOUR TRUE DESIRES. AND UNTIL YOU ARE HONEST AND ACCEPT WHO YOU REALLY ARE...
WISH I COULDN'T HEAR THEM. WHAT MYLES IS DESCRIBING IS VERY SIMILAR TO A PROBLEM EDIE HAD A WHILE AGO.
SHE HAD TROUBLE WITH HER 'PORTING... UNTIL SHE FACED UP TO HER PAST... HER LITTLE GIRL.
MY GOD. I'VE WALLOWED IN SO MUCH SELF-PITY... WORRYING SO MUCH ABOUT MY STATE OF MIND... THAT I HAVEN'T THOUGHT ABOUT THEM.
EDIE'S MOTHER. AND HER DAUGHTER, WHO THINKS SHE'S EDIE'S KID SISTER.

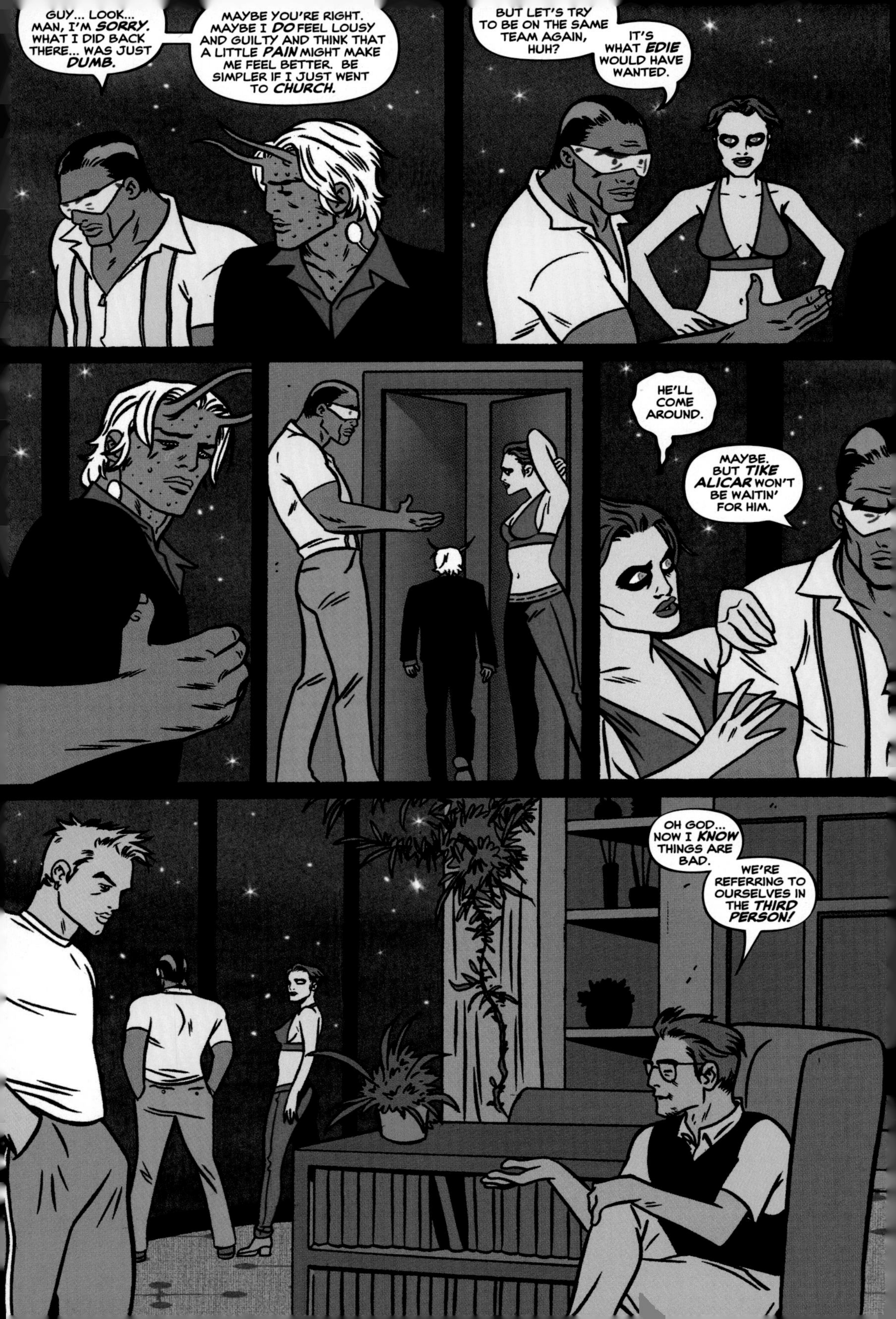
GUY... LOOK... MAN, I'M SORRY. WHAT I DID BACK THERE... WAS JUST DUMB.
MAYBE YOU'RE RIGHT. MAYBE I DO FEEL LOUSY AND GUILTY AND THINK THAT A LITTLE PAIN MIGHT MAKE ME FEEL BETTER. BE SIMPLER IF I JUST WENT TO CHURCH.
BUT LET'S TRY TO BE ON THE SAME TEAM AGAIN, HUH?
IT'S WHAT EDIE WOULD HAVE WANTED.
HE'LL COME AROUND.
MAYBE. BUT TIKE ALICAR WON'T BE WAITIN' FOR HIM.
OH GOD... NOW I KNOW THINGS ARE BAD.
WE'RE REFERRING TO OURSELVES IN THE THIRD PERSON!

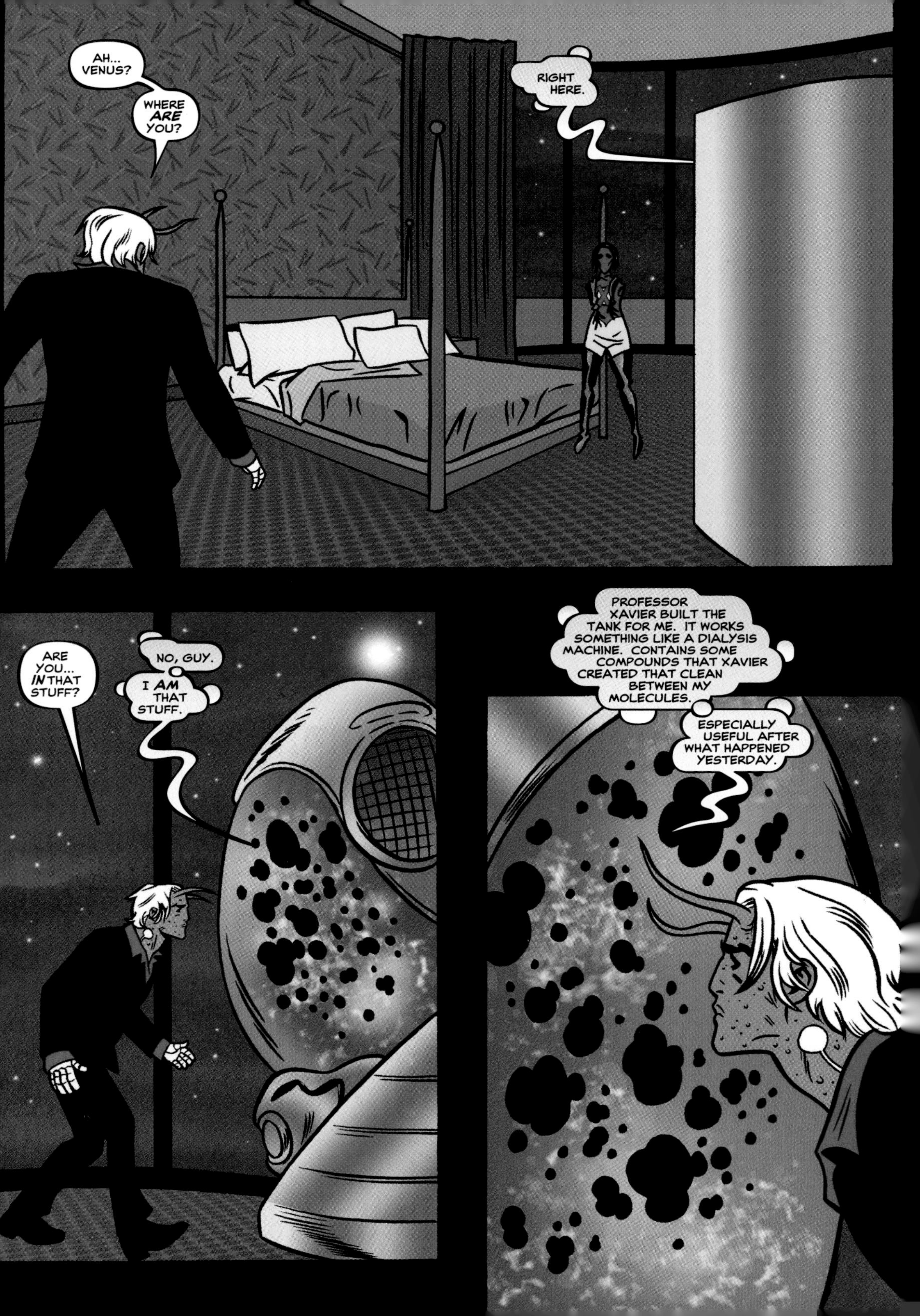
AH... VENUS?
WHERE ARE YOU?
RIGHT HERE.
ARE YOU... IN THAT STUFF?
NO, GUY.
I AM THAT STUFF.
PROFESSOR XAVIER BUILT THE TANK FOR ME. IT WORKS SOMETHING LIKE A DIALYSIS MACHINE. CONTAINS SOME COMPOUNDS THAT XAVIER CREATED THAT CLEAN BETWEEN MY MOLECULES.
ESPECIALLY USEFUL AFTER WHAT HAPPENED YESTERDAY.

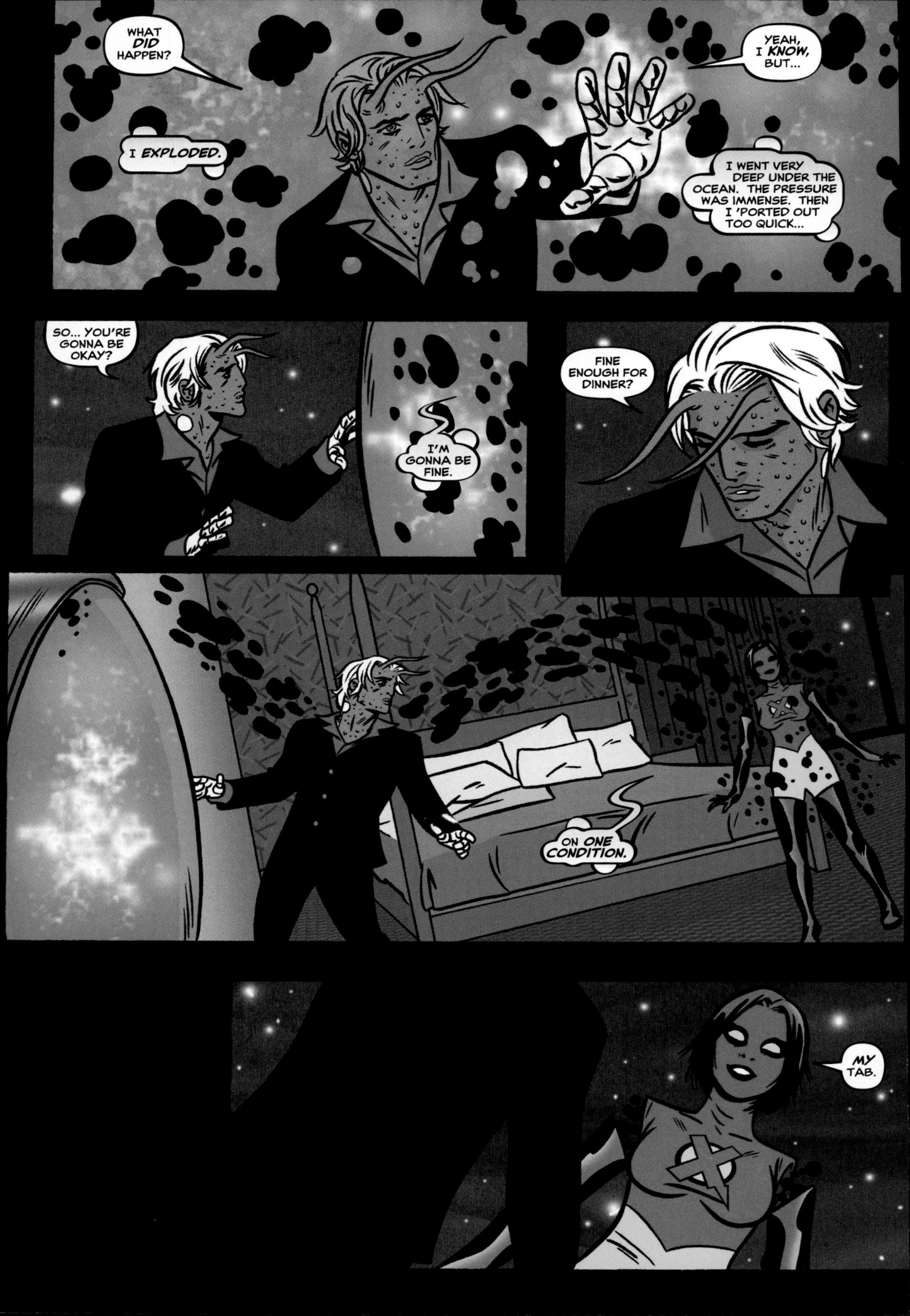
WHAT *DID* HAPPEN?
I *EXPLODED.*
YEAH, I *KNOW,* BUT...
I WENT VERY DEEP UNDER THE OCEAN. THE PRESSURE WAS IMMENSE. THEN I 'PORTED OUT TOO QUICK...
SO... YOU'RE GONNA BE OKAY?
I'M GONNA BE FINE.
FINE ENOUGH FOR DINNER?
ON *ONE CONDITION.*
MY TAB.

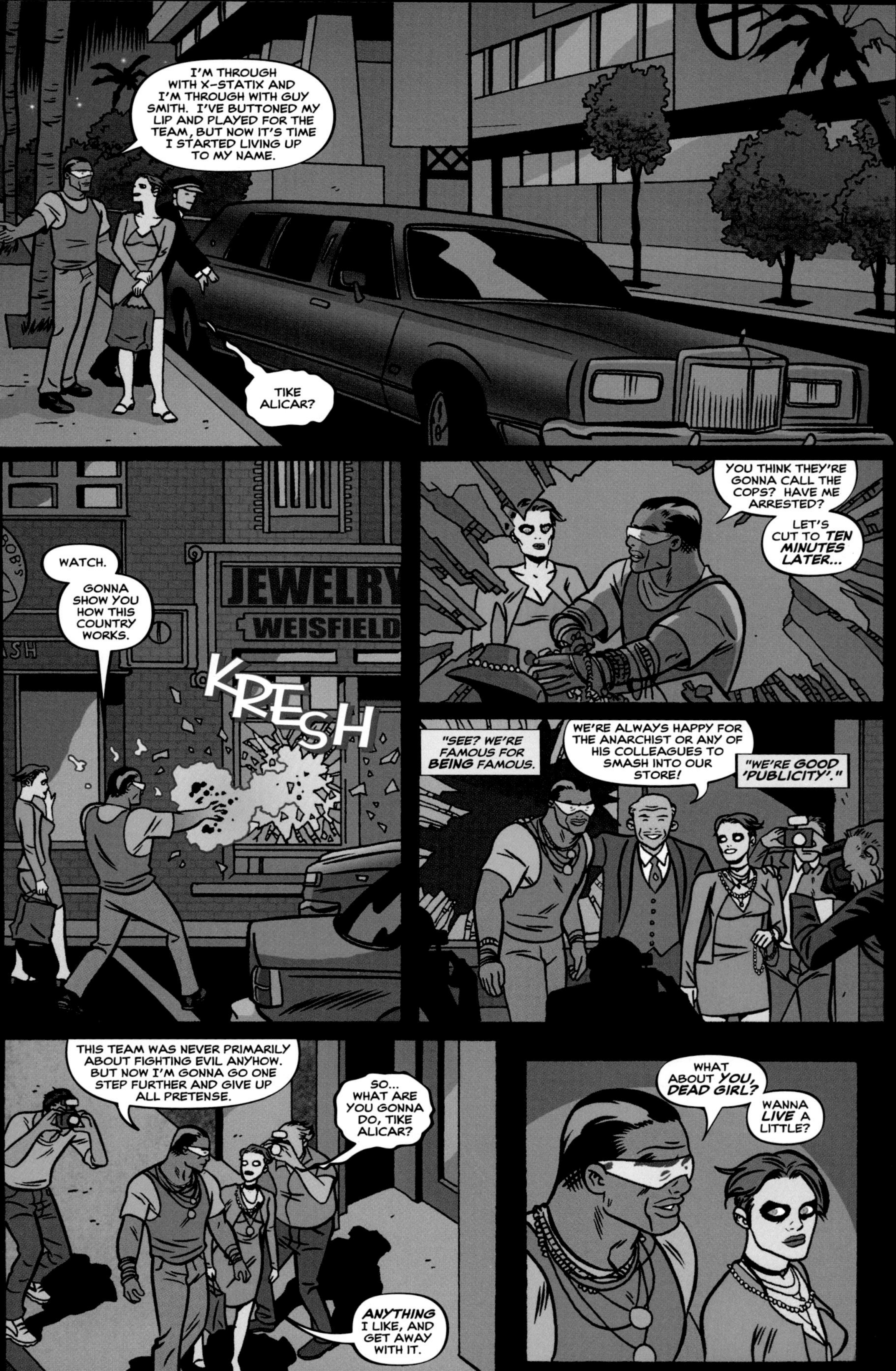

I'M THROUGH WITH X-STATIX AND I'M THROUGH WITH GUY SMITH. I'VE BUTTONED MY LIP AND PLAYED FOR THE TEAM, BUT NOW IT'S TIME I STARTED LIVING UP TO MY NAME.
TIKE ALICAR?
WATCH.
GONNA SHOW YOU HOW THIS COUNTRY WORKS.
JEWELRY
WEISFIELD
KRESH
YOU THINK THEY'RE GONNA CALL THE COPS? HAVE ME ARRESTED?
LET'S CUT TO TEN MINUTES LATER...
"SEE? WE'RE FAMOUS FOR BEING FAMOUS.
WE'RE ALWAYS HAPPY FOR THE ANARCHIST OR ANY OF HIS COLLEAGUES TO SMASH INTO OUR STORE!
"WE'RE GOOD 'PUBLICITY'."
THIS TEAM WAS NEVER PRIMARILY ABOUT FIGHTING EVIL ANYHOW. BUT NOW I'M GONNA GO ONE STEP FURTHER AND GIVE UP ALL PRETENSE.
SO... WHAT ARE YOU GONNA DO, TIKE ALICAR?
ANYTHING I LIKE, AND GET AWAY WITH IT.
WHAT ABOUT YOU, DEAD GIRL?
WANNA LIVE A LITTLE?

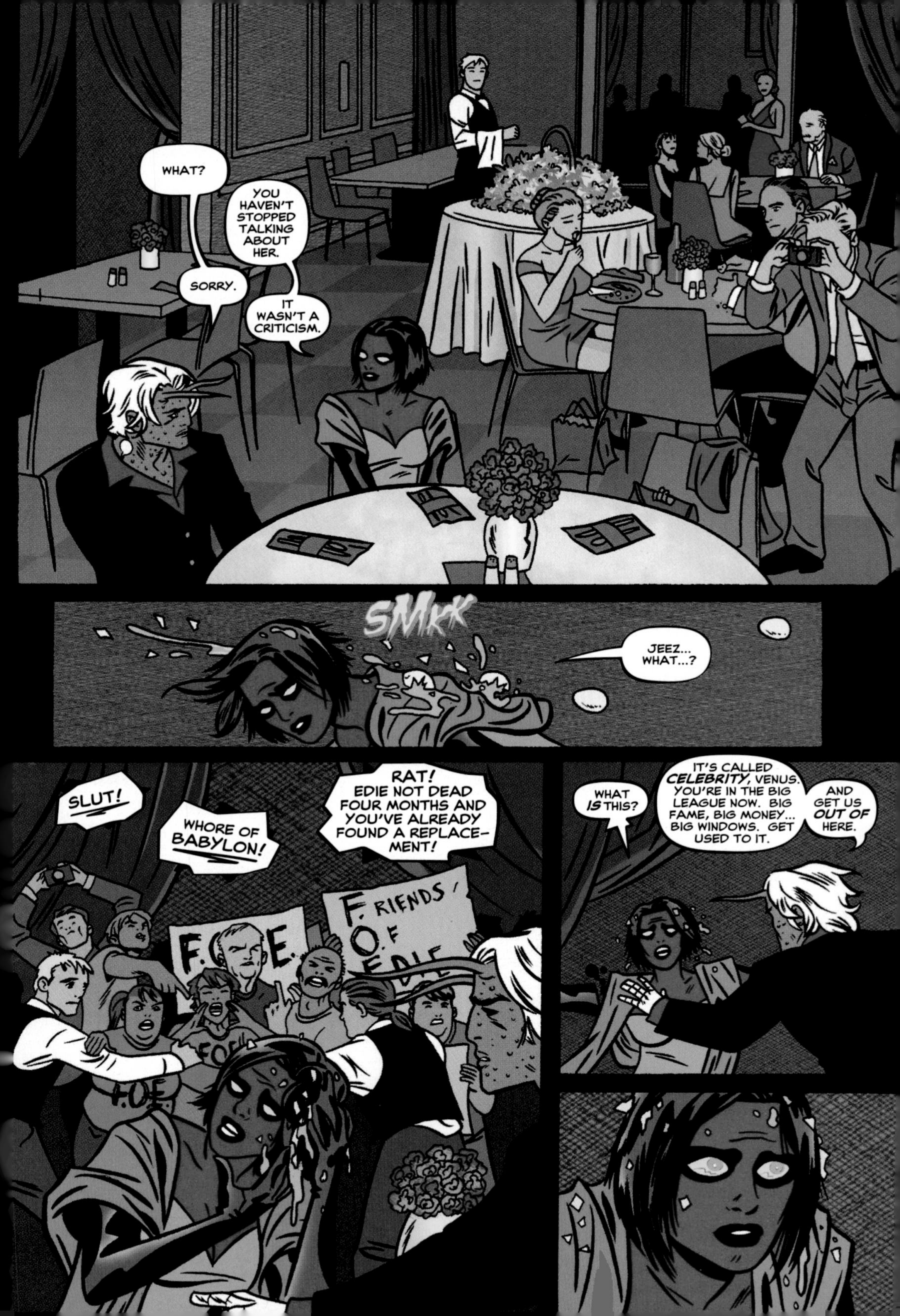
WHAT?
YOU HAVEN'T STOPPED TALKING ABOUT HER.
SORRY.
IT WASN'T A CRITICISM.
SMKK
JEEZ... WHAT...?
SLUT!
WHORE OF BABYLON!
RAT! EDIE NOT DEAD FOUR MONTHS AND YOU'VE ALREADY FOUND A REPLACEMENT!
F.O.E.
F.RIENDS O.F EDIE
F.O.E.
WHAT IS THIS?
IT'S CALLED CELEBRITY, VENUS. YOU'RE IN THE BIG LEAGUE NOW. BIG FAME, BIG MONEY... BIG WINDOWS. GET USED TO IT.
AND GET US OUT OF HERE.

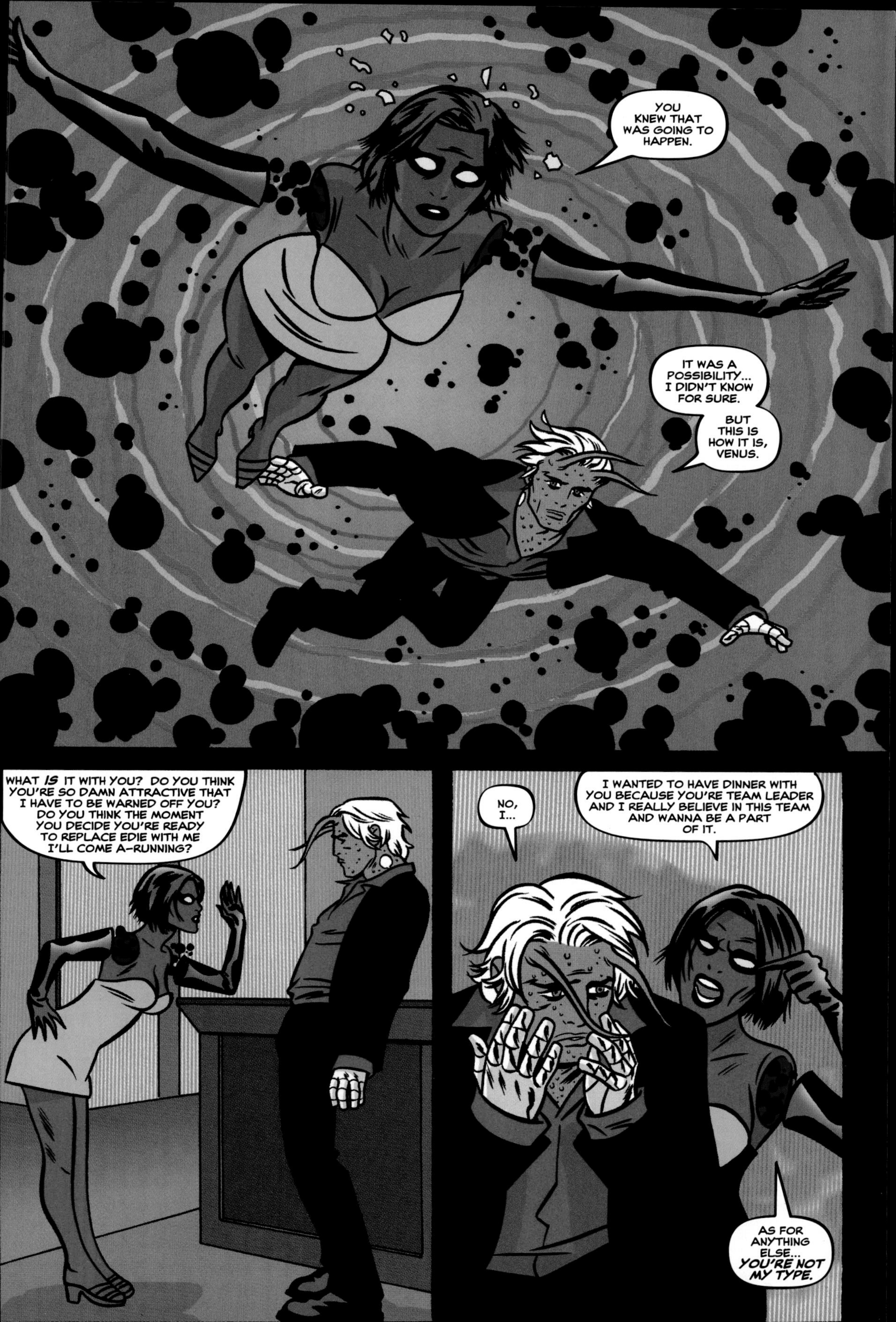

YOU KNEW THAT WAS GOING TO HAPPEN.
IT WAS A POSSIBILITY... I DIDN'T KNOW FOR SURE.
BUT THIS IS HOW IT IS, VENUS.
WHAT *IS* IT WITH YOU? DO YOU THINK YOU'RE SO DAMN ATTRACTIVE THAT I HAVE TO BE WARNED OFF YOU? DO YOU THINK THE MOMENT YOU DECIDE YOU'RE READY TO REPLACE EDIE WITH ME I'LL COME A-RUNNING?
NO, I...
I WANTED TO HAVE DINNER WITH YOU BECAUSE YOU'RE TEAM LEADER AND I REALLY BELIEVE IN THIS TEAM AND WANNA BE A PART OF IT.
AS FOR ANYTHING ELSE... ***YOU'RE NOT MY TYPE.***

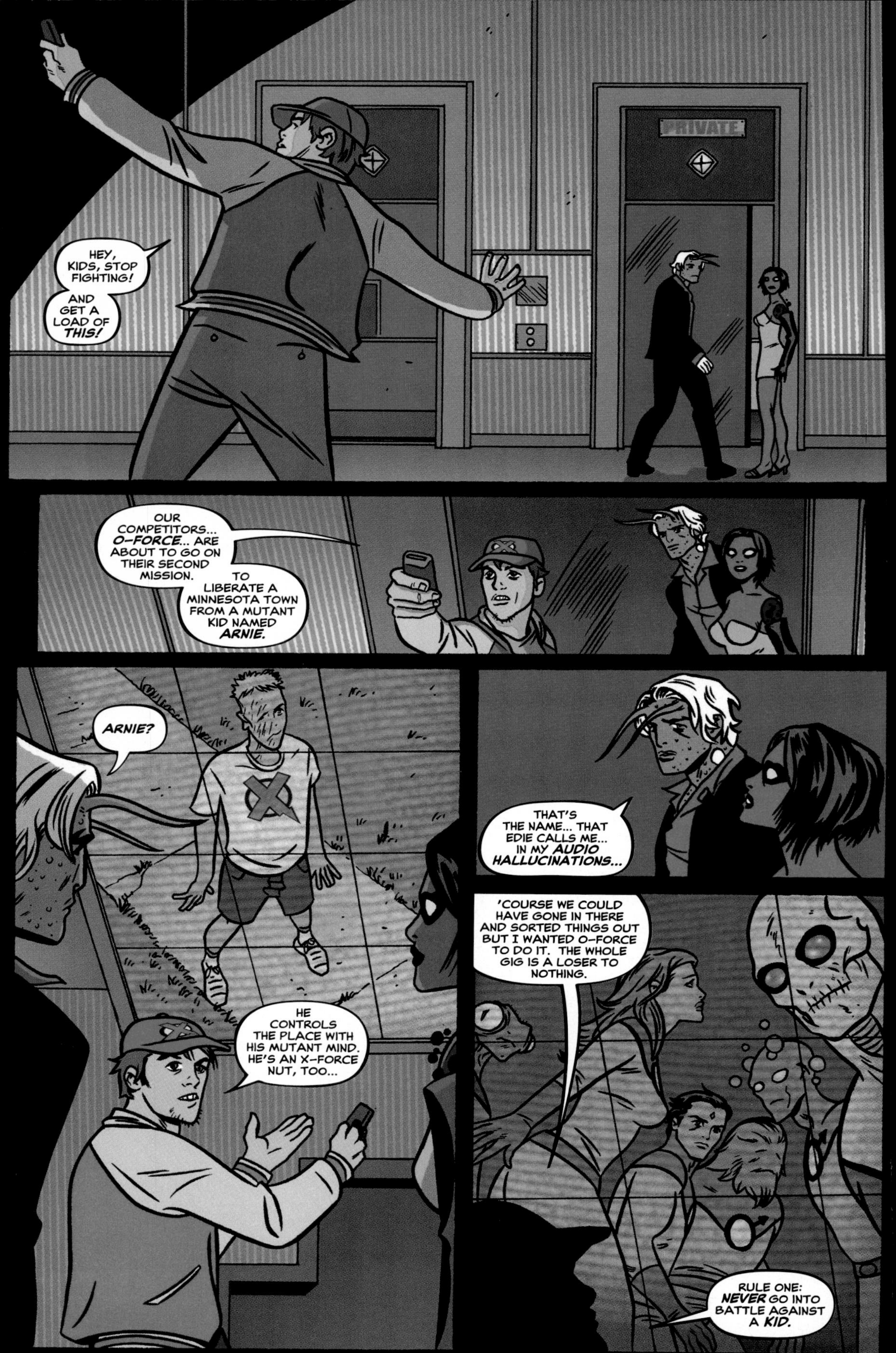
PRIVATE
HEY, KIDS, STOP FIGHTING!
AND GET A LOAD OF THIS!
OUR COMPETITORS... O-FORCE... ARE ABOUT TO GO ON THEIR SECOND MISSION.
TO LIBERATE A MINNESOTA TOWN FROM A MUTANT KID NAMED ARNIE.
ARNIE?
THAT'S THE NAME... THAT EDIE CALLS ME... IN MY AUDIO HALLUCINATIONS...
HE CONTROLS THE PLACE WITH HIS MUTANT MIND. HE'S AN X-FORCE NUT, TOO...
'COURSE WE COULD HAVE GONE IN THERE AND SORTED THINGS OUT BUT I WANTED O-FORCE TO DO IT. THE WHOLE GIG IS A LOSER TO NOTHING.
RULE ONE: NEVER GO INTO BATTLE AGAINST A KID.

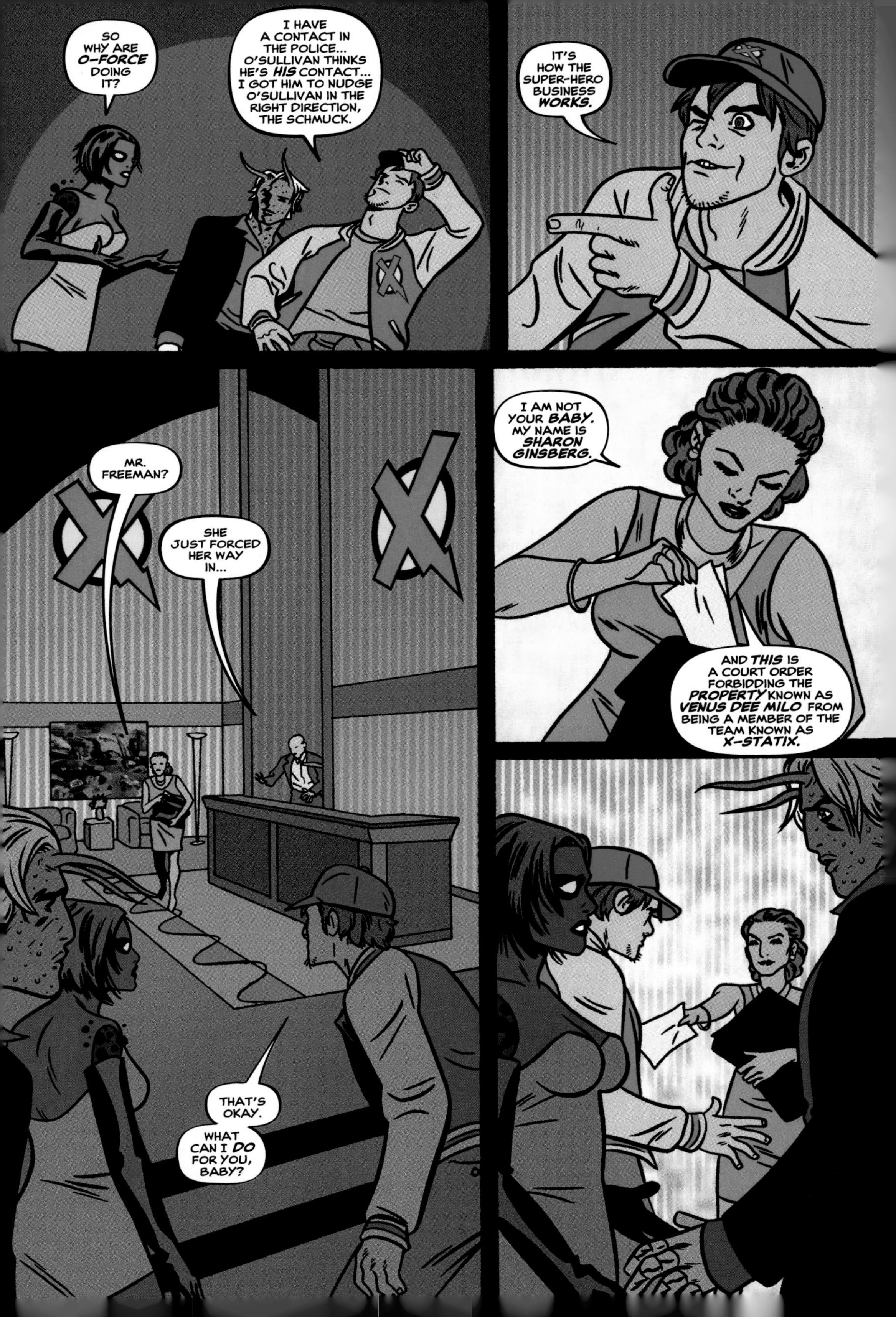
SO WHY ARE O-FORCE DOING IT?
I HAVE A CONTACT IN THE POLICE... O'SULLIVAN THINKS HE'S HIS CONTACT... I GOT HIM TO NUDGE O'SULLIVAN IN THE RIGHT DIRECTION, THE SCHMUCK.
IT'S HOW THE SUPER-HERO BUSINESS WORKS.
MR. FREEMAN?
SHE JUST FORCED HER WAY IN...
THAT'S OKAY.
WHAT CAN I DO FOR YOU, BABY?
I AM NOT YOUR BABY. MY NAME IS SHARON GINSBERG.
AND THIS IS A COURT ORDER FORBIDDING THE PROPERTY KNOWN AS VENUS DEE MILO FROM BEING A MEMBER OF THE TEAM KNOWN AS X-STATIX.

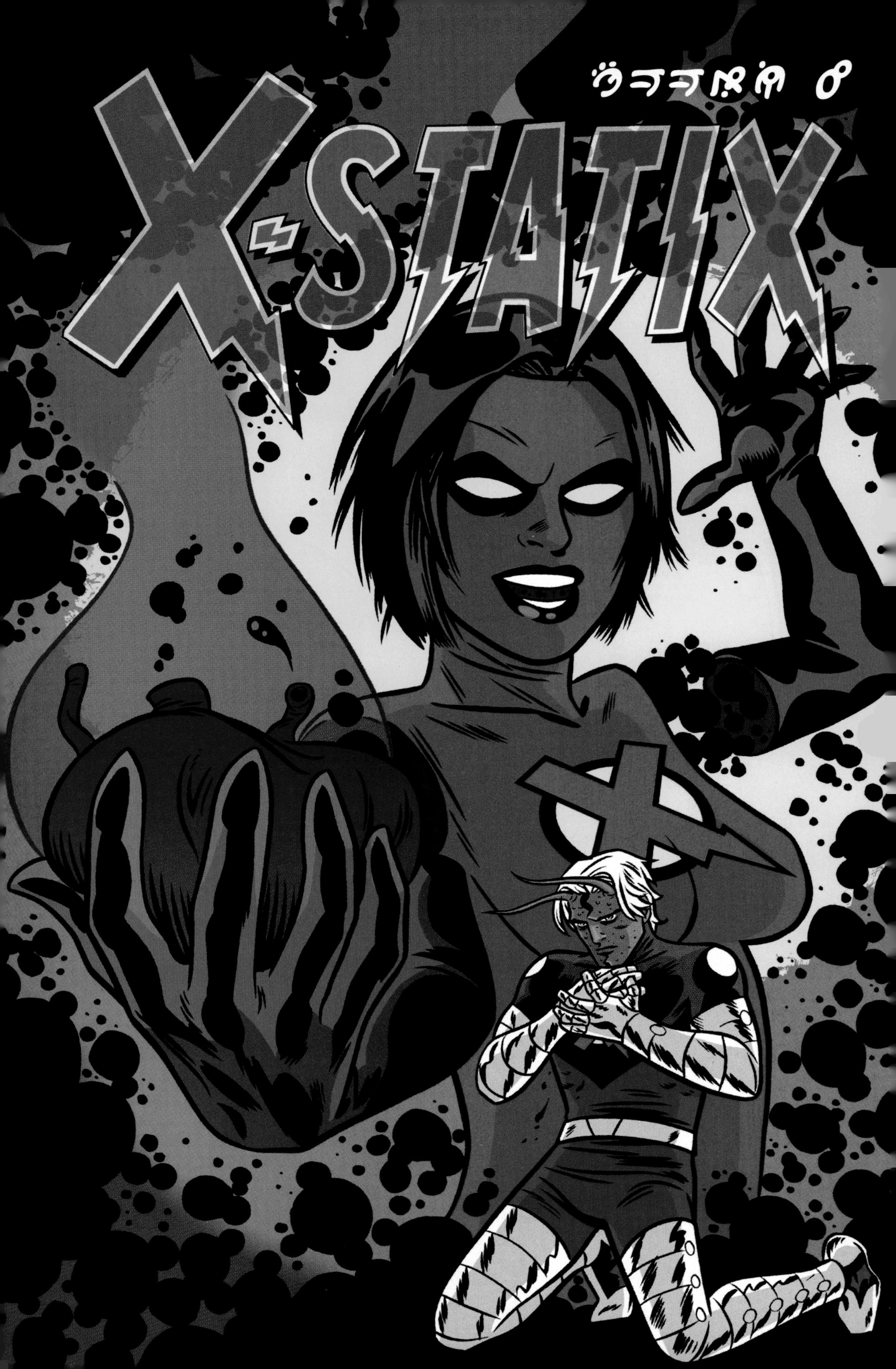
X-STATIX

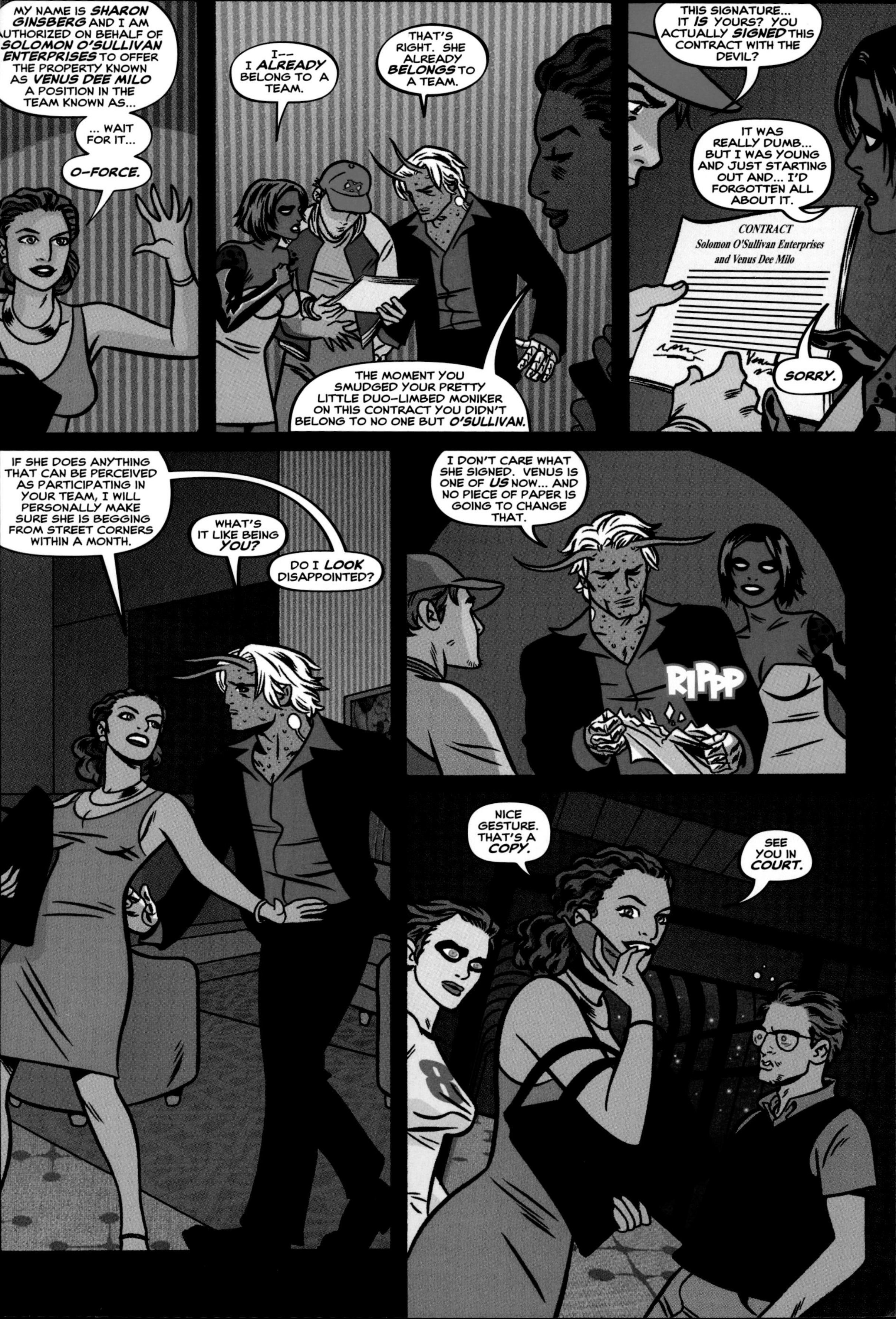

MY NAME IS SHARON GINSBERG AND I AM AUTHORIZED ON BEHALF OF SOLOMON O'SULLIVAN ENTERPRISES TO OFFER THE PROPERTY KNOWN AS VENUS DEE MILO A POSITION IN THE TEAM KNOWN AS...
... WAIT FOR IT...
O-FORCE.
I-- I ALREADY BELONG TO A TEAM.
THAT'S RIGHT. SHE ALREADY BELONGS TO A TEAM.
THE MOMENT YOU SMUDGED YOUR PRETTY LITTLE DUO-LIMBED MONIKER ON THIS CONTRACT YOU DIDN'T BELONG TO NO ONE BUT O'SULLIVAN.
THIS SIGNATURE... IT IS YOURS? YOU ACTUALLY SIGNED THIS CONTRACT WITH THE DEVIL?
IT WAS REALLY DUMB... BUT I WAS YOUNG AND JUST STARTING OUT AND... I'D FORGOTTEN ALL ABOUT IT.
CONTRACT
Solomon O'Sullivan Enterprises
and Venus Dee Milo
SORRY.
IF SHE DOES ANYTHING THAT CAN BE PERCEIVED AS PARTICIPATING IN YOUR TEAM, I WILL PERSONALLY MAKE SURE SHE IS BEGGING FROM STREET CORNERS WITHIN A MONTH.
WHAT'S IT LIKE BEING YOU?
DO I LOOK DISAPPOINTED?
I DON'T CARE WHAT SHE SIGNED. VENUS IS ONE OF US NOW... AND NO PIECE OF PAPER IS GOING TO CHANGE THAT.
RIPPP
NICE GESTURE. THAT'S A COPY.
SEE YOU IN COURT.

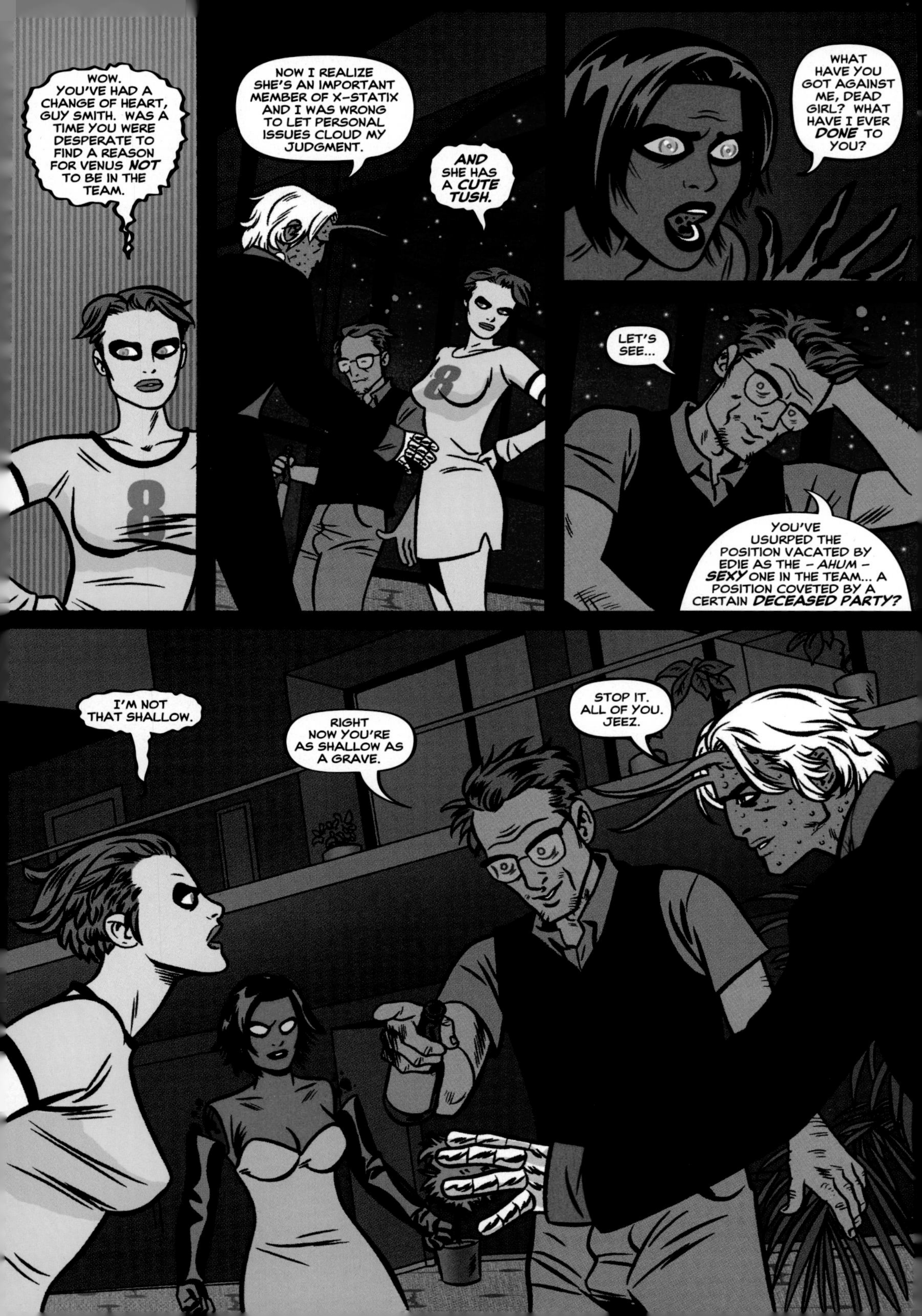
WOW. YOU'VE HAD A CHANGE OF HEART, GUY SMITH. WAS A TIME YOU WERE DESPERATE TO FIND A REASON FOR VENUS *NOT* TO BE IN THE TEAM.
NOW I REALIZE SHE'S AN IMPORTANT MEMBER OF X-STATIX AND I WAS WRONG TO LET PERSONAL ISSUES CLOUD MY JUDGMENT.
AND SHE HAS A *CUTE TUSH.*
WHAT HAVE YOU GOT AGAINST ME, DEAD GIRL? WHAT HAVE I EVER *DONE* TO YOU?
LET'S SEE...
YOU'VE USURPED THE POSITION VACATED BY EDIE AS THE *– AHUM – SEXY* ONE IN THE TEAM... A POSITION COVETED BY A CERTAIN *DECEASED PARTY?*
I'M NOT THAT SHALLOW.
RIGHT NOW YOU'RE AS SHALLOW AS A GRAVE.
STOP IT. ALL OF YOU. JEEZ.

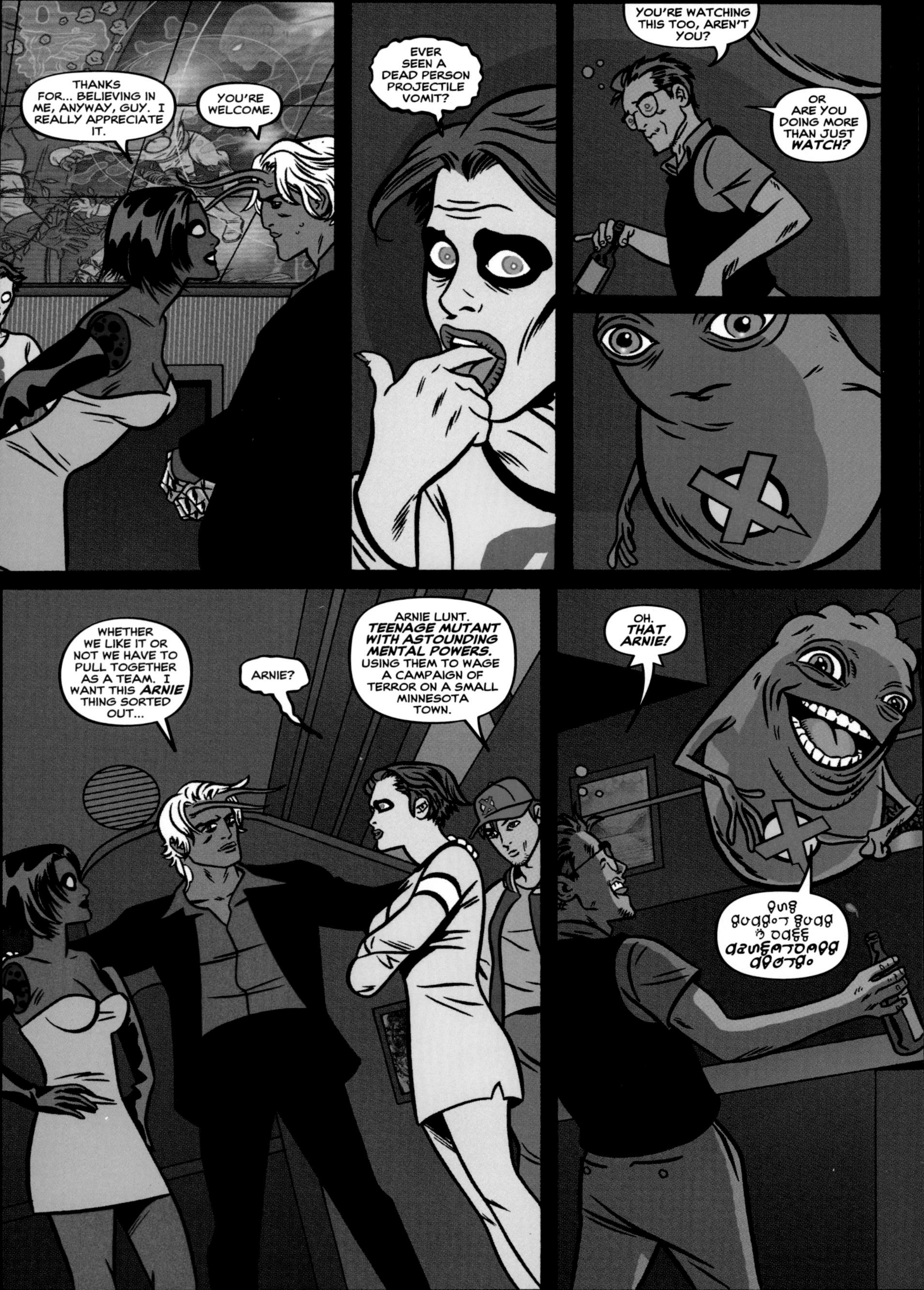
THANKS FOR... BELIEVING IN ME, ANYWAY, GUY. I REALLY APPRECIATE IT.
YOU'RE WELCOME.
EVER SEEN A DEAD PERSON PROJECTILE VOMIT?
YOU'RE WATCHING THIS TOO, AREN'T YOU?
OR ARE YOU DOING MORE THAN JUST *WATCH?*
WHETHER WE LIKE IT OR NOT WE HAVE TO PULL TOGETHER AS A TEAM. I WANT THIS *ARNIE* THING SORTED OUT...
ARNIE?
ARNIE LUNT. *TEENAGE MUTANT WITH ASTOUNDING MENTAL POWERS.* USING THEM TO WAGE A CAMPAIGN OF TERROR ON A SMALL MINNESOTA TOWN.
OH. *THAT ARNIE!*

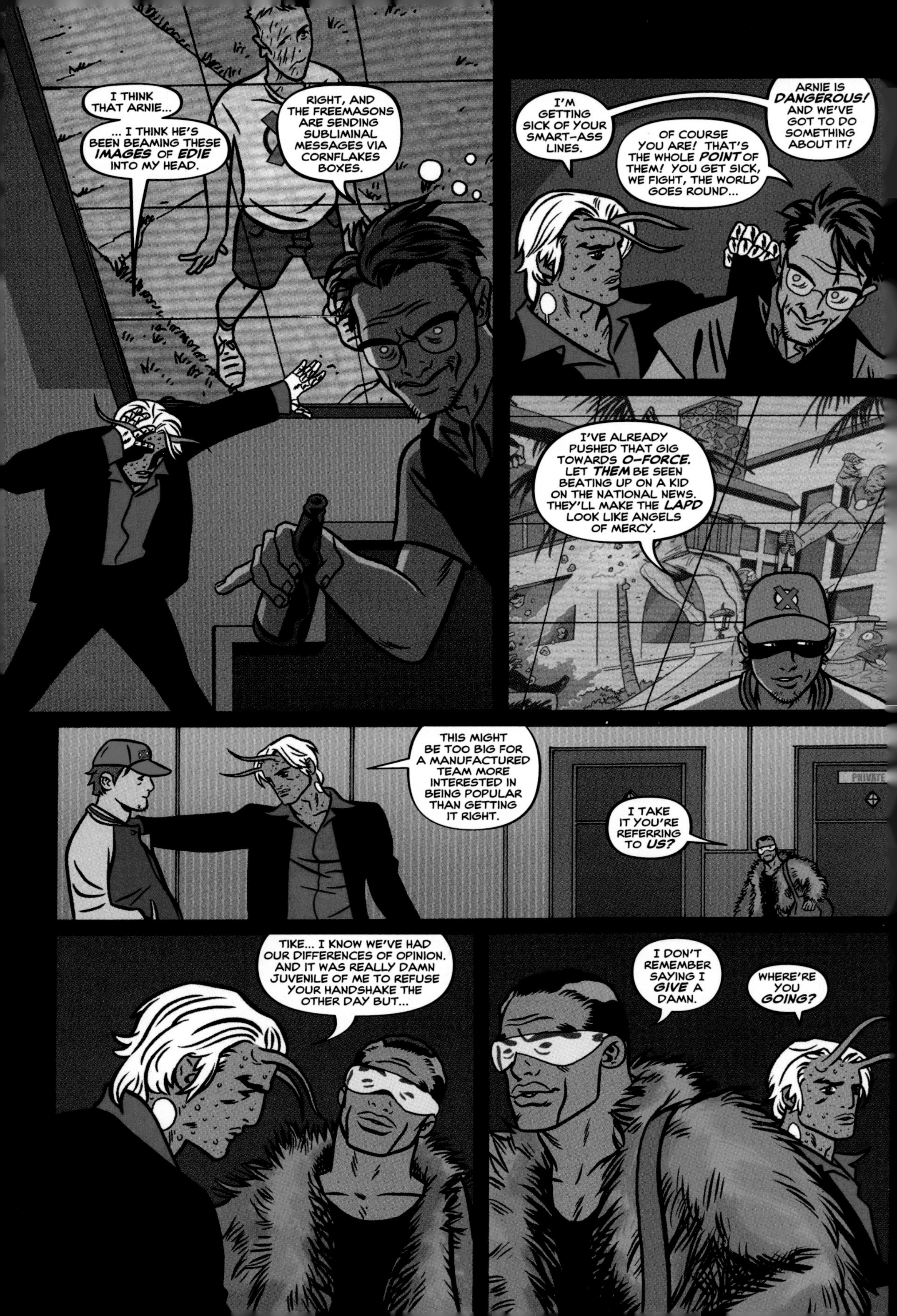
I THINK THAT ARNIE...
... I THINK HE'S BEEN BEAMING THESE IMAGES OF EDIE INTO MY HEAD.
RIGHT, AND THE FREEMASONS ARE SENDING SUBLIMINAL MESSAGES VIA CORNFLAKES BOXES.
I'M GETTING SICK OF YOUR SMART-ASS LINES.
ARNIE IS DANGEROUS! AND WE'VE GOT TO DO SOMETHING ABOUT IT!
OF COURSE YOU ARE! THAT'S THE WHOLE POINT OF THEM! YOU GET SICK, WE FIGHT, THE WORLD GOES ROUND...
I'VE ALREADY PUSHED THAT GIG TOWARDS O-FORCE. LET THEM BE SEEN BEATING UP ON A KID ON THE NATIONAL NEWS. THEY'LL MAKE THE LAPD LOOK LIKE ANGELS OF MERCY.
THIS MIGHT BE TOO BIG FOR A MANUFACTURED TEAM MORE INTERESTED IN BEING POPULAR THAN GETTING IT RIGHT.
PRIVATE
I TAKE IT YOU'RE REFERRING TO US?
TIKE... I KNOW WE'VE HAD OUR DIFFERENCES OF OPINION. AND IT WAS REALLY DAMN JUVENILE OF ME TO REFUSE YOUR HANDSHAKE THE OTHER DAY BUT...
I DON'T REMEMBER SAYING I GIVE A DAMN.
WHERE'RE YOU GOING?

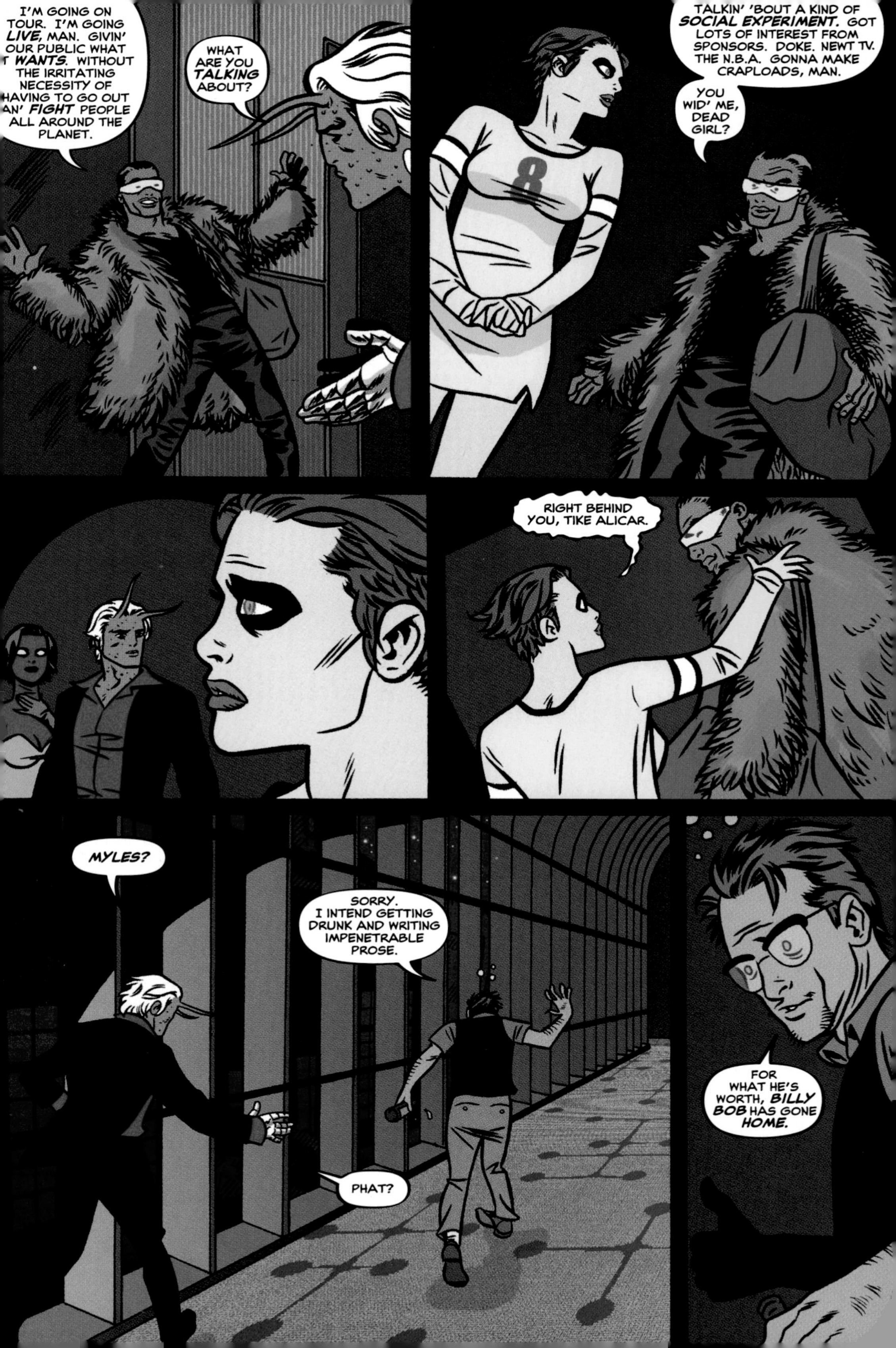
I'M GOING ON TOUR. I'M GOING LIVE, MAN. GIVIN' OUR PUBLIC WHAT IT WANTS. WITHOUT THE IRRITATING NECESSITY OF HAVING TO GO OUT AN' FIGHT PEOPLE ALL AROUND THE PLANET.
WHAT ARE YOU TALKING ABOUT?
TALKIN' 'BOUT A KIND OF SOCIAL EXPERIMENT. GOT LOTS OF INTEREST FROM SPONSORS. DOKE. NEWT TV. THE N.B.A. GONNA MAKE CRAPLOADS, MAN.
YOU WID' ME, DEAD GIRL?
RIGHT BEHIND YOU, TIKE ALICAR.
MYLES?
SORRY. I INTEND GETTING DRUNK AND WRITING IMPENETRABLE PROSE.
PHAT?
FOR WHAT HE'S WORTH, BILLY BOB HAS GONE HOME.

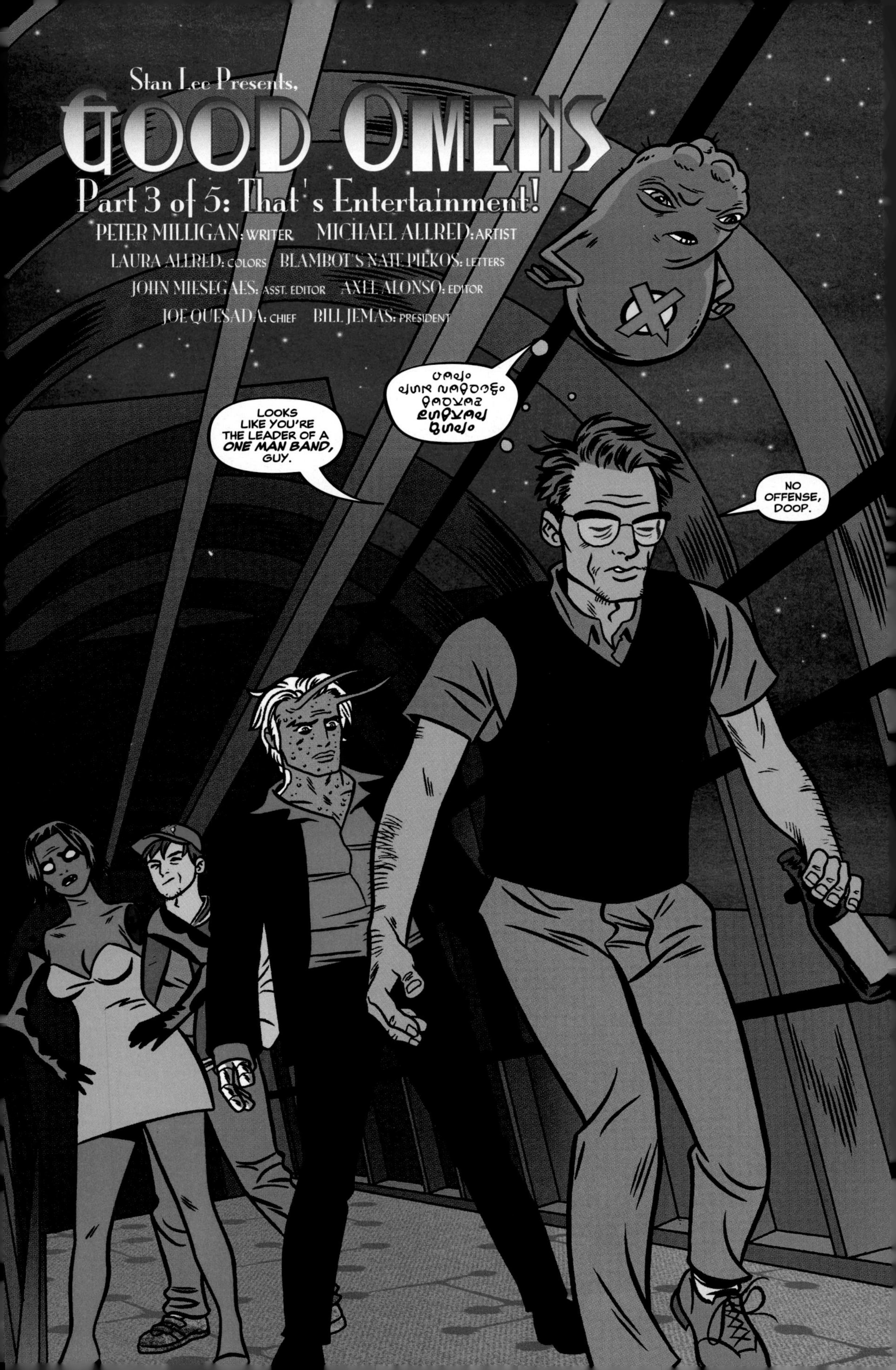
Stan Lee Presents,
GOOD OMENS
Part 3 of 5: That's Entertainment!
PETER MILLIGAN: WRITER MICHAEL ALLRED: ARTIST
LAURA ALLRED: COLORS BLAMBOT'S NATE PIEKOS: LETTERS
JOHN MIESEGAES: ASST. EDITOR AXEL ALONSO: EDITOR
JOE QUESADA: CHIEF BILL JEMAS: PRESIDENT
LOOKS LIKE YOU'RE THE LEADER OF A ONE MAN BAND, GUY.
NO OFFENSE, DOOP.

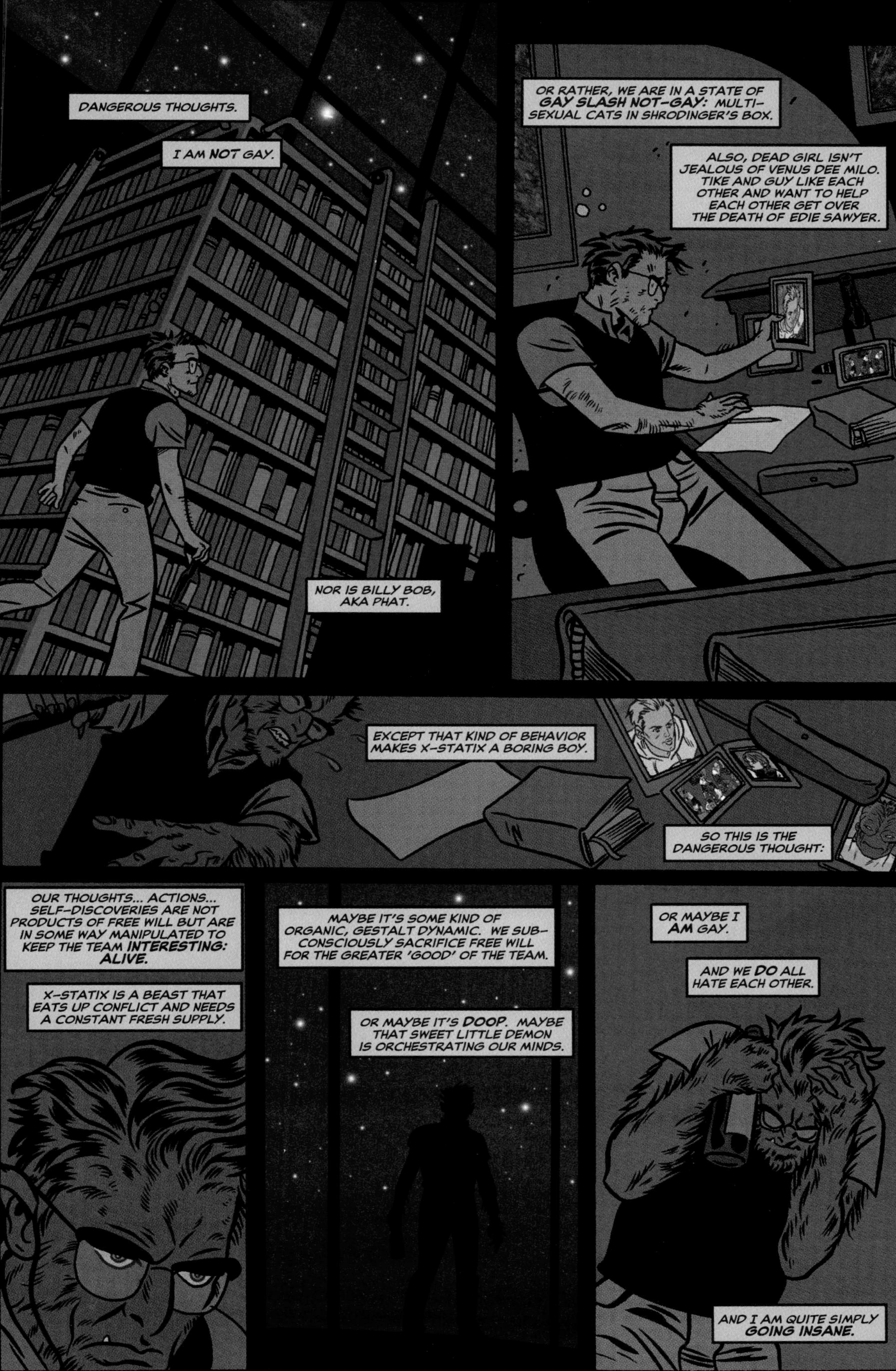
DANGEROUS THOUGHTS.
I AM NOT GAY.
NOR IS BILLY BOB, AKA PHAT.
OR RATHER, WE ARE IN A STATE OF GAY SLASH NOT-GAY: MULTI-SEXUAL CATS IN SHRODINGER'S BOX.
ALSO, DEAD GIRL ISN'T JEALOUS OF VENUS DEE MILO. TIKE AND GUY LIKE EACH OTHER AND WANT TO HELP EACH OTHER GET OVER THE DEATH OF EDIE SAWYER.
EXCEPT THAT KIND OF BEHAVIOR MAKES X-STATIX A BORING BOY.
SO THIS IS THE DANGEROUS THOUGHT:
OUR THOUGHTS... ACTIONS... SELF-DISCOVERIES ARE NOT PRODUCTS OF FREE WILL BUT ARE IN SOME WAY MANIPULATED TO KEEP THE TEAM INTERESTING: ALIVE.
X-STATIX IS A BEAST THAT EATS UP CONFLICT AND NEEDS A CONSTANT FRESH SUPPLY.
MAYBE IT'S SOME KIND OF ORGANIC, GESTALT DYNAMIC. WE SUB-CONSCIOUSLY SACRIFICE FREE WILL FOR THE GREATER 'GOOD' OF THE TEAM.
OR MAYBE IT'S DOOP. MAYBE THAT SWEET LITTLE DEMON IS ORCHESTRATING OUR MINDS.
OR MAYBE I AM GAY.
AND WE DO ALL HATE EACH OTHER.
AND I AM QUITE SIMPLY GOING INSANE.

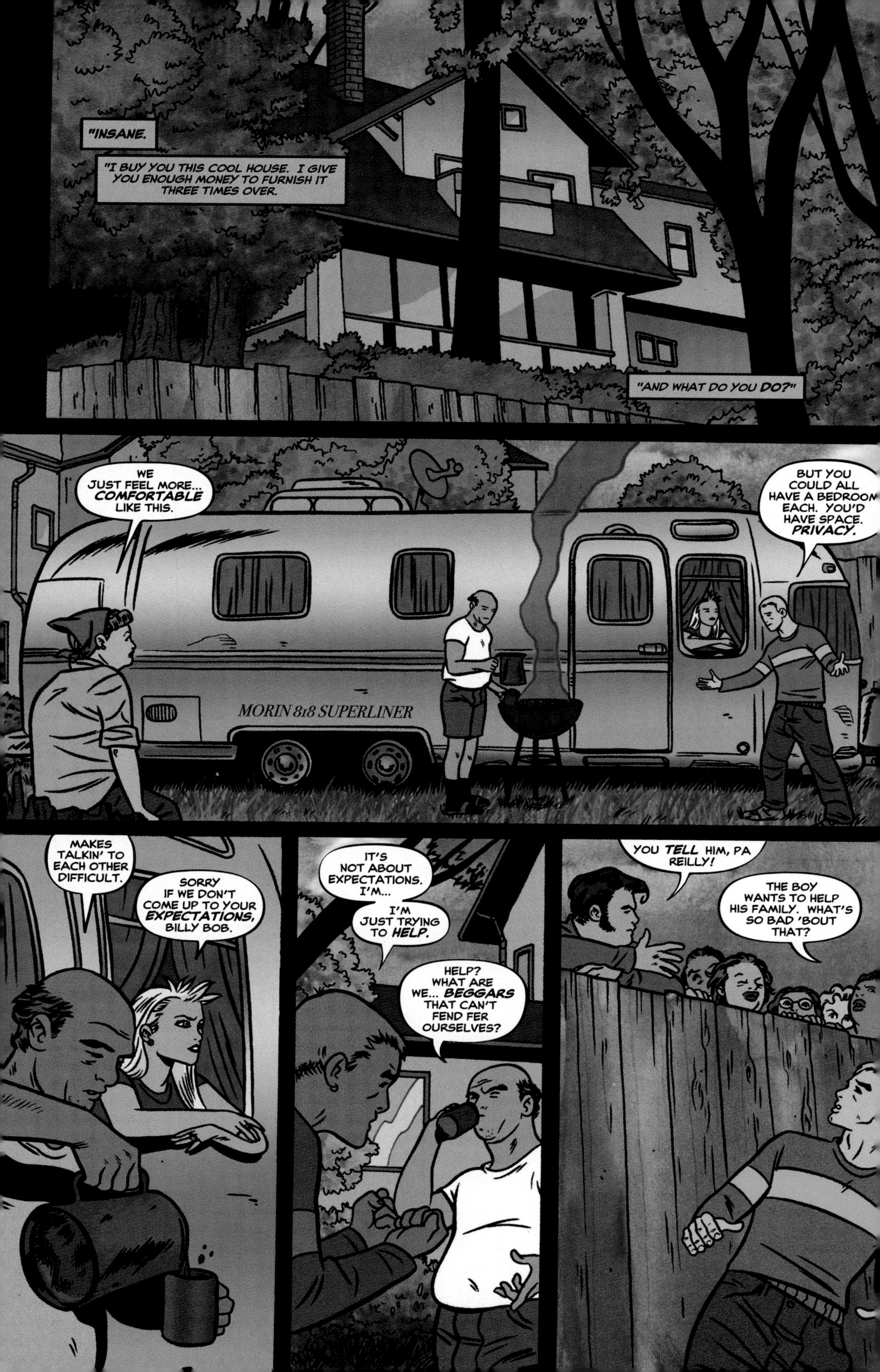
"INSANE.
"I BUY YOU THIS COOL HOUSE. I GIVE YOU ENOUGH MONEY TO FURNISH IT THREE TIMES OVER.
"AND WHAT DO YOU DO?"
WE JUST FEEL MORE... COMFORTABLE LIKE THIS.
BUT YOU COULD ALL HAVE A BEDROOM EACH. YOU'D HAVE SPACE. PRIVACY.
MORIN 818 SUPERLINER
MAKES TALKIN' TO EACH OTHER DIFFICULT.
SORRY IF WE DON'T COME UP TO YOUR EXPECTATIONS, BILLY BOB.
IT'S NOT ABOUT EXPECTATIONS. I'M...
I'M JUST TRYING TO HELP.
HELP? WHAT ARE WE... BEGGARS THAT CAN'T FEND FER OURSELVES?
YOU TELL HIM, PA REILLY!
THE BOY WANTS TO HELP HIS FAMILY. WHAT'S SO BAD 'BOUT THAT?

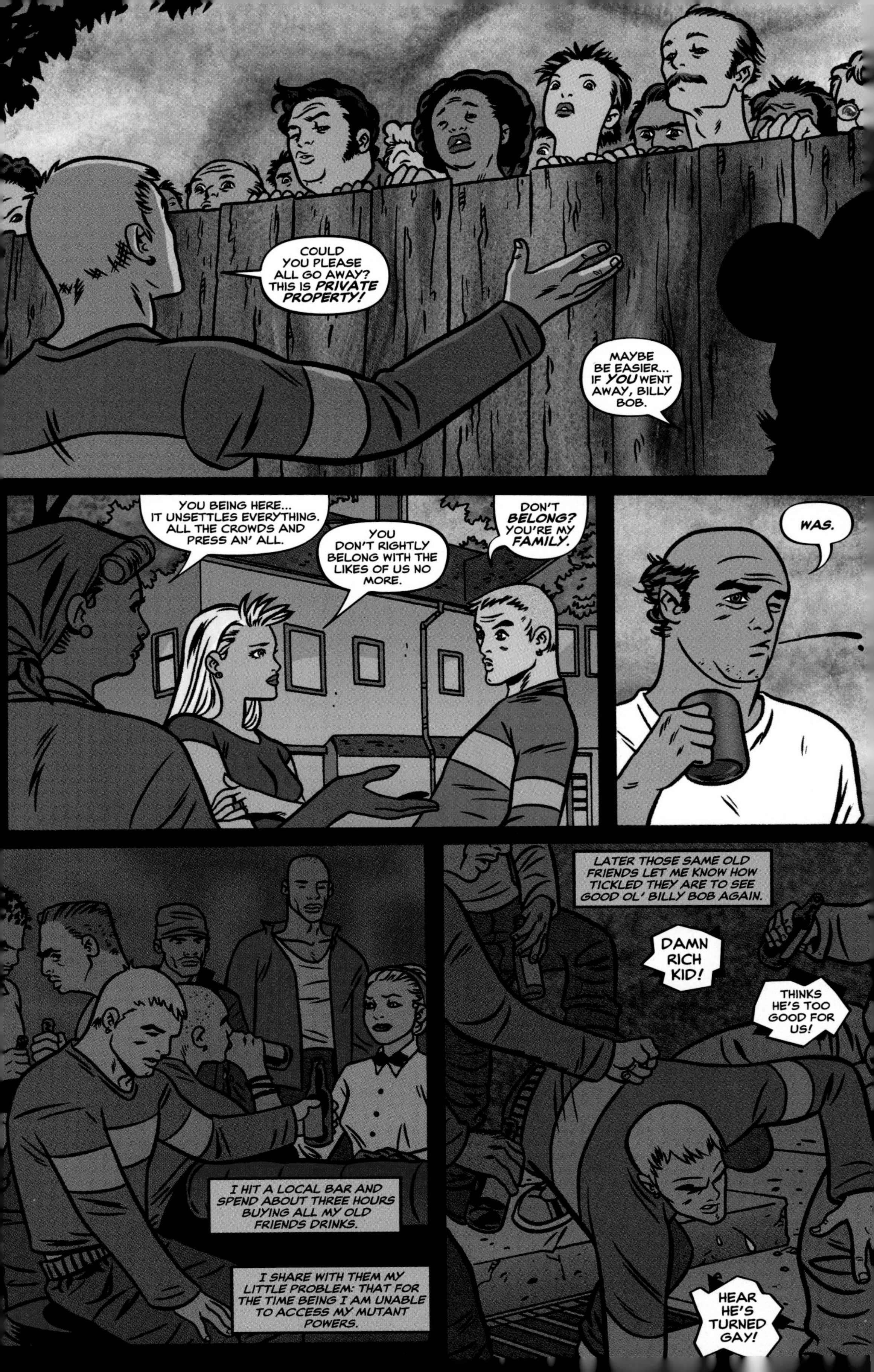
COULD YOU PLEASE ALL GO AWAY? THIS IS PRIVATE PROPERTY!
MAYBE BE EASIER... IF YOU WENT AWAY, BILLY BOB.
YOU BEING HERE... IT UNSETTLES EVERYTHING. ALL THE CROWDS AND PRESS AN' ALL.
YOU DON'T RIGHTLY BELONG WITH THE LIKES OF US NO MORE.
DON'T BELONG? YOU'RE MY FAMILY.
WAS.
I HIT A LOCAL BAR AND SPEND ABOUT THREE HOURS BUYING ALL MY OLD FRIENDS DRINKS.
I SHARE WITH THEM MY LITTLE PROBLEM: THAT FOR THE TIME BEING I AM UNABLE TO ACCESS MY MUTANT POWERS.
LATER THOSE SAME OLD FRIENDS LET ME KNOW HOW TICKLED THEY ARE TO SEE GOOD OL' BILLY BOB AGAIN.
DAMN RICH KID!
THINKS HE'S TOO GOOD FOR US!
HEAR HE'S TURNED GAY!

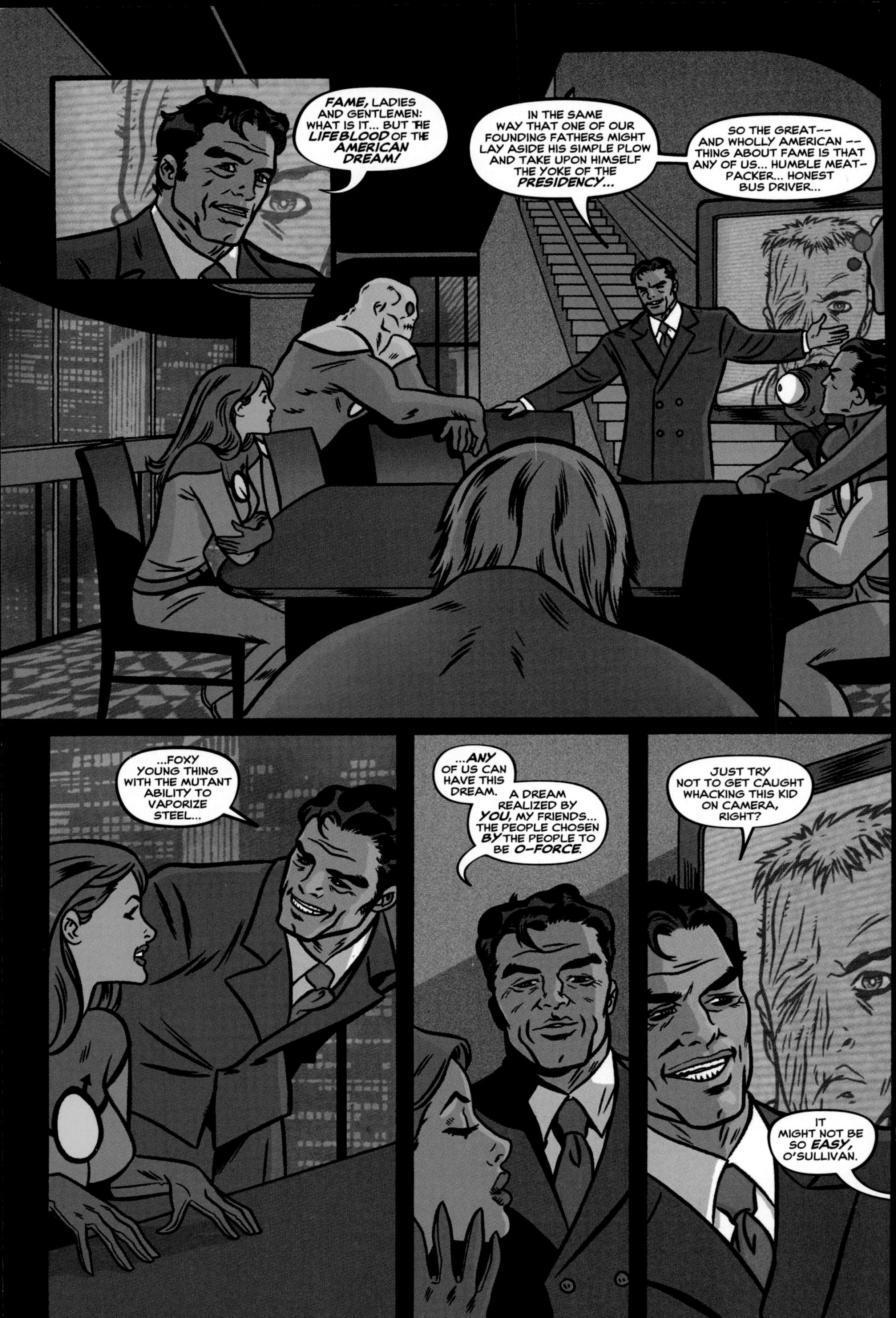
FAME, LADIES AND GENTLEMEN: WHAT IS IT... BUT THE LIFEBLOOD OF THE AMERICAN DREAM!
IN THE SAME WAY THAT ONE OF OUR FOUNDING FATHERS MIGHT LAY ASIDE HIS SIMPLE PLOW AND TAKE UPON HIMSELF THE YOKE OF THE PRESIDENCY...
SO THE GREAT-- AND WHOLLY AMERICAN -- THING ABOUT FAME IS THAT ANY OF US... HUMBLE MEAT-PACKER... HONEST BUS DRIVER...
...FOXY YOUNG THING WITH THE MUTANT ABILITY TO VAPORIZE STEEL...
...ANY OF US CAN HAVE THIS DREAM.
A DREAM REALIZED BY YOU, MY FRIENDS... THE PEOPLE CHOSEN BY THE PEOPLE TO BE O-FORCE.
JUST TRY NOT TO GET CAUGHT WHACKING THIS KID ON CAMERA, RIGHT?
IT MIGHT NOT BE SO EASY, O'SULLIVAN.

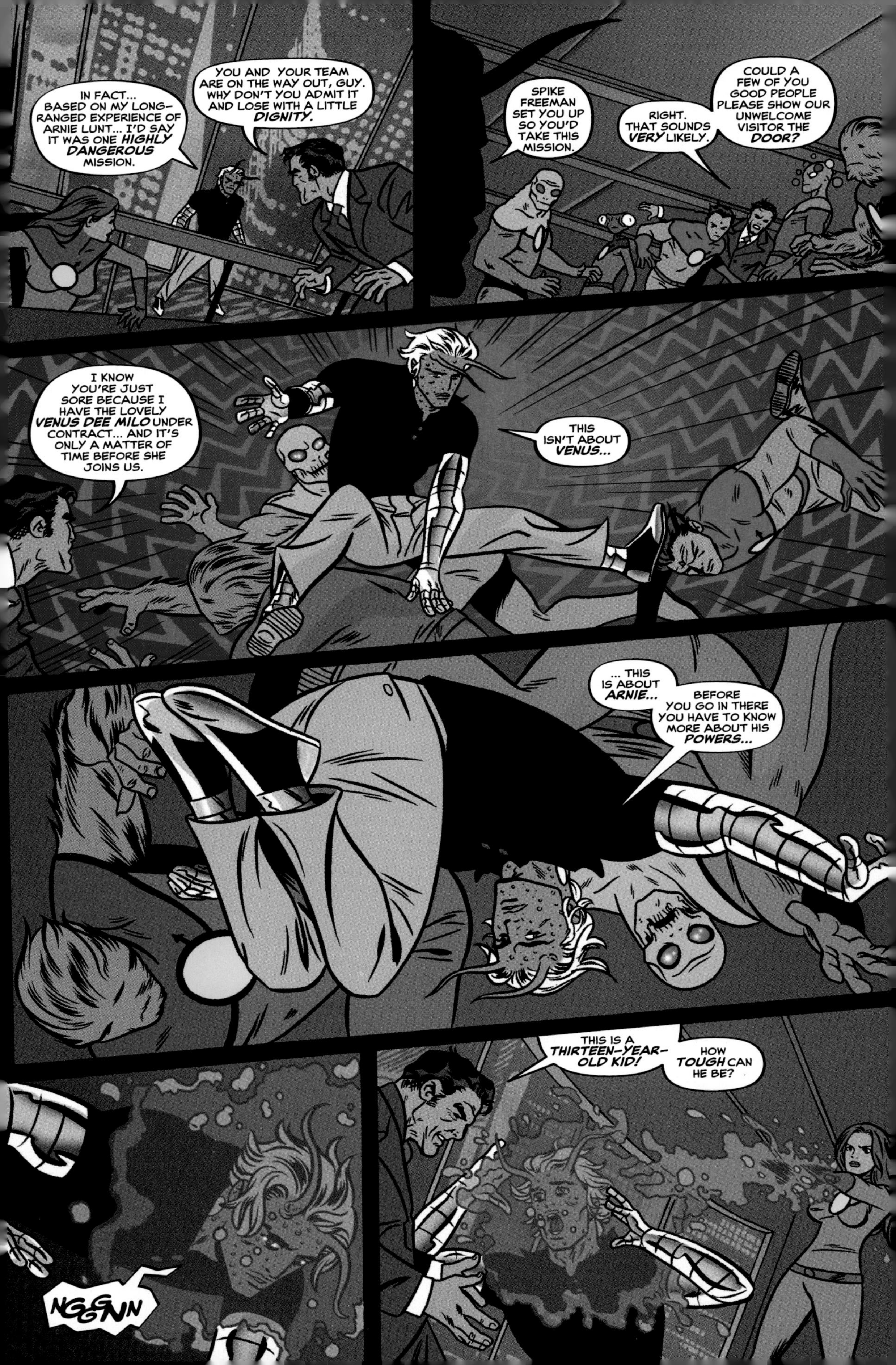
IN FACT... BASED ON MY LONG-RANGED EXPERIENCE OF ARNIE LUNT... I'D SAY IT WAS ONE HIGHLY DANGEROUS MISSION.
YOU AND YOUR TEAM ARE ON THE WAY OUT, GUY. WHY DON'T YOU ADMIT IT AND LOSE WITH A LITTLE DIGNITY.
SPIKE FREEMAN SET YOU UP SO YOU'D TAKE THIS MISSION.
RIGHT. THAT SOUNDS VERY LIKELY.
COULD A FEW OF YOU GOOD PEOPLE PLEASE SHOW OUR UNWELCOME VISITOR THE DOOR?
I KNOW YOU'RE JUST SORE BECAUSE I HAVE THE LOVELY VENUS DEE MILO UNDER CONTRACT... AND IT'S ONLY A MATTER OF TIME BEFORE SHE JOINS US.
THIS ISN'T ABOUT VENUS...
... THIS IS ABOUT ARNIE...
BEFORE YOU GO IN THERE YOU HAVE TO KNOW MORE ABOUT HIS POWERS...
NGGGNN
THIS IS A THIRTEEN-YEAR-OLD KID!
HOW TOUGH CAN HE BE?

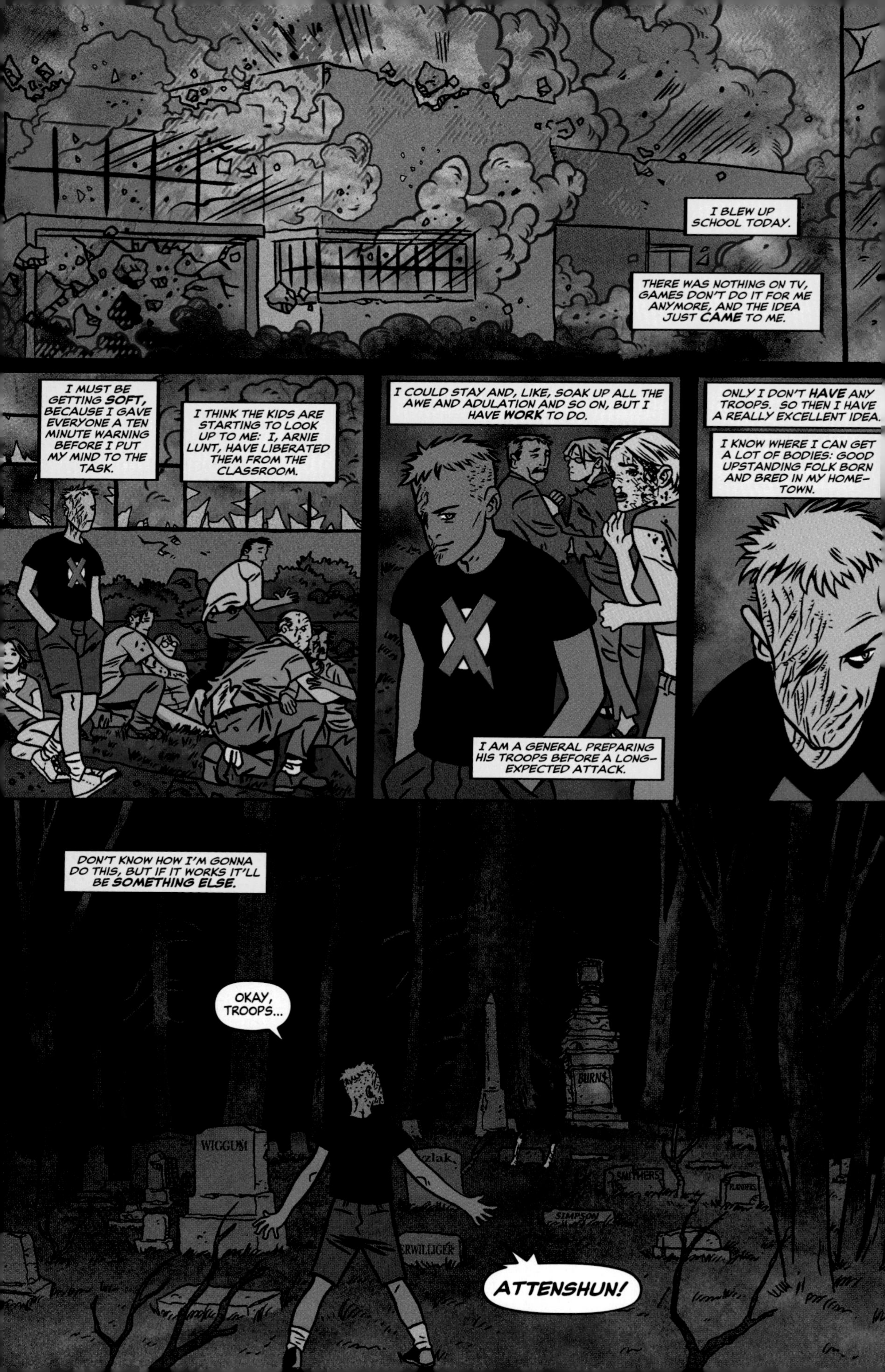

I BLEW UP SCHOOL TODAY.
THERE WAS NOTHING ON TV, GAMES DON'T DO IT FOR ME ANYMORE, AND THE IDEA JUST CAME TO ME.
I MUST BE GETTING SOFT, BECAUSE I GAVE EVERYONE A TEN MINUTE WARNING BEFORE I PUT MY MIND TO THE TASK.
I THINK THE KIDS ARE STARTING TO LOOK UP TO ME: I, ARNIE LUNT, HAVE LIBERATED THEM FROM THE CLASSROOM.
I COULD STAY AND, LIKE, SOAK UP ALL THE AWE AND ADULATION AND SO ON, BUT I HAVE WORK TO DO.
I AM A GENERAL PREPARING HIS TROOPS BEFORE A LONG-EXPECTED ATTACK.
ONLY I DON'T HAVE ANY TROOPS. SO THEN I HAVE A REALLY EXCELLENT IDEA.
I KNOW WHERE I CAN GET A LOT OF BODIES: GOOD UPSTANDING FOLK BORN AND BRED IN MY HOME-TOWN.
DON'T KNOW HOW I'M GONNA DO THIS, BUT IF IT WORKS IT'LL BE SOMETHING ELSE.
OKAY, TROOPS...
WIGGUM
BURNS
SMITHERS
SIMPSON
FLANDERS
ATTENSHUN!

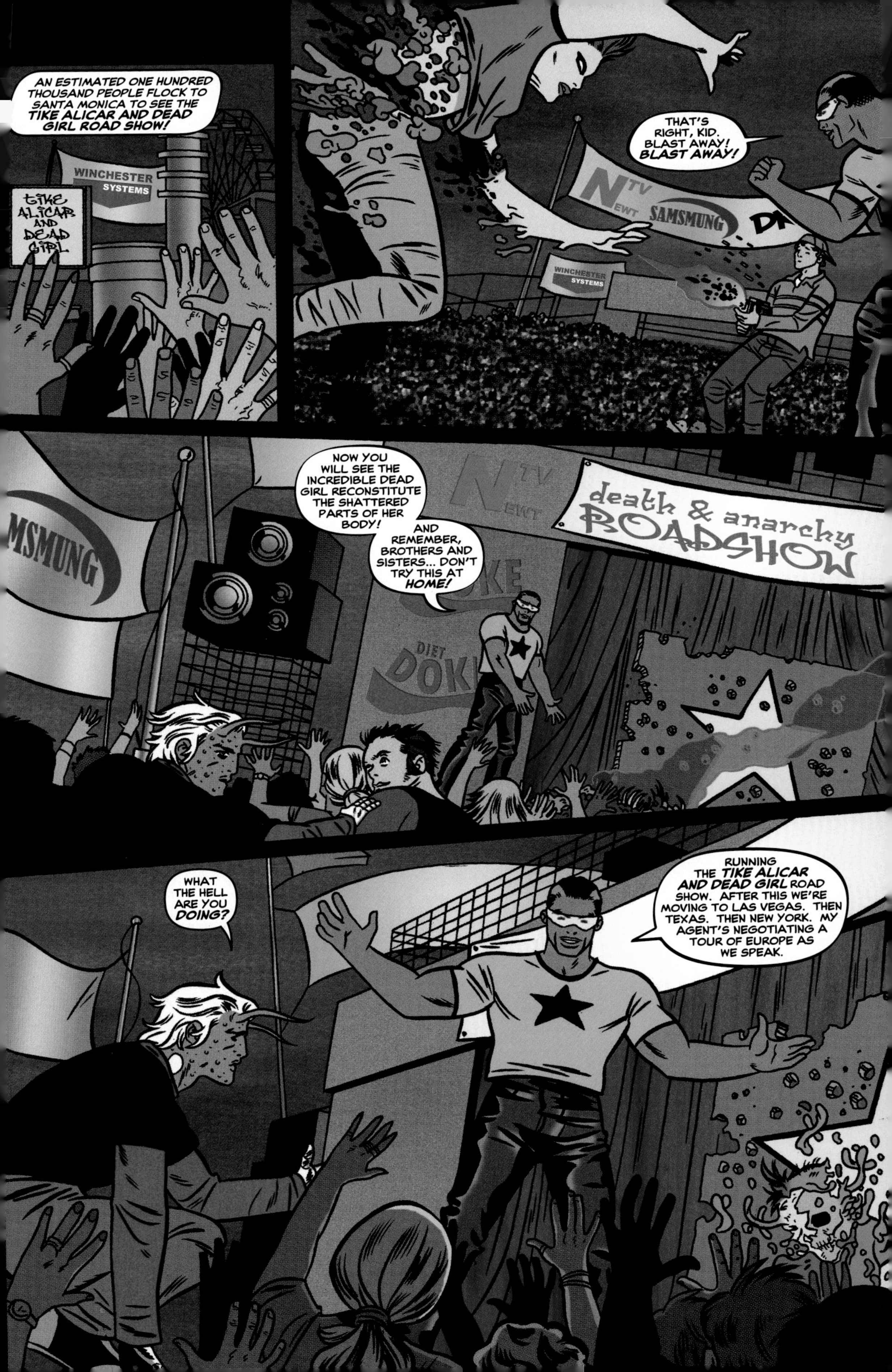
AN ESTIMATED ONE HUNDRED THOUSAND PEOPLE FLOCK TO SANTA MONICA TO SEE THE TIKE ALICAR AND DEAD GIRL ROAD SHOW!
WINCHESTER SYSTEMS
TIKE ALICAR AND DEAD GIRL
THAT'S RIGHT, KID. BLAST AWAY! BLAST AWAY!
N TV NEWT
SAMSMUNG
WINCHESTER SYSTEMS
NOW YOU WILL SEE THE INCREDIBLE DEAD GIRL RECONSTITUTE THE SHATTERED PARTS OF HER BODY!
AND REMEMBER, BROTHERS AND SISTERS... DON'T TRY THIS AT HOME!
death & anarchy ROADSHOW
MSMUNG
DIET DOK
WHAT THE HELL ARE YOU DOING?
RUNNING THE TIKE ALICAR AND DEAD GIRL ROAD SHOW. AFTER THIS WE'RE MOVING TO LAS VEGAS. THEN TEXAS. THEN NEW YORK. MY AGENT'S NEGOTIATING A TOUR OF EUROPE AS WE SPEAK.

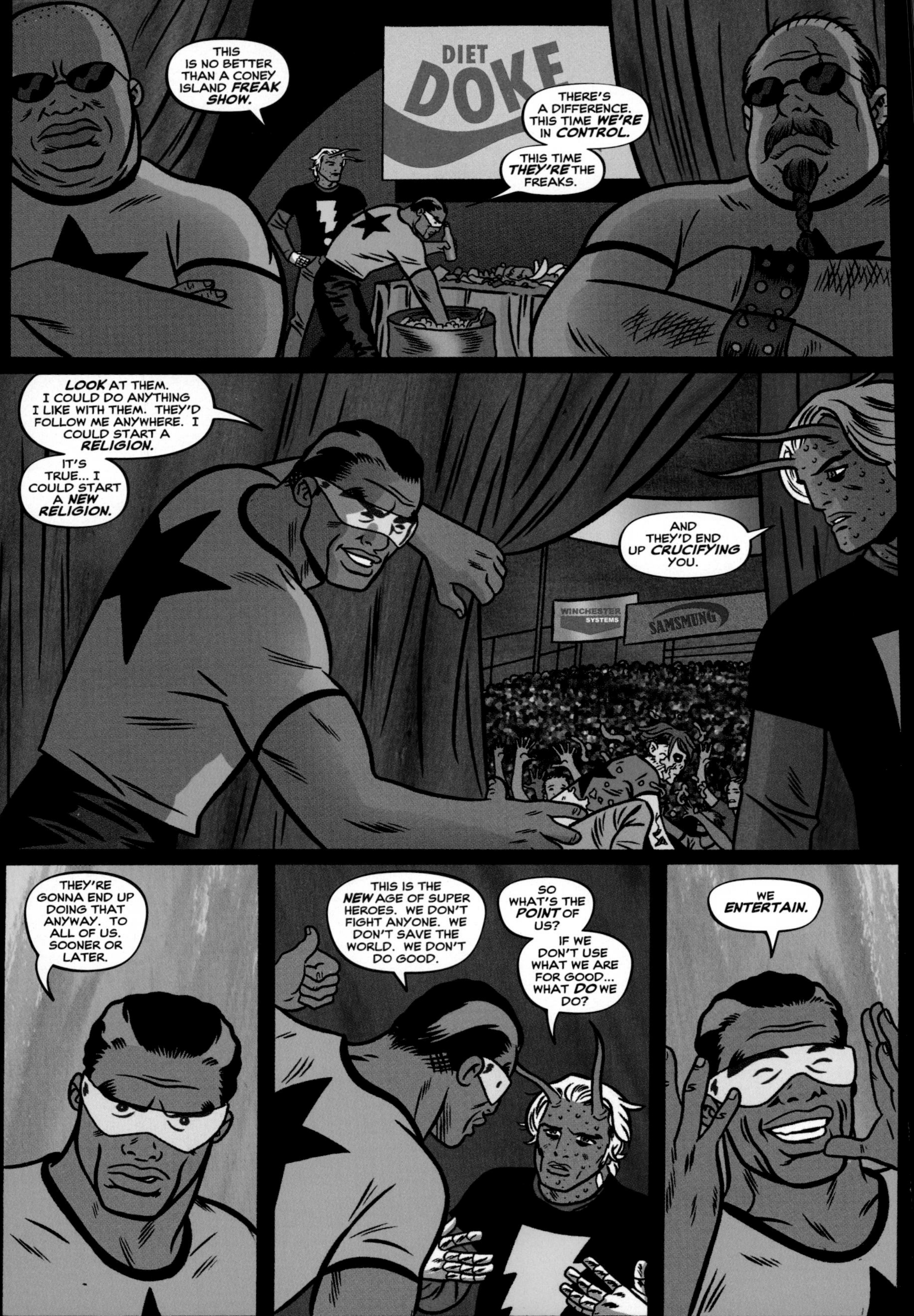
DIET DOKE
THIS IS NO BETTER THAN A CONEY ISLAND FREAK SHOW.
THERE'S A DIFFERENCE. THIS TIME WE'RE IN CONTROL.
THIS TIME THEY'RE THE FREAKS.
LOOK AT THEM. I COULD DO ANYTHING I LIKE WITH THEM. THEY'D FOLLOW ME ANYWHERE. I COULD START A RELIGION.
IT'S TRUE... I COULD START A NEW RELIGION.
AND THEY'D END UP CRUCIFYING YOU.
WINCHESTER SYSTEMS
SAMSMUNG
THEY'RE GONNA END UP DOING THAT ANYWAY. TO ALL OF US. SOONER OR LATER.
THIS IS THE NEW AGE OF SUPER HEROES. WE DON'T FIGHT ANYONE. WE DON'T SAVE THE WORLD. WE DON'T DO GOOD.
SO WHAT'S THE POINT OF US?
IF WE DON'T USE WHAT WE ARE FOR GOOD... WHAT DO WE DO?
WE ENTERTAIN.

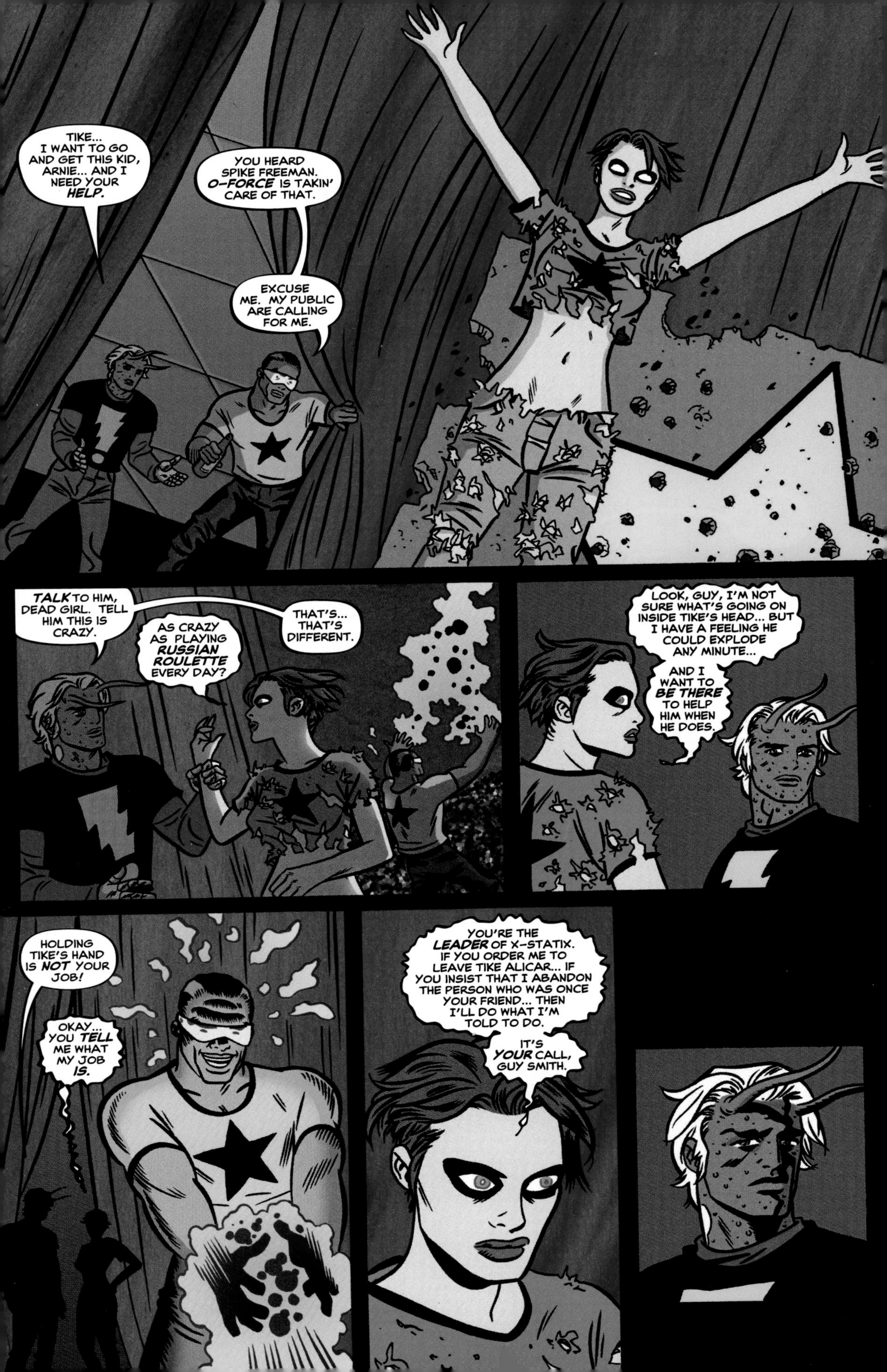
TIKE... I WANT TO GO AND GET THIS KID, ARNIE... AND I NEED YOUR HELP.
YOU HEARD SPIKE FREEMAN. O-FORCE IS TAKIN' CARE OF THAT.
EXCUSE ME. MY PUBLIC ARE CALLING FOR ME.
TALK TO HIM, DEAD GIRL. TELL HIM THIS IS CRAZY.
THAT'S... THAT'S DIFFERENT.
AS CRAZY AS PLAYING RUSSIAN ROULETTE EVERY DAY?
LOOK, GUY, I'M NOT SURE WHAT'S GOING ON INSIDE TIKE'S HEAD... BUT I HAVE A FEELING HE COULD EXPLODE ANY MINUTE...
AND I WANT TO BE THERE TO HELP HIM WHEN HE DOES.
HOLDING TIKE'S HAND IS NOT YOUR JOB!
OKAY... YOU TELL ME WHAT MY JOB IS.
YOU'RE THE LEADER OF X-STATIX. IF YOU ORDER ME TO LEAVE TIKE ALICAR... IF YOU INSIST THAT I ABANDON THE PERSON WHO WAS ONCE YOUR FRIEND... THEN I'LL DO WHAT I'M TOLD TO DO.
IT'S YOUR CALL, GUY SMITH.

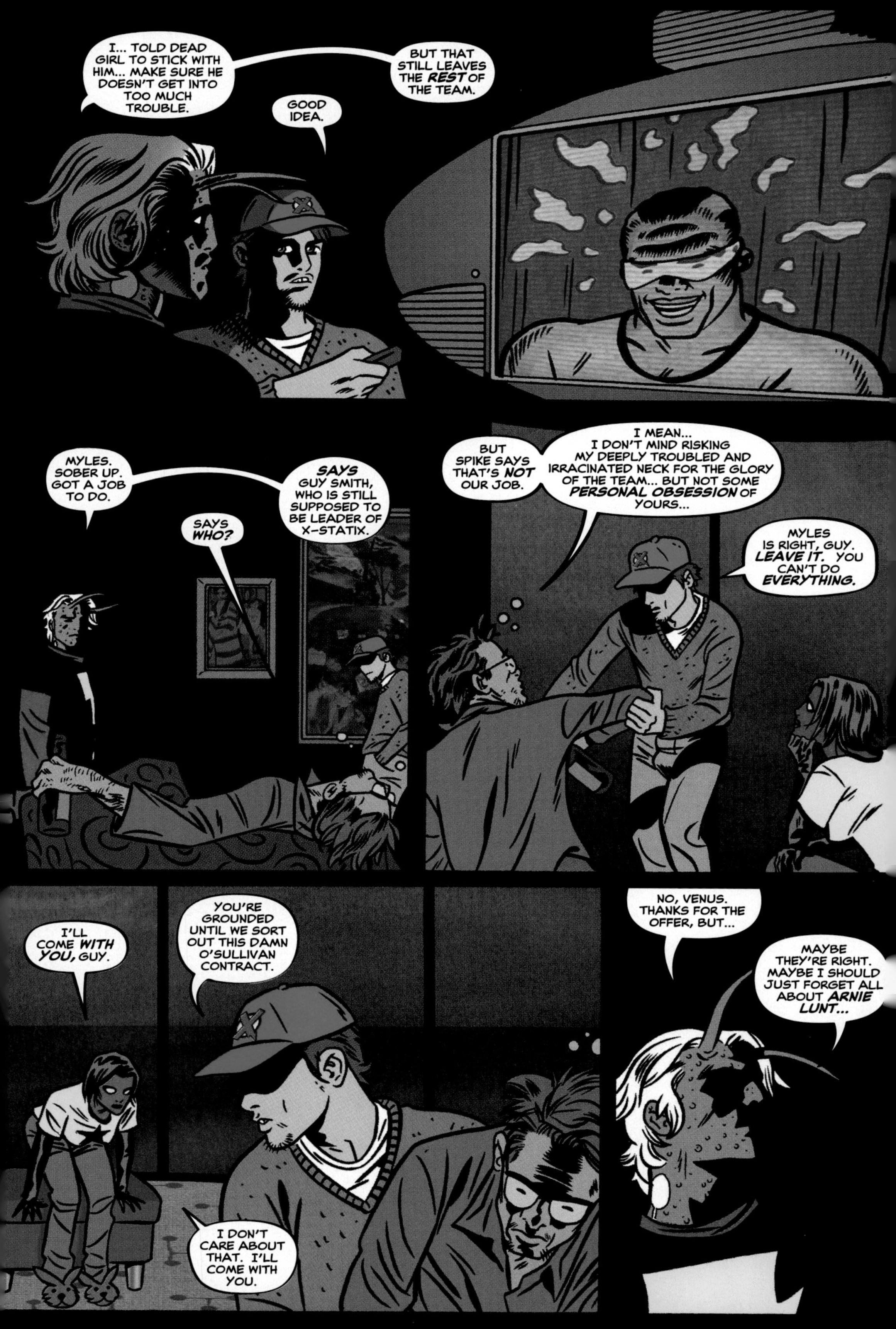

I... TOLD DEAD GIRL TO STICK WITH HIM... MAKE SURE HE DOESN'T GET INTO TOO MUCH TROUBLE.
GOOD IDEA.
BUT THAT STILL LEAVES THE *REST* OF THE TEAM.
MYLES. SOBER UP. GOT A JOB TO DO.
SAYS *WHO?*
SAYS GUY SMITH, WHO IS STILL SUPPOSED TO BE LEADER OF X-STATIX.
BUT SPIKE SAYS THAT'S *NOT* OUR JOB.
I MEAN... I DON'T MIND RISKING MY DEEPLY TROUBLED AND IRRACINATED NECK FOR THE GLORY OF THE TEAM... BUT NOT SOME *PERSONAL OBSESSION* OF YOURS...
MYLES IS RIGHT, GUY. *LEAVE IT.* YOU CAN'T DO *EVERYTHING.*
I'LL COME *WITH YOU,* GUY.
YOU'RE GROUNDED UNTIL WE SORT OUT THIS DAMN O'SULLIVAN CONTRACT.
I DON'T CARE ABOUT THAT. I'LL COME WITH YOU.
NO, VENUS. THANKS FOR THE OFFER, BUT...
MAYBE THEY'RE RIGHT. MAYBE I SHOULD JUST FORGET ALL ABOUT *ARNIE LUNT...*

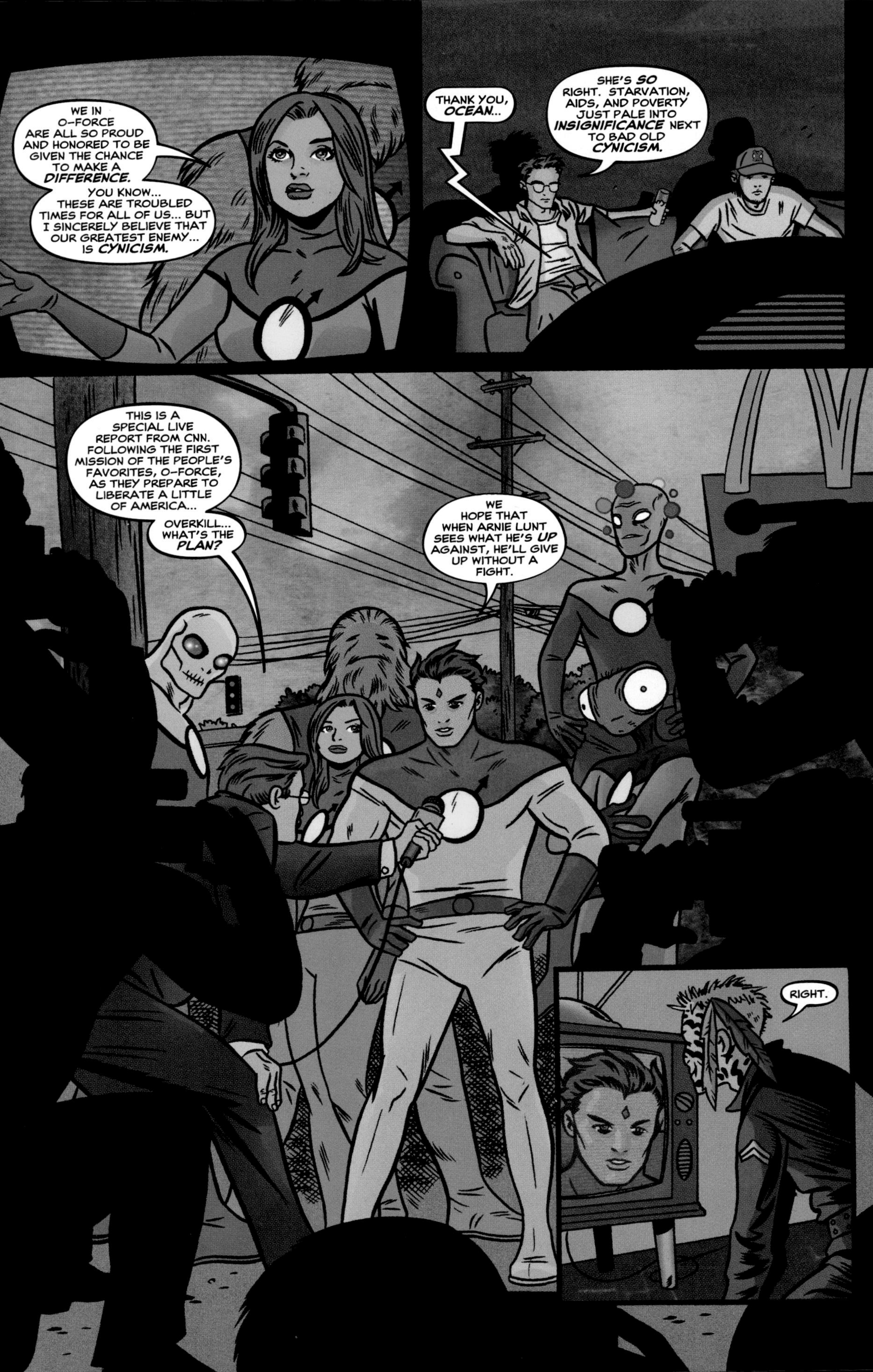
WE IN O-FORCE ARE ALL SO PROUD AND HONORED TO BE GIVEN THE CHANCE TO MAKE A DIFFERENCE.
YOU KNOW... THESE ARE TROUBLED TIMES FOR ALL OF US... BUT I SINCERELY BELIEVE THAT OUR GREATEST ENEMY... IS CYNICISM.
THANK YOU, OCEAN...
SHE'S SO RIGHT. STARVATION, AIDS, AND POVERTY JUST PALE INTO INSIGNIFICANCE NEXT TO BAD OLD CYNICISM.
THIS IS A SPECIAL LIVE REPORT FROM CNN. FOLLOWING THE FIRST MISSION OF THE PEOPLE'S FAVORITES, O-FORCE, AS THEY PREPARE TO LIBERATE A LITTLE OF AMERICA...
OVERKILL... WHAT'S THE PLAN?
WE HOPE THAT WHEN ARNIE LUNT SEES WHAT HE'S UP AGAINST, HE'LL GIVE UP WITHOUT A FIGHT.
RIGHT.

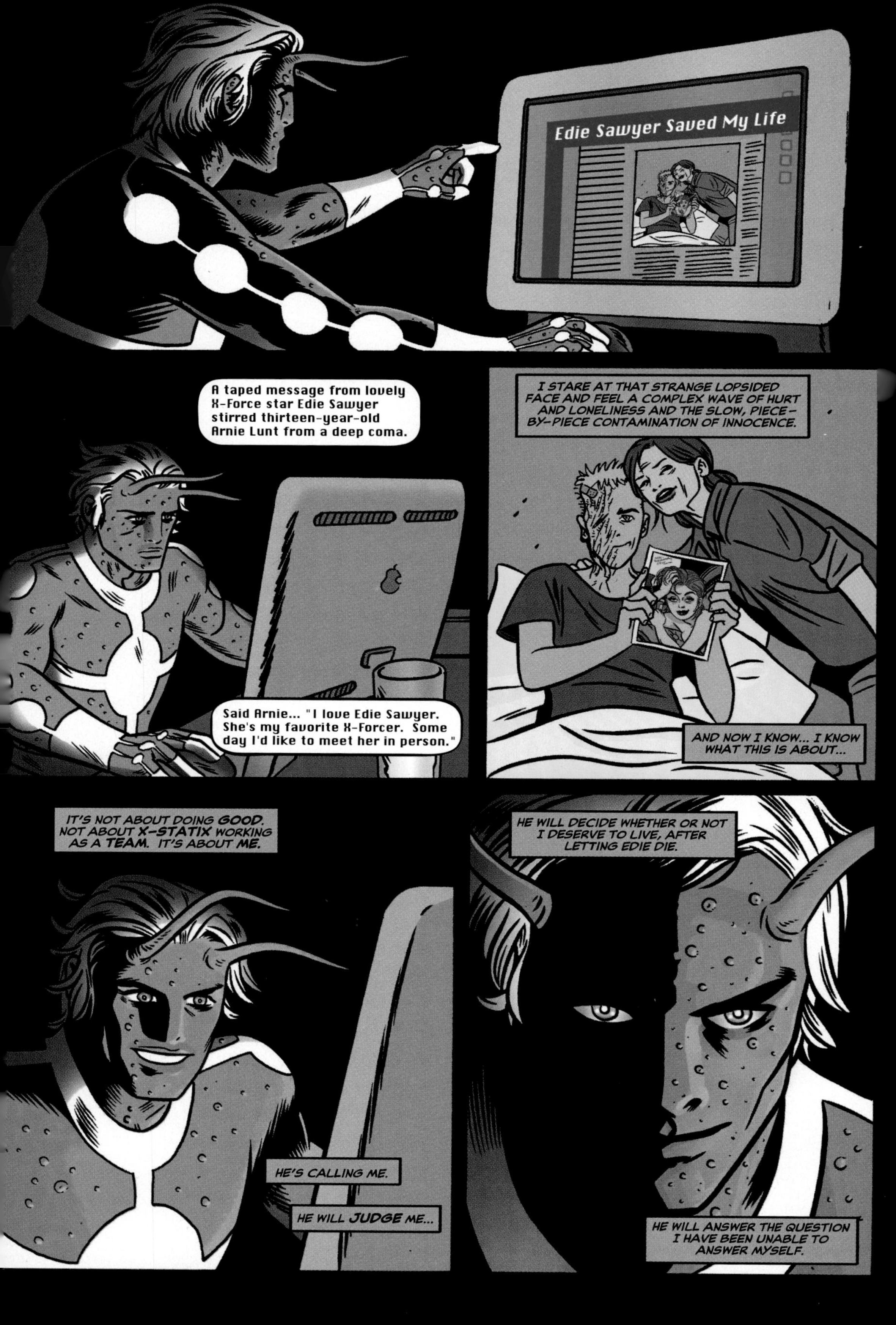
Edie Sawyer Saved My Life
A taped message from lovely X-Force star Edie Sawyer stirred thirteen-year-old Arnie Lunt from a deep coma.
Said Arnie... "I love Edie Sawyer. She's my favorite X-Forcer. Some day I'd like to meet her in person."
I STARE AT THAT STRANGE LOPSIDED FACE AND FEEL A COMPLEX WAVE OF HURT AND LONELINESS AND THE SLOW, PIECE-BY-PIECE CONTAMINATION OF INNOCENCE.
AND NOW I KNOW... I KNOW WHAT THIS IS ABOUT...
IT'S NOT ABOUT DOING GOOD. NOT ABOUT X-STATIX WORKING AS A TEAM. IT'S ABOUT ME.
HE'S CALLING ME.
HE WILL JUDGE ME...
HE WILL DECIDE WHETHER OR NOT I DESERVE TO LIVE, AFTER LETTING EDIE DIE.
HE WILL ANSWER THE QUESTION I HAVE BEEN UNABLE TO ANSWER MYSELF.

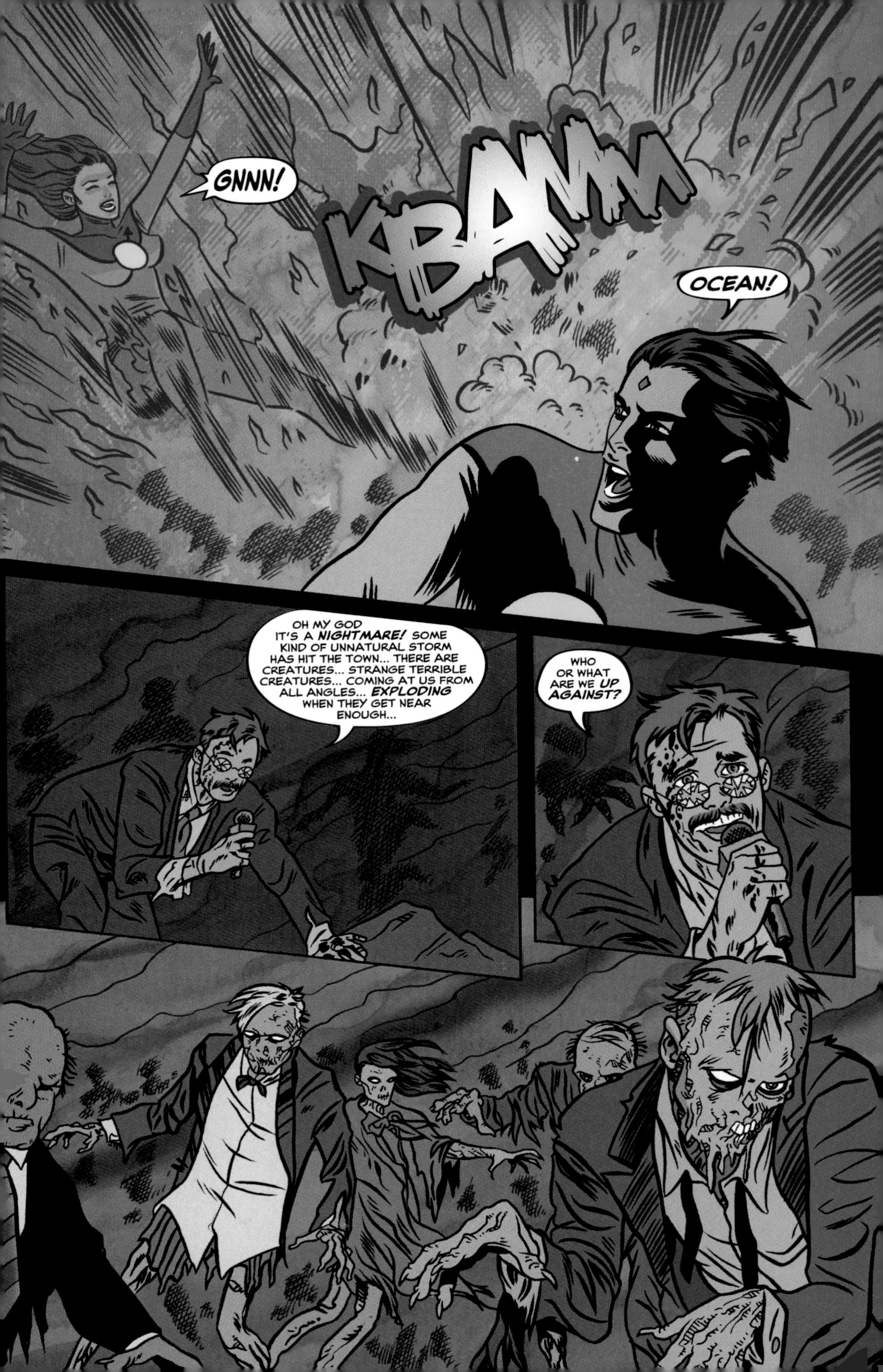
GNNN!
KBAMM
OCEAN!
OH MY GOD IT'S A NIGHTMARE! SOME KIND OF UNNATURAL STORM HAS HIT THE TOWN... THERE ARE CREATURES... STRANGE TERRIBLE CREATURES... COMING AT US FROM ALL ANGLES... EXPLODING WHEN THEY GET NEAR ENOUGH...
WHO OR WHAT ARE WE UP AGAINST?

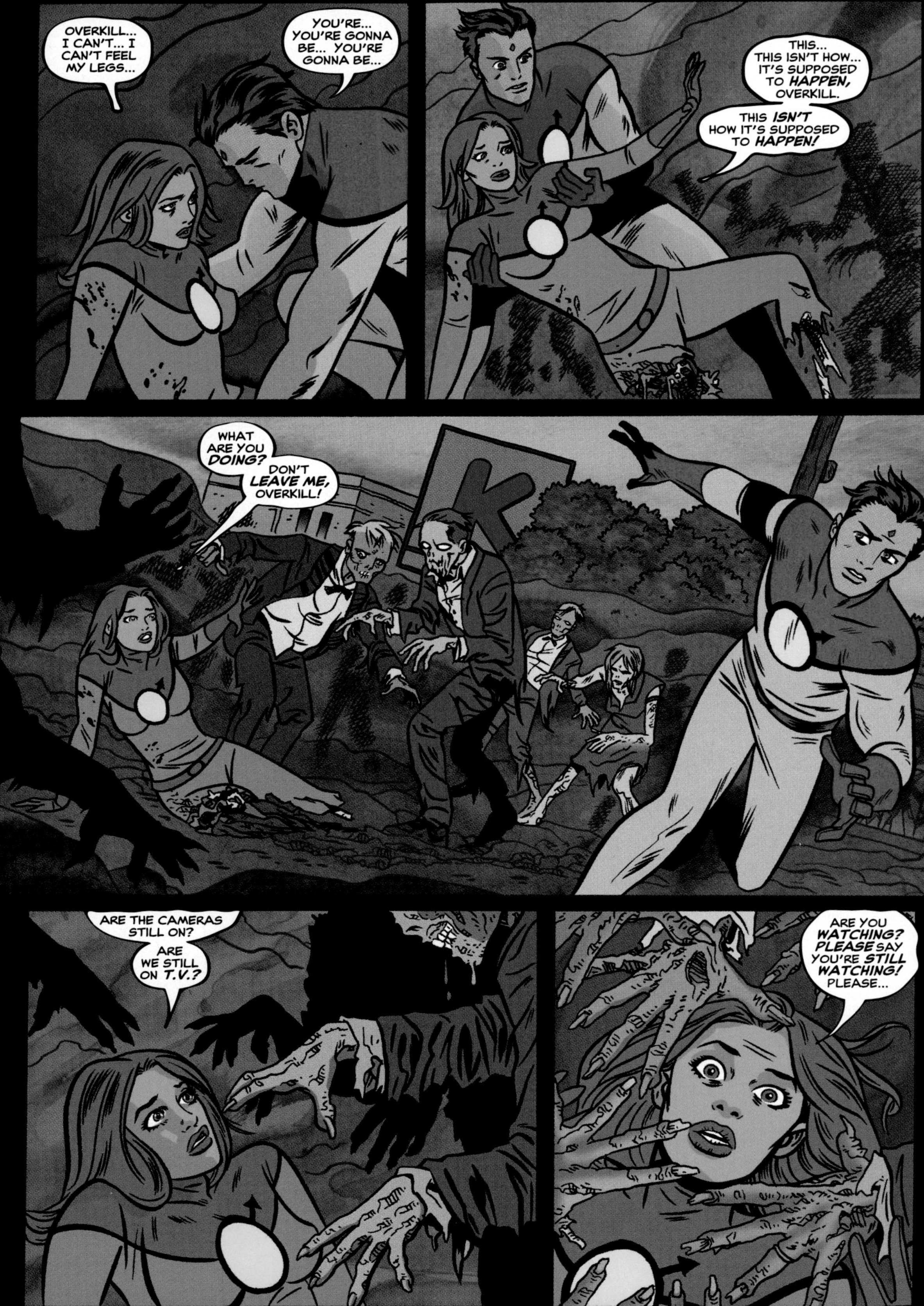
OVERKILL... I CAN'T... I CAN'T FEEL MY LEGS...
YOU'RE... YOU'RE GONNA BE... YOU'RE GONNA BE...
THIS... THIS ISN'T HOW... IT'S SUPPOSED TO HAPPEN, OVERKILL.
THIS ISN'T HOW IT'S SUPPOSED TO HAPPEN!
WHAT ARE YOU DOING?
DON'T LEAVE ME, OVERKILL!
ARE THE CAMERAS STILL ON?
ARE WE STILL ON T.V.?
ARE YOU WATCHING? PLEASE SAY YOU'RE STILL WATCHING! PLEASE...

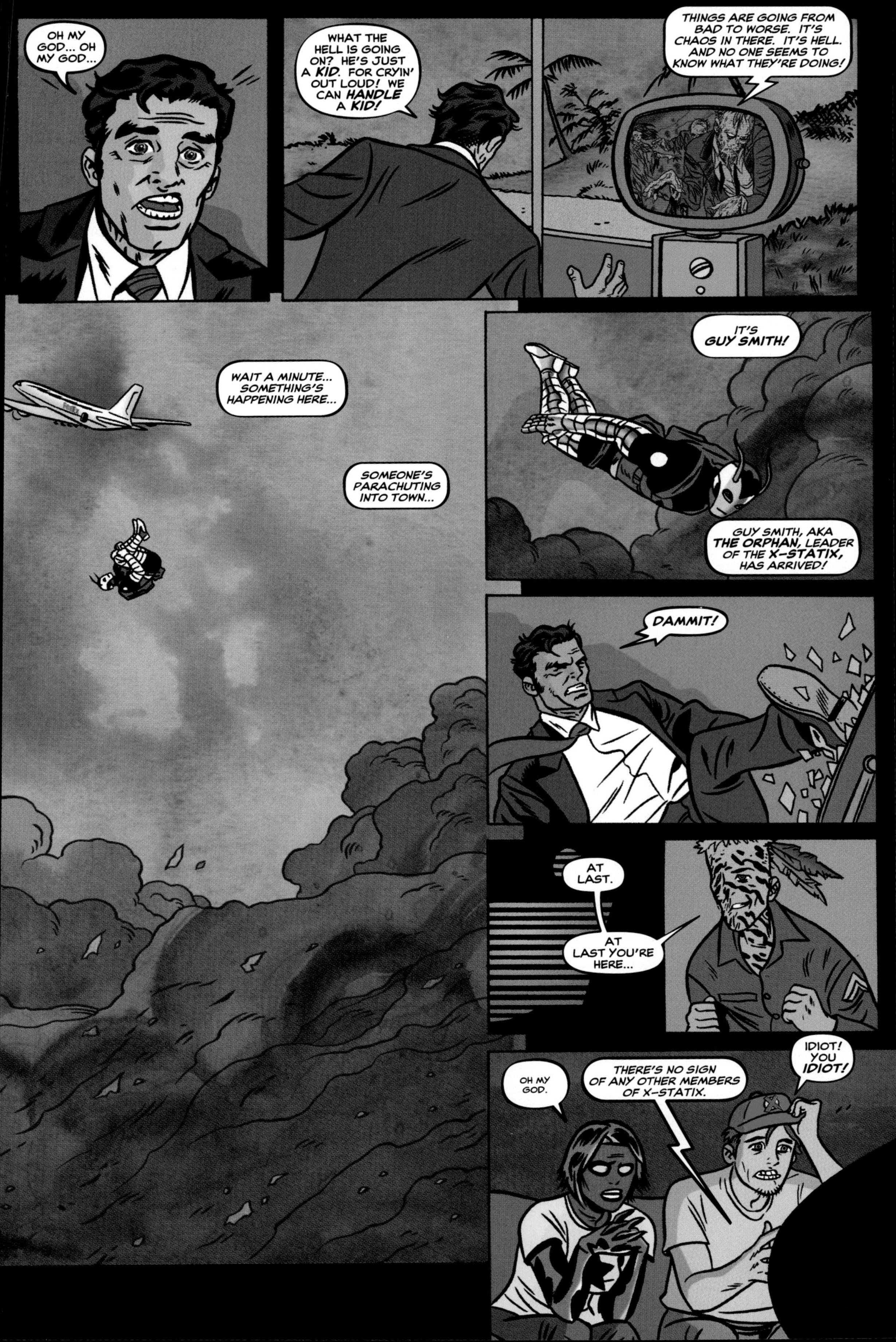
OH MY GOD... OH MY GOD...
WHAT THE HELL IS GOING ON? HE'S JUST A KID. FOR CRYIN' OUT LOUD! WE CAN HANDLE A KID!
THINGS ARE GOING FROM BAD TO WORSE. IT'S CHAOS IN THERE. IT'S HELL. AND NO ONE SEEMS TO KNOW WHAT THEY'RE DOING!
WAIT A MINUTE... SOMETHING'S HAPPENING HERE...
SOMEONE'S PARACHUTING INTO TOWN...
IT'S GUY SMITH!
GUY SMITH, AKA THE ORPHAN, LEADER OF THE X-STATIX, HAS ARRIVED!
DAMMIT!
AT LAST.
AT LAST YOU'RE HERE...
OH MY GOD.
THERE'S NO SIGN OF ANY OTHER MEMBERS OF X-STATIX.
IDIOT! YOU IDIOT!

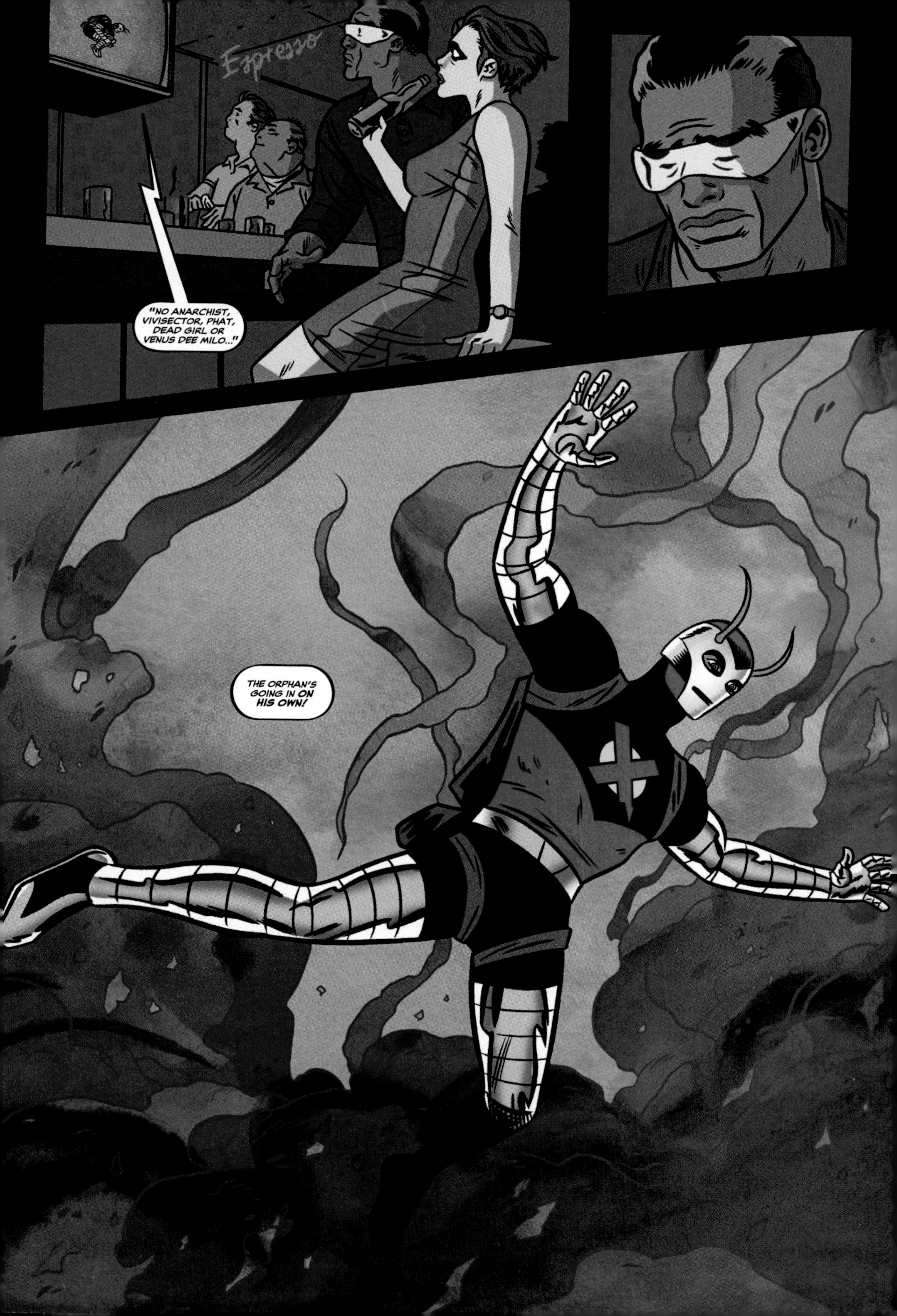
Espresso
"NO ANARCHIST, VIVISECTOR, PHAT, DEAD GIRL OR VENUS DEE MILO..."
THE ORPHAN'S GOING IN ON HIS OWN!

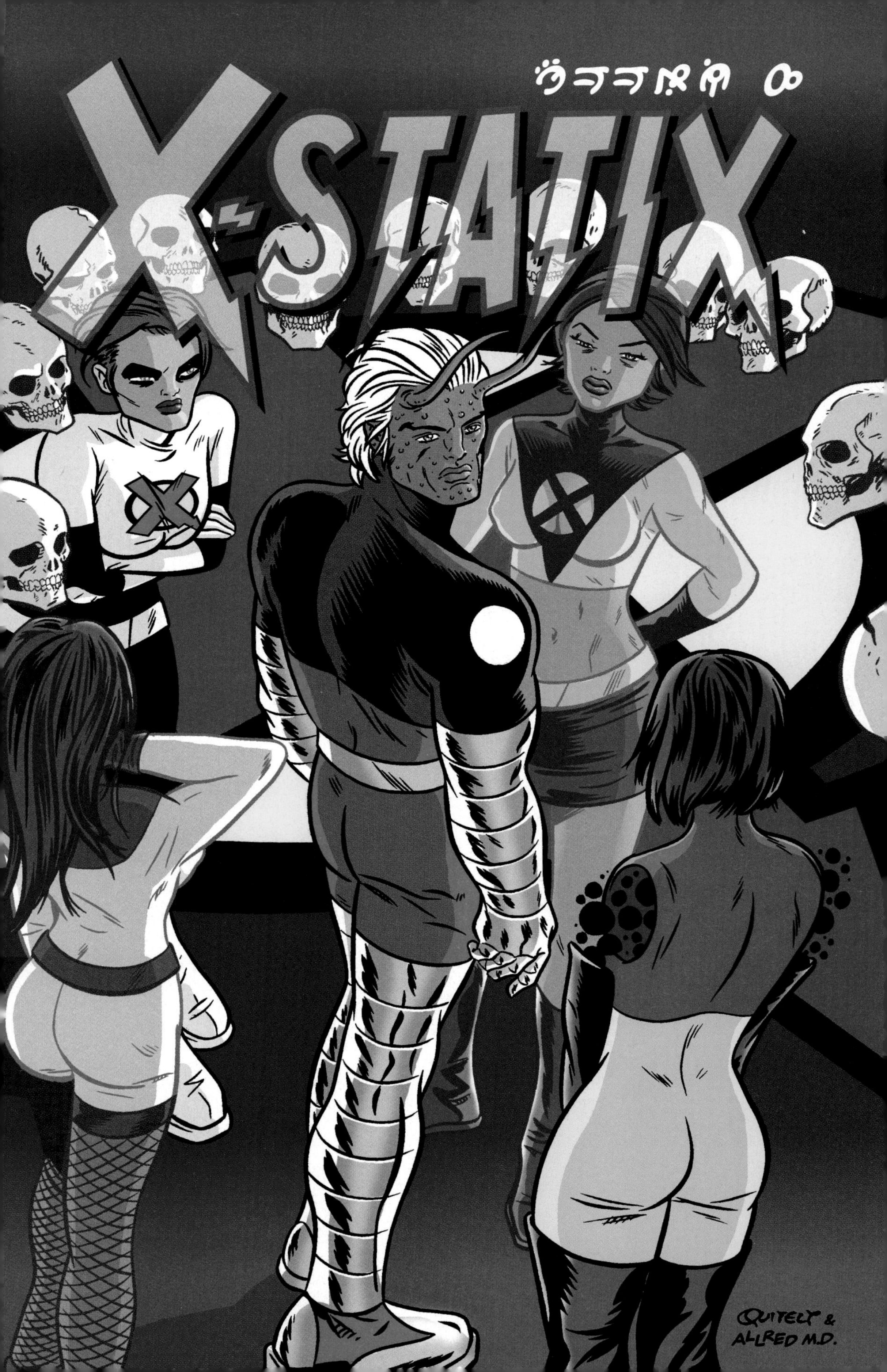
X-STATIX
QUITELY &
ALLRED M.D.

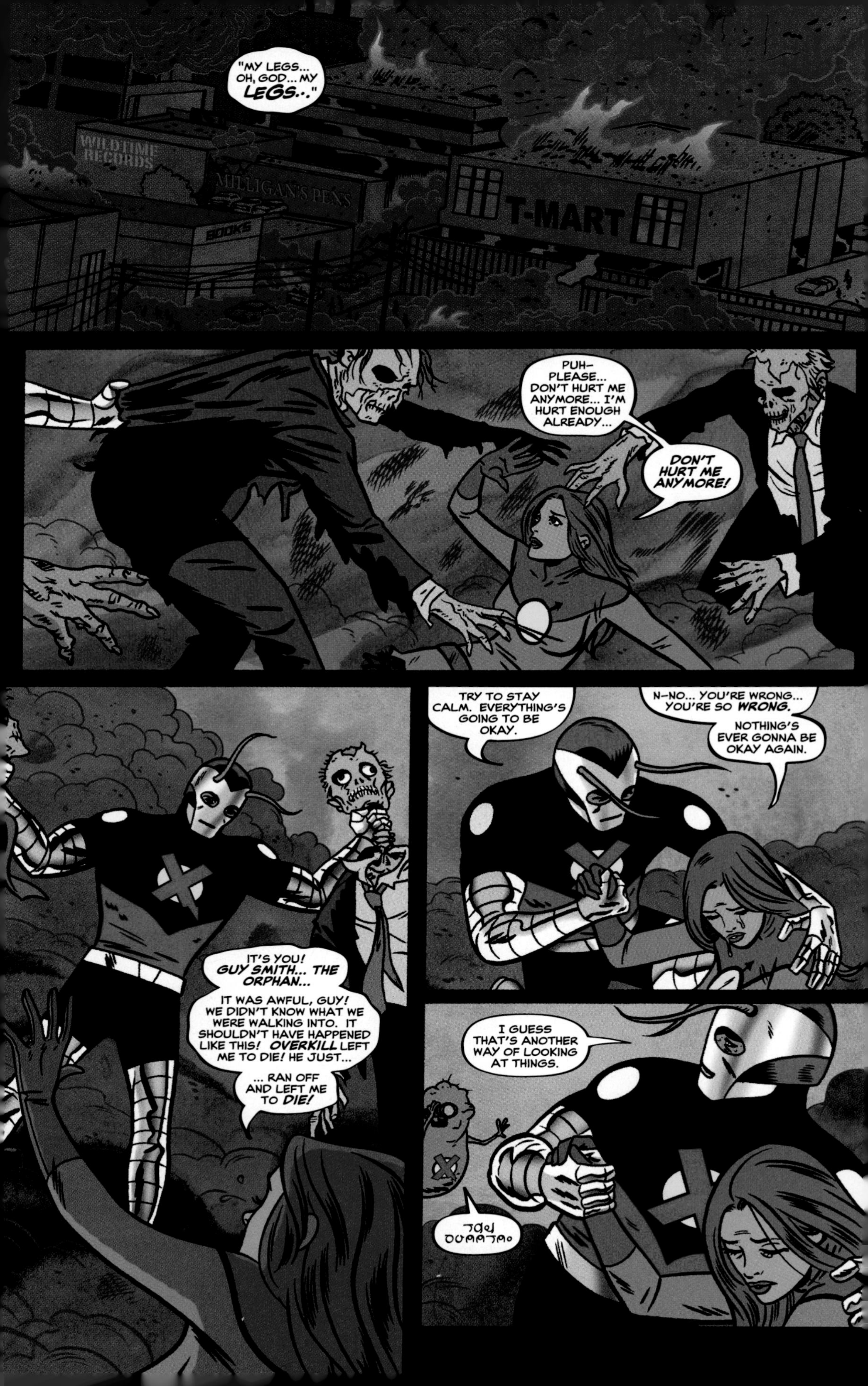
"MY LEGS... OH, GOD... MY LEGS..."
WILDTIME RECORDS
MILLIGAN'S PENS
BOOKS
T-MART
PUH-PLEASE... DON'T HURT ME ANYMORE... I'M HURT ENOUGH ALREADY...
DON'T HURT ME ANYMORE!
IT'S YOU! GUY SMITH... THE ORPHAN...
IT WAS AWFUL, GUY! WE DIDN'T KNOW WHAT WE WERE WALKING INTO. IT SHOULDN'T HAVE HAPPENED LIKE THIS! OVERKILL LEFT ME TO DIE! HE JUST...
... RAN OFF AND LEFT ME TO DIE!
TRY TO STAY CALM. EVERYTHING'S GOING TO BE OKAY.
N-NO... YOU'RE WRONG... YOU'RE SO WRONG.
NOTHING'S EVER GONNA BE OKAY AGAIN.
I GUESS THAT'S ANOTHER WAY OF LOOKING AT THINGS.

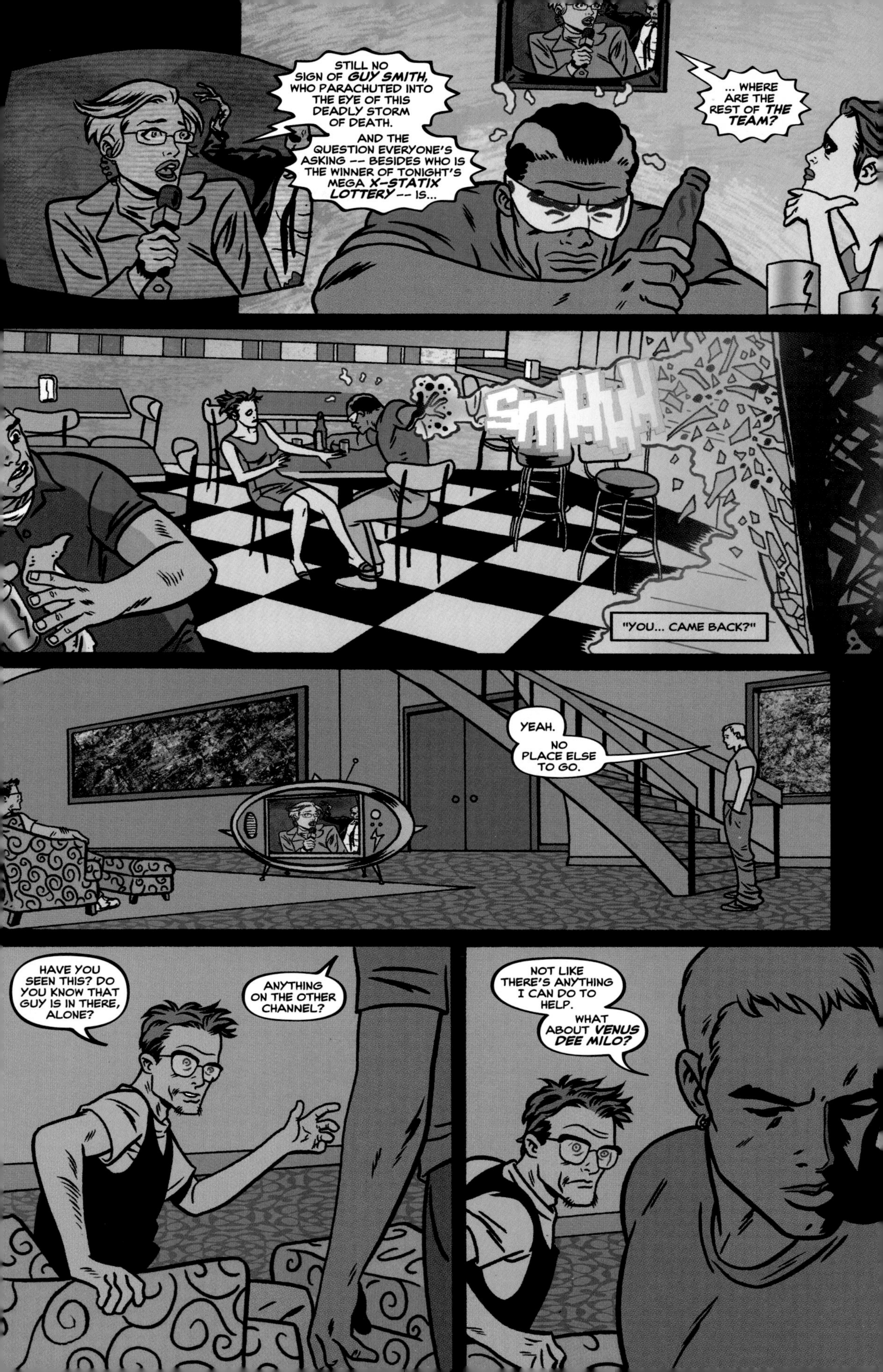
STILL NO SIGN OF GUY SMITH, WHO PARACHUTED INTO THE EYE OF THIS DEADLY STORM OF DEATH.
AND THE QUESTION EVERYONE'S ASKING -- BESIDES WHO IS THE WINNER OF TONIGHT'S MEGA X-STATIX LOTTERY -- IS...
... WHERE ARE THE REST OF THE TEAM?
SMHHH
"YOU... CAME BACK?"
YEAH.
NO PLACE ELSE TO GO.
HAVE YOU SEEN THIS? DO YOU KNOW THAT GUY IS IN THERE, ALONE?
ANYTHING ON THE OTHER CHANNEL?
NOT LIKE THERE'S ANYTHING I CAN DO TO HELP.
WHAT ABOUT VENUS DEE MILO?

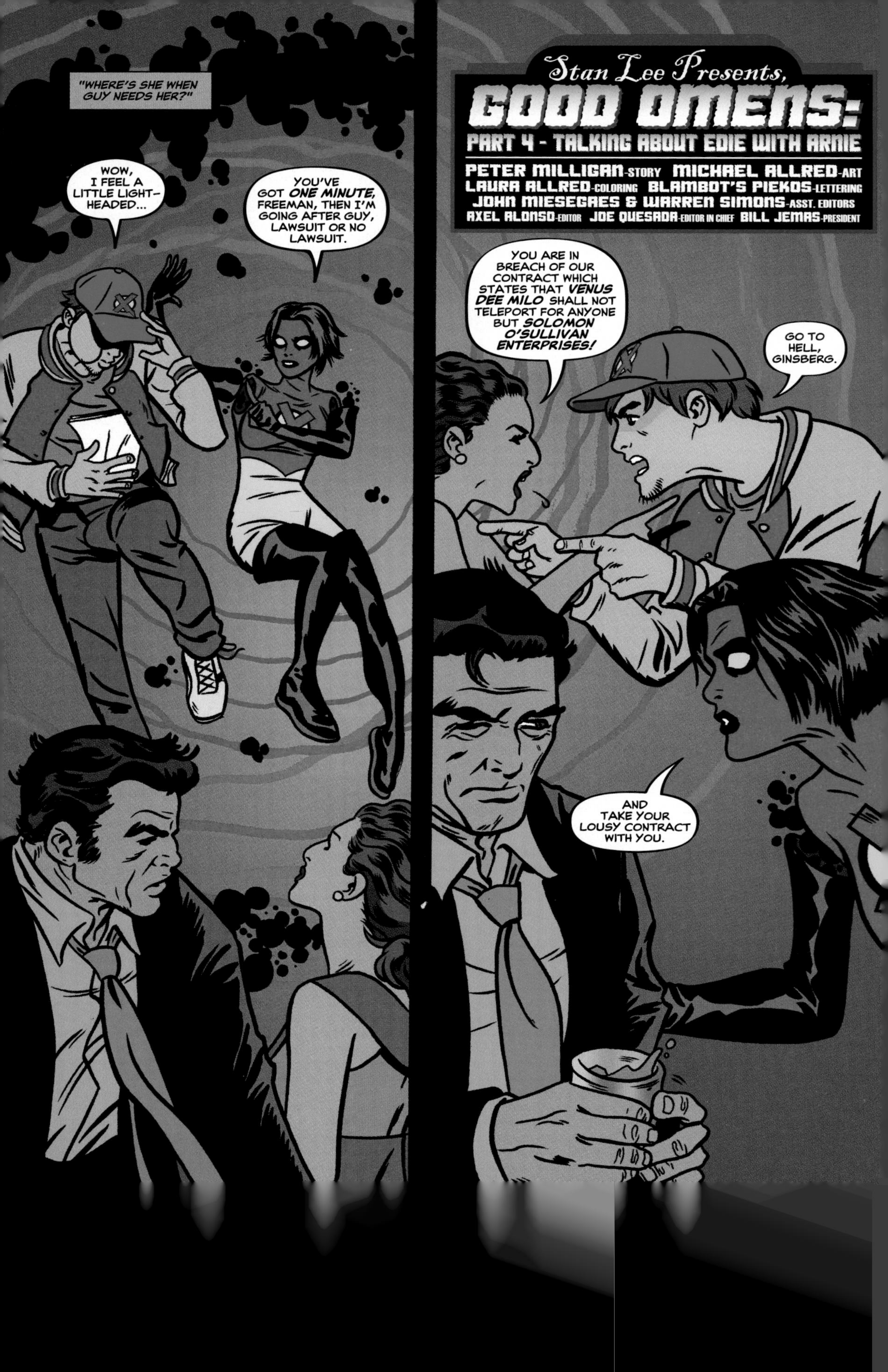
"WHERE'S SHE WHEN GUY NEEDS HER?"
WOW, I FEEL A LITTLE LIGHT-HEADED...
YOU'VE GOT ONE MINUTE, FREEMAN, THEN I'M GOING AFTER GUY, LAWSUIT OR NO LAWSUIT.
Stan Lee Presents,
GOOD OMENS:
PART 4 - TALKING ABOUT EDIE WITH ARNIE
PETER MILLIGAN-STORY MICHAEL ALLRED-ART
LAURA ALLRED-COLORING BLAMBOT'S PIEKOS-LETTERING
JOHN MIESEGAES & WARREN SIMONS-ASST. EDITORS
AXEL ALONSO-EDITOR JOE QUESADA-EDITOR IN CHIEF BILL JEMAS-PRESIDENT
YOU ARE IN BREACH OF OUR CONTRACT WHICH STATES THAT VENUS DEE MILO SHALL NOT TELEPORT FOR ANYONE BUT SOLOMON O'SULLIVAN ENTERPRISES!
GO TO HELL, GINSBERG.
AND TAKE YOUR LOUSY CONTRACT WITH YOU.

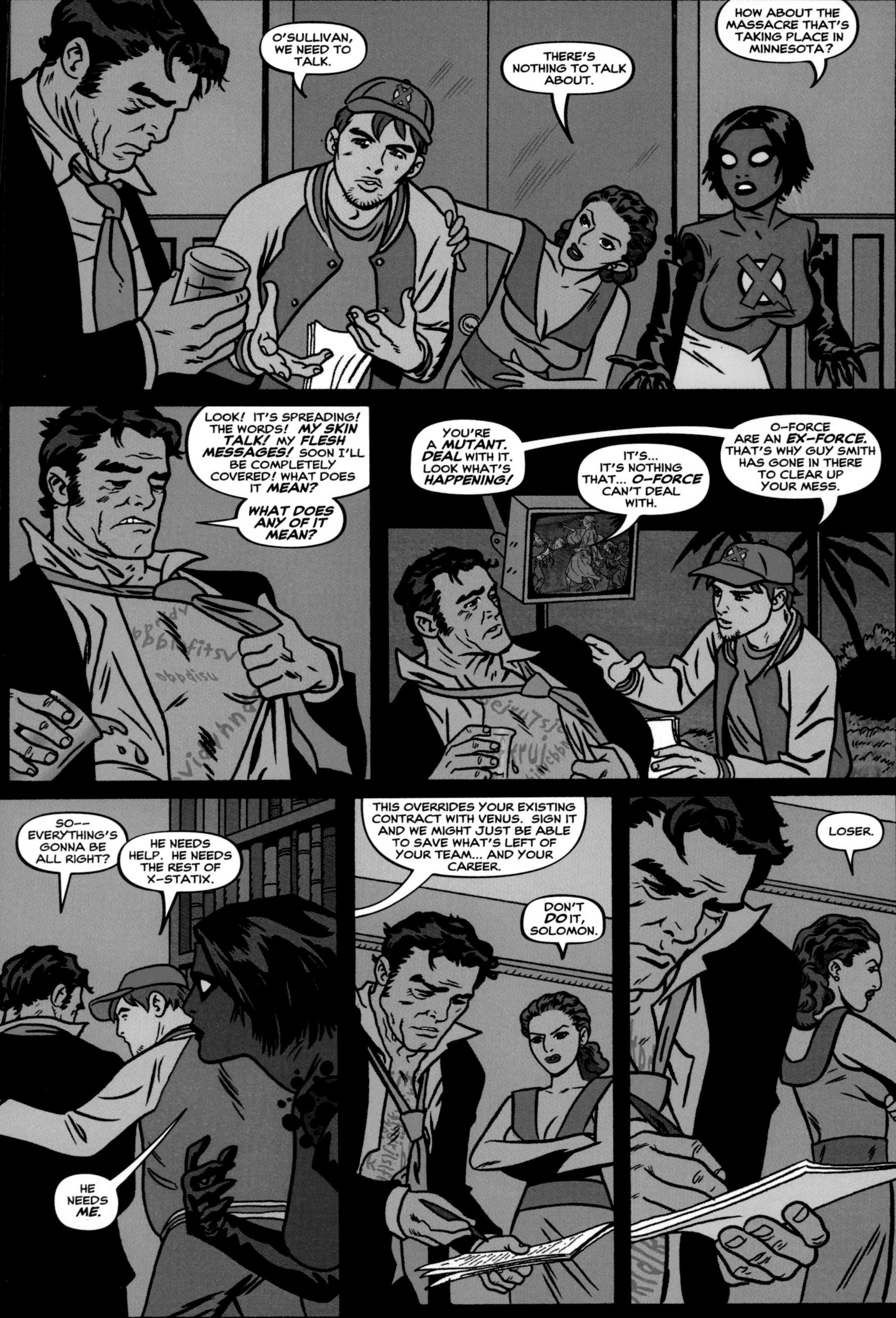

O'SULLIVAN, WE NEED TO TALK.
THERE'S NOTHING TO TALK ABOUT.
HOW ABOUT THE MASSACRE THAT'S TAKING PLACE IN MINNESOTA?
LOOK! IT'S SPREADING! THE WORDS! MY SKIN TALK! MY FLESH MESSAGES! SOON I'LL BE COMPLETELY COVERED! WHAT DOES IT MEAN?
WHAT DOES ANY OF IT MEAN?
YOU'RE A MUTANT. DEAL WITH IT. LOOK WHAT'S HAPPENING!
IT'S... IT'S NOTHING THAT... O-FORCE CAN'T DEAL WITH.
O-FORCE ARE AN EX-FORCE. THAT'S WHY GUY SMITH HAS GONE IN THERE TO CLEAR UP YOUR MESS.
SO-- EVERYTHING'S GONNA BE ALL RIGHT?
HE NEEDS HELP. HE NEEDS THE REST OF X-STATIX.
HE NEEDS ME.
THIS OVERRIDES YOUR EXISTING CONTRACT WITH VENUS. SIGN IT AND WE MIGHT JUST BE ABLE TO SAVE WHAT'S LEFT OF YOUR TEAM... AND YOUR CAREER.
DON'T DO IT, SOLOMON.
LOSER.

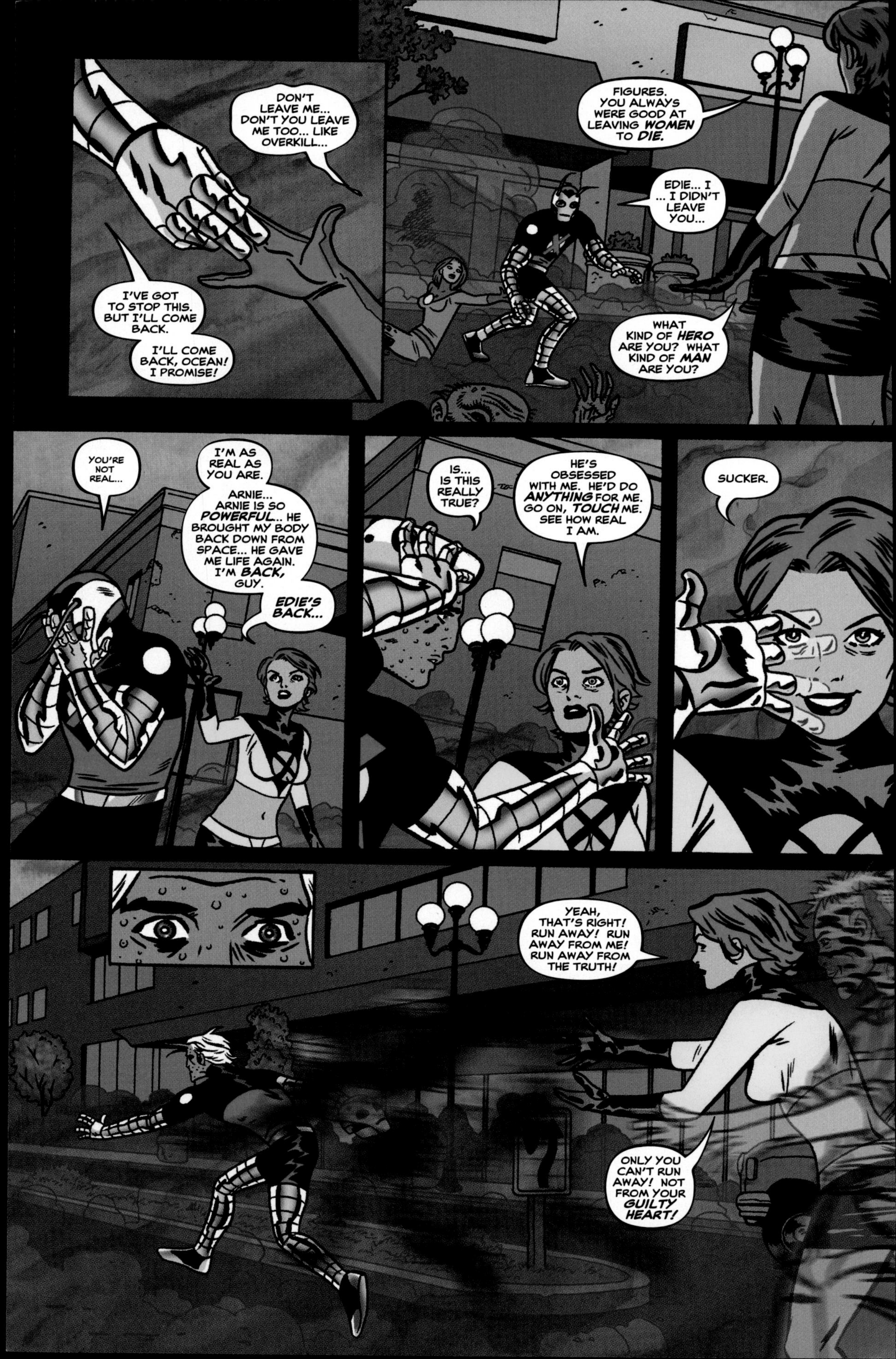
DON'T LEAVE ME... DON'T YOU LEAVE ME TOO... LIKE OVERKILL...
I'VE GOT TO STOP THIS. BUT I'LL COME BACK.
I'LL COME BACK, OCEAN! I PROMISE!
FIGURES. YOU ALWAYS WERE GOOD AT LEAVING WOMEN TO DIE.
EDIE... I ... I DIDN'T LEAVE YOU...
WHAT KIND OF HERO ARE YOU? WHAT KIND OF MAN ARE YOU?
YOU'RE NOT REAL...
I'M AS REAL AS YOU ARE.
ARNIE... ARNIE IS SO POWERFUL... HE BROUGHT MY BODY BACK DOWN FROM SPACE... HE GAVE ME LIFE AGAIN. I'M BACK, GUY.
EDIE'S BACK...
IS... IS THIS REALLY TRUE?
HE'S OBSESSED WITH ME. HE'D DO ANYTHING FOR ME. GO ON, TOUCH ME. SEE HOW REAL I AM.
SUCKER.
YEAH, THAT'S RIGHT! RUN AWAY! RUN AWAY FROM ME! RUN AWAY FROM THE TRUTH!
ONLY YOU CAN'T RUN AWAY! NOT FROM YOUR GUILTY HEART!

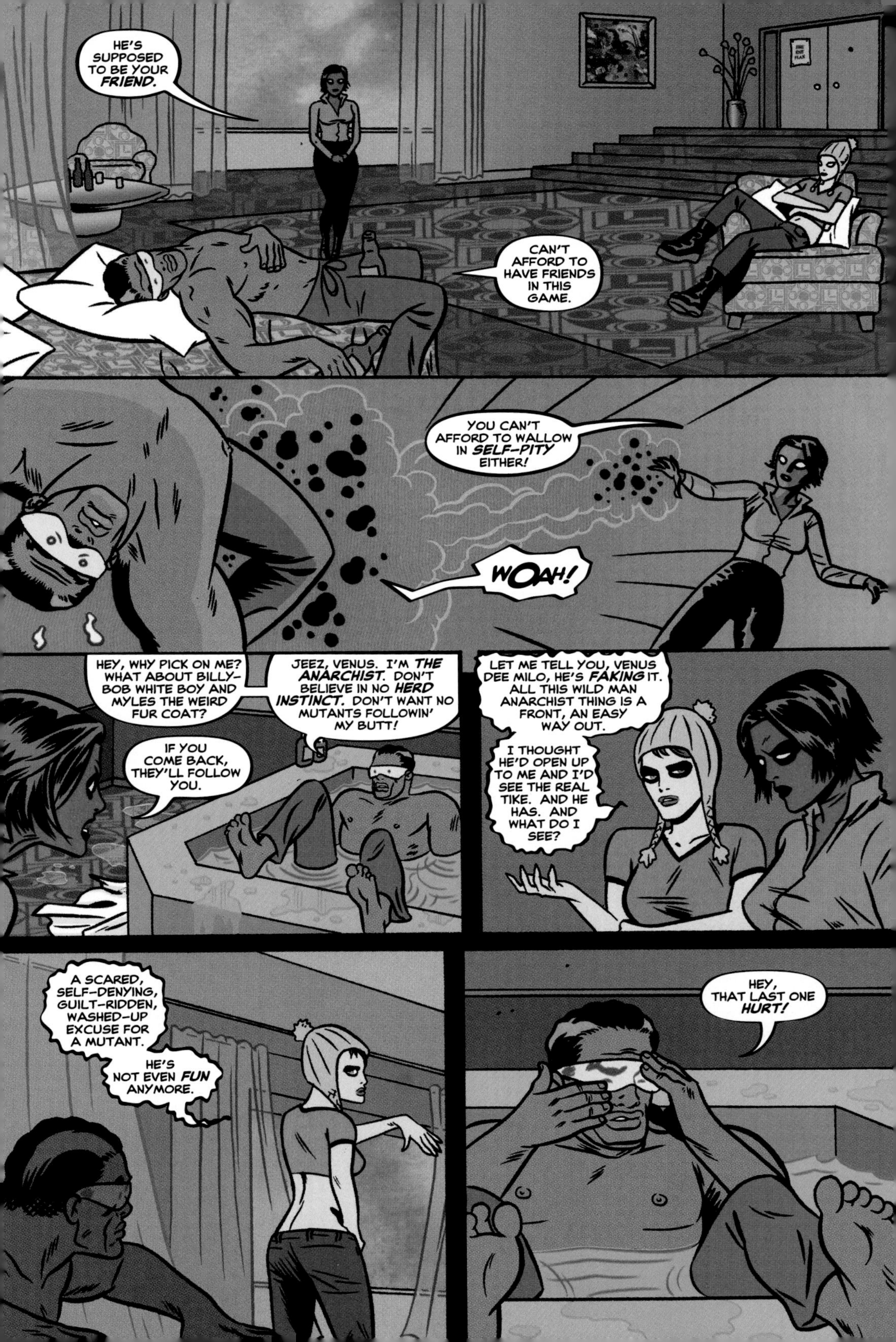
HE'S SUPPOSED TO BE YOUR FRIEND.
CAN'T AFFORD TO HAVE FRIENDS IN THIS GAME.
YOU CAN'T AFFORD TO WALLOW IN SELF-PITY EITHER!
WOAH!
HEY, WHY PICK ON ME? WHAT ABOUT BILLY-BOB WHITE BOY AND MYLES THE WEIRD FUR COAT?
JEEZ, VENUS. I'M THE ANARCHIST. DON'T BELIEVE IN NO HERD INSTINCT. DON'T WANT NO MUTANTS FOLLOWIN' MY BUTT!
IF YOU COME BACK, THEY'LL FOLLOW YOU.
LET ME TELL YOU, VENUS DEE MILO, HE'S FAKING IT. ALL THIS WILD MAN ANARCHIST THING IS A FRONT, AN EASY WAY OUT.
I THOUGHT HE'D OPEN UP TO ME AND I'D SEE THE REAL TIKE. AND HE HAS. AND WHAT DO I SEE?
A SCARED, SELF-DENYING, GUILT-RIDDEN, WASHED-UP EXCUSE FOR A MUTANT.
HE'S NOT EVEN FUN ANYMORE.
HEY, THAT LAST ONE HURT!

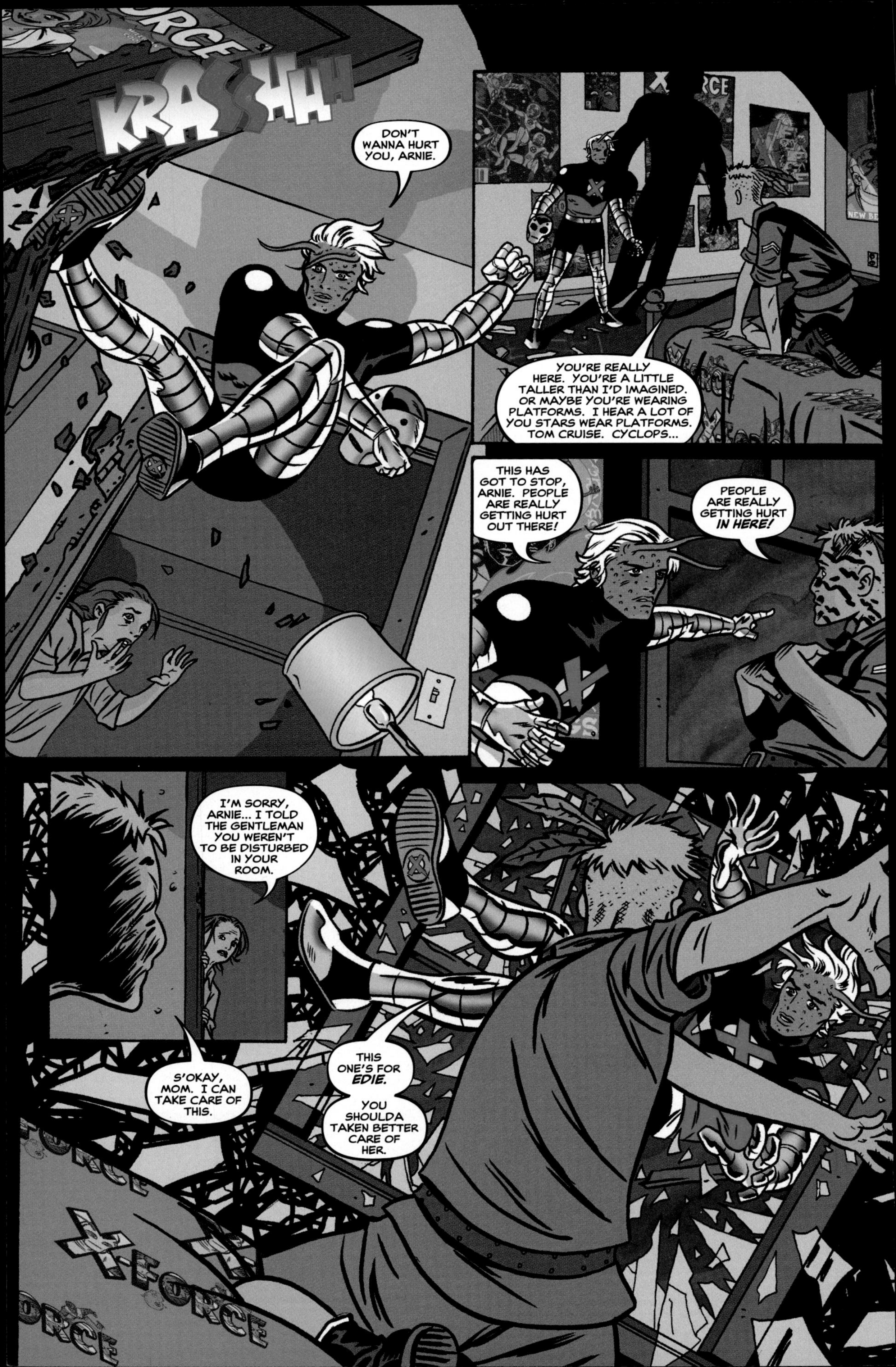
KRASSHHH
DON'T WANNA HURT YOU, ARNIE.
YOU'RE REALLY HERE. YOU'RE A LITTLE TALLER THAN I'D IMAGINED. OR MAYBE YOU'RE WEARING PLATFORMS. I HEAR A LOT OF YOU STARS WEAR PLATFORMS. TOM CRUISE. CYCLOPS...
THIS HAS GOT TO STOP, ARNIE. PEOPLE ARE REALLY GETTING HURT OUT THERE!
PEOPLE ARE REALLY GETTING HURT *IN HERE!*
I'M SORRY, ARNIE... I TOLD THE GENTLEMAN YOU WEREN'T TO BE DISTURBED IN YOUR ROOM.
S'OKAY, MOM. I CAN TAKE CARE OF THIS.
THIS ONE'S FOR *EDIE.*
YOU SHOULDA TAKEN BETTER CARE OF HER.
X-FORCE

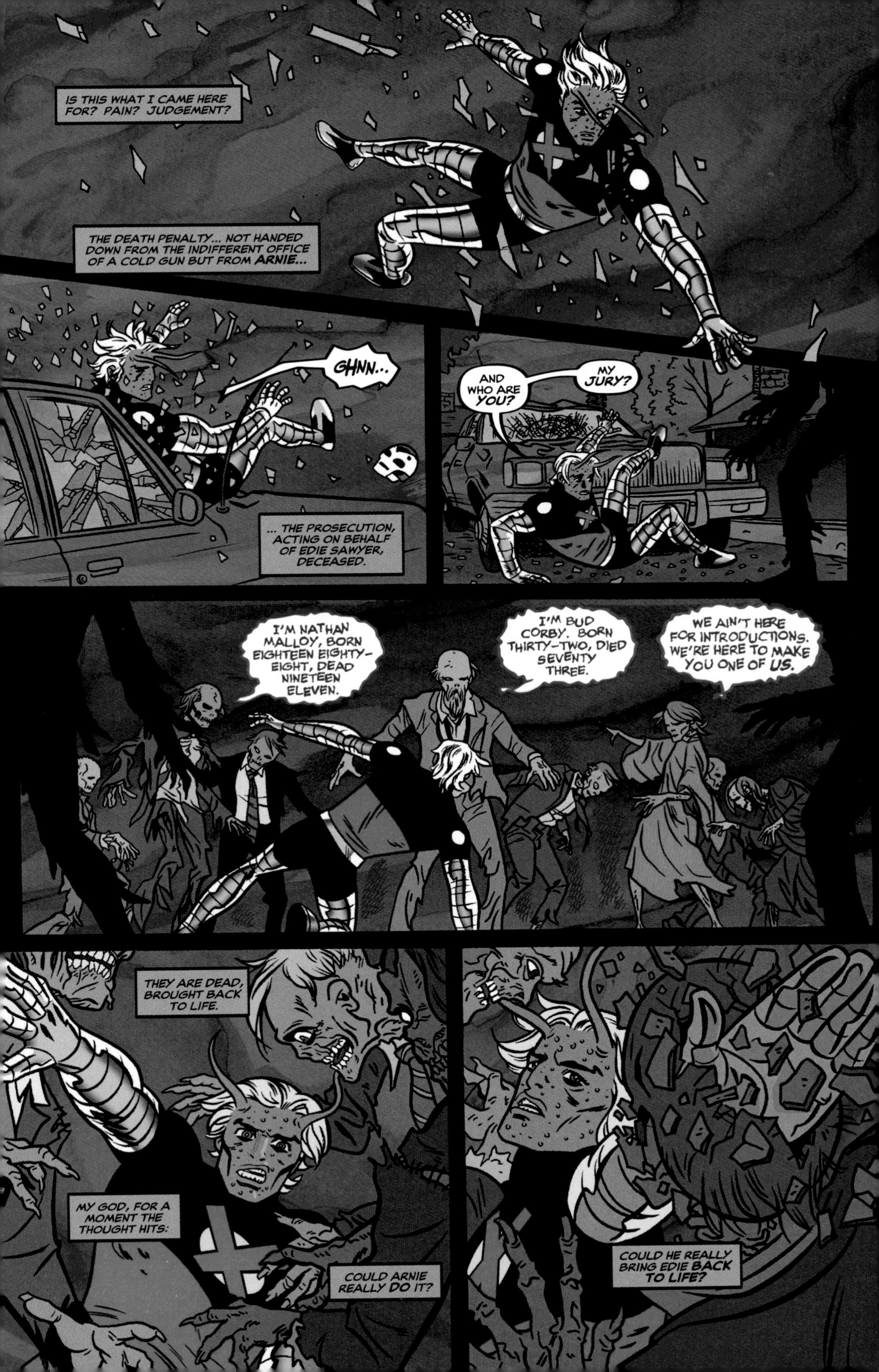
IS THIS WHAT I CAME HERE FOR? PAIN? JUDGEMENT?
THE DEATH PENALTY... NOT HANDED DOWN FROM THE INDIFFERENT OFFICE OF A COLD GUN BUT FROM ARNIE...
GHNN...
... THE PROSECUTION, ACTING ON BEHALF OF EDIE SAWYER, DECEASED.
AND WHO ARE YOU?
MY JURY?
I'M NATHAN MALLOY, BORN EIGHTEEN EIGHTY-EIGHT, DEAD NINETEEN ELEVEN.
I'M BUD CORBY. BORN THIRTY-TWO, DIED SEVENTY THREE.
WE AIN'T HERE FOR INTRODUCTIONS. WE'RE HERE TO MAKE YOU ONE OF US.
THEY ARE DEAD, BROUGHT BACK TO LIFE.
MY GOD, FOR A MOMENT THE THOUGHT HITS:
COULD ARNIE REALLY DO IT?
COULD HE REALLY BRING EDIE BACK TO LIFE?

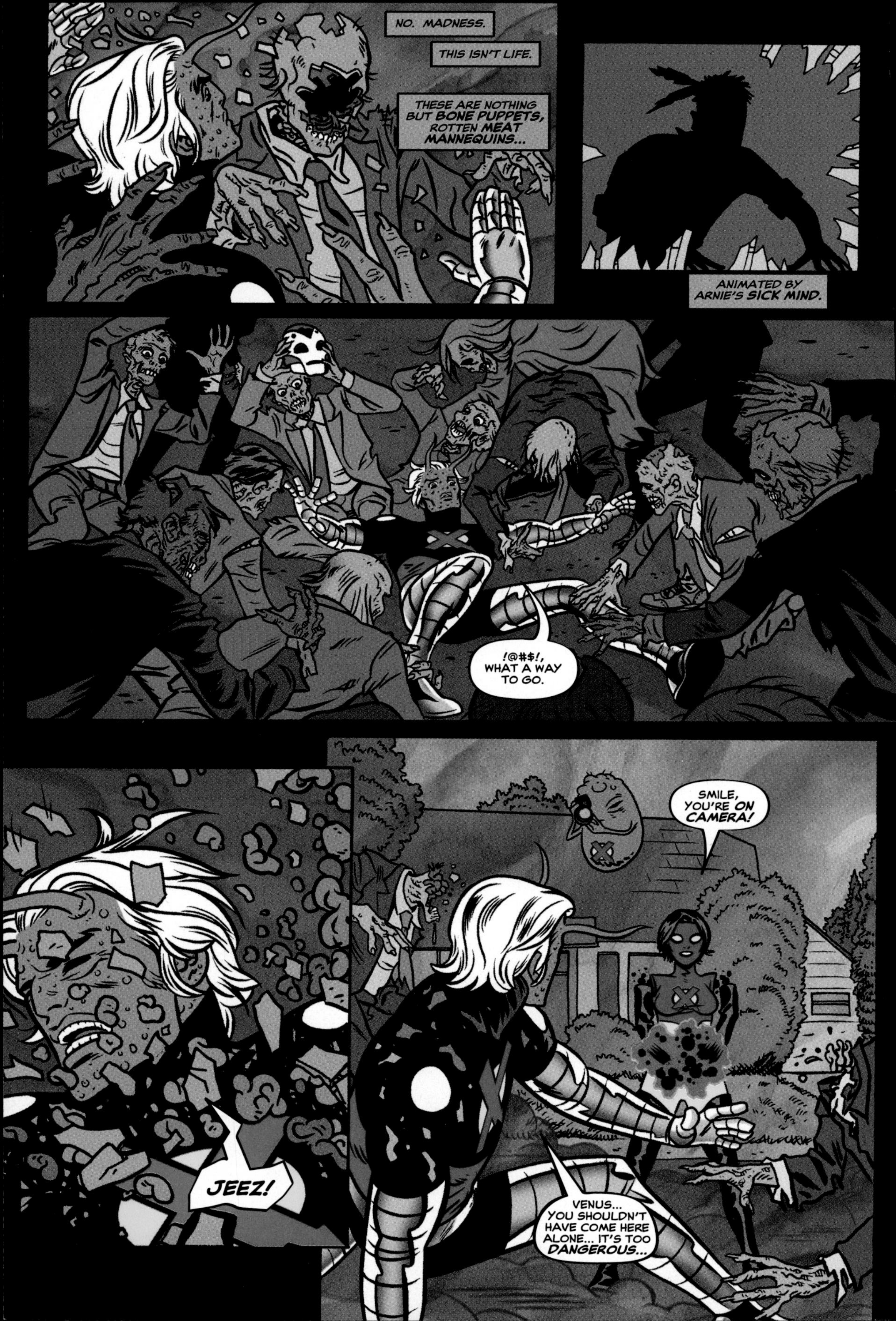
NO. MADNESS.
THIS ISN'T LIFE.
THESE ARE NOTHING BUT BONE PUPPETS, ROTTEN MEAT MANNEQUINS...
ANIMATED BY ARNIE'S SICK MIND.
!@#$!, WHAT A WAY TO GO.
JEEZ!
SMILE, YOU'RE ON CAMERA!
VENUS... YOU SHOULDN'T HAVE COME HERE ALONE... IT'S TOO DANGEROUS...

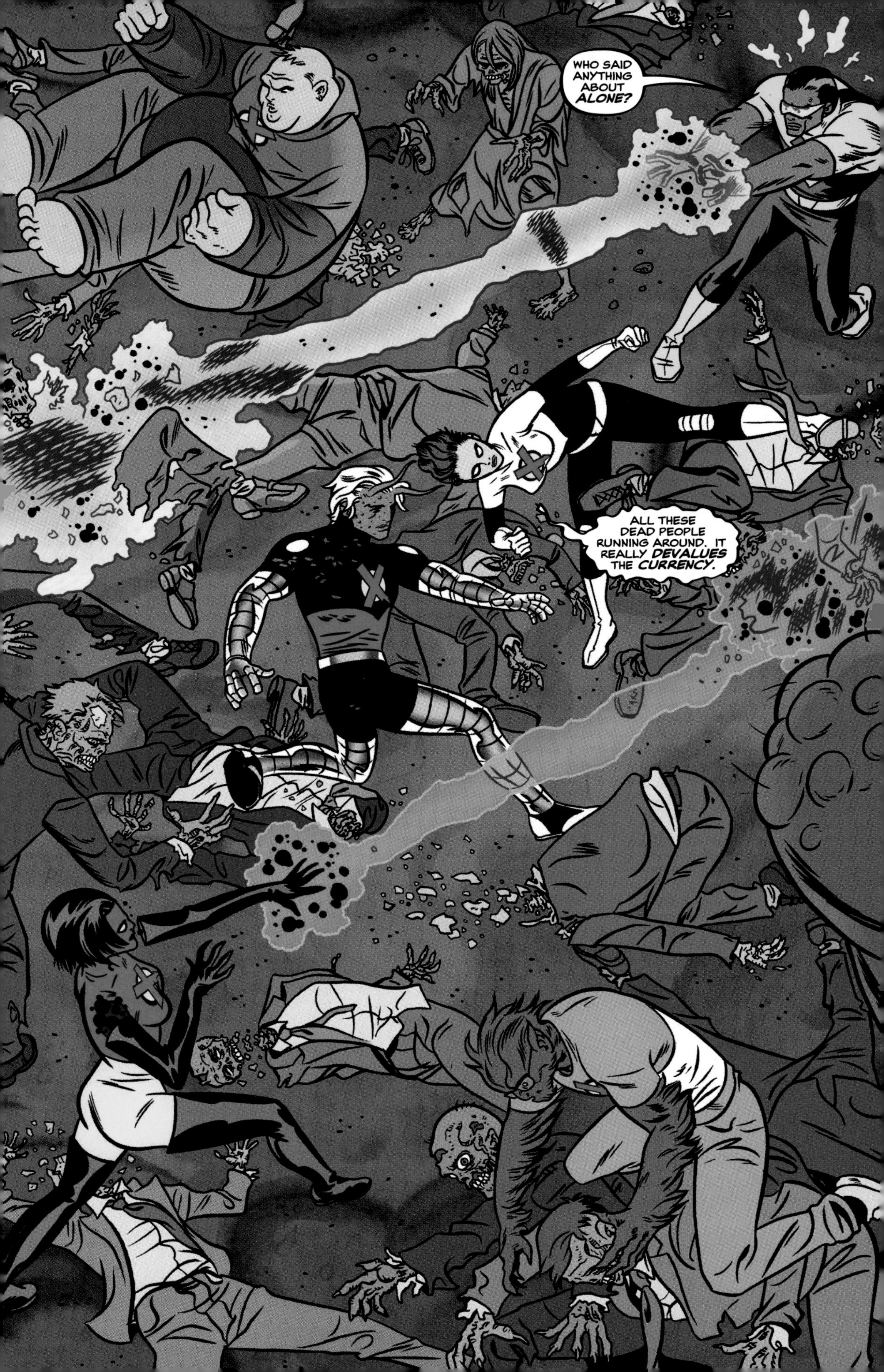
WHO SAID ANYTHING ABOUT *ALONE?*
ALL THESE DEAD PEOPLE RUNNING AROUND. IT REALLY *DEVALUES* THE *CURRENCY.*

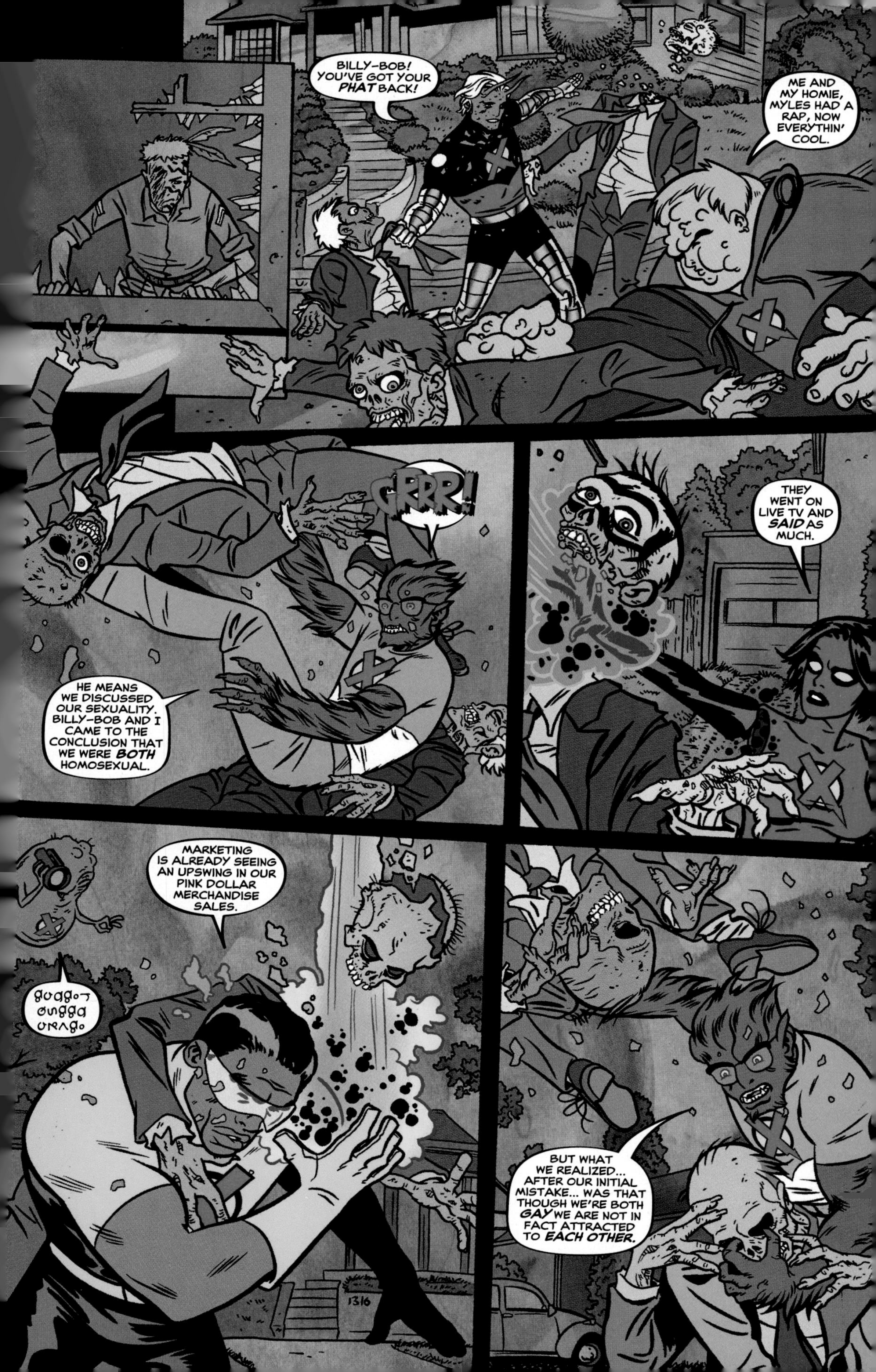
BILLY-BOB! YOU'VE GOT YOUR PHAT BACK!
ME AND MY HOMIE, MYLES HAD A RAP, NOW EVERYTHIN' COOL.
GRRR!
HE MEANS WE DISCUSSED OUR SEXUALITY. BILLY-BOB AND I CAME TO THE CONCLUSION THAT WE WERE BOTH HOMOSEXUAL.
THEY WENT ON LIVE TV AND SAID AS MUCH.
MARKETING IS ALREADY SEEING AN UPSWING IN OUR PINK DOLLAR MERCHANDISE SALES.
BUT WHAT WE REALIZED... AFTER OUR INITIAL MISTAKE... WAS THAT THOUGH WE'RE BOTH GAY WE ARE NOT IN FACT ATTRACTED TO EACH OTHER.
1316

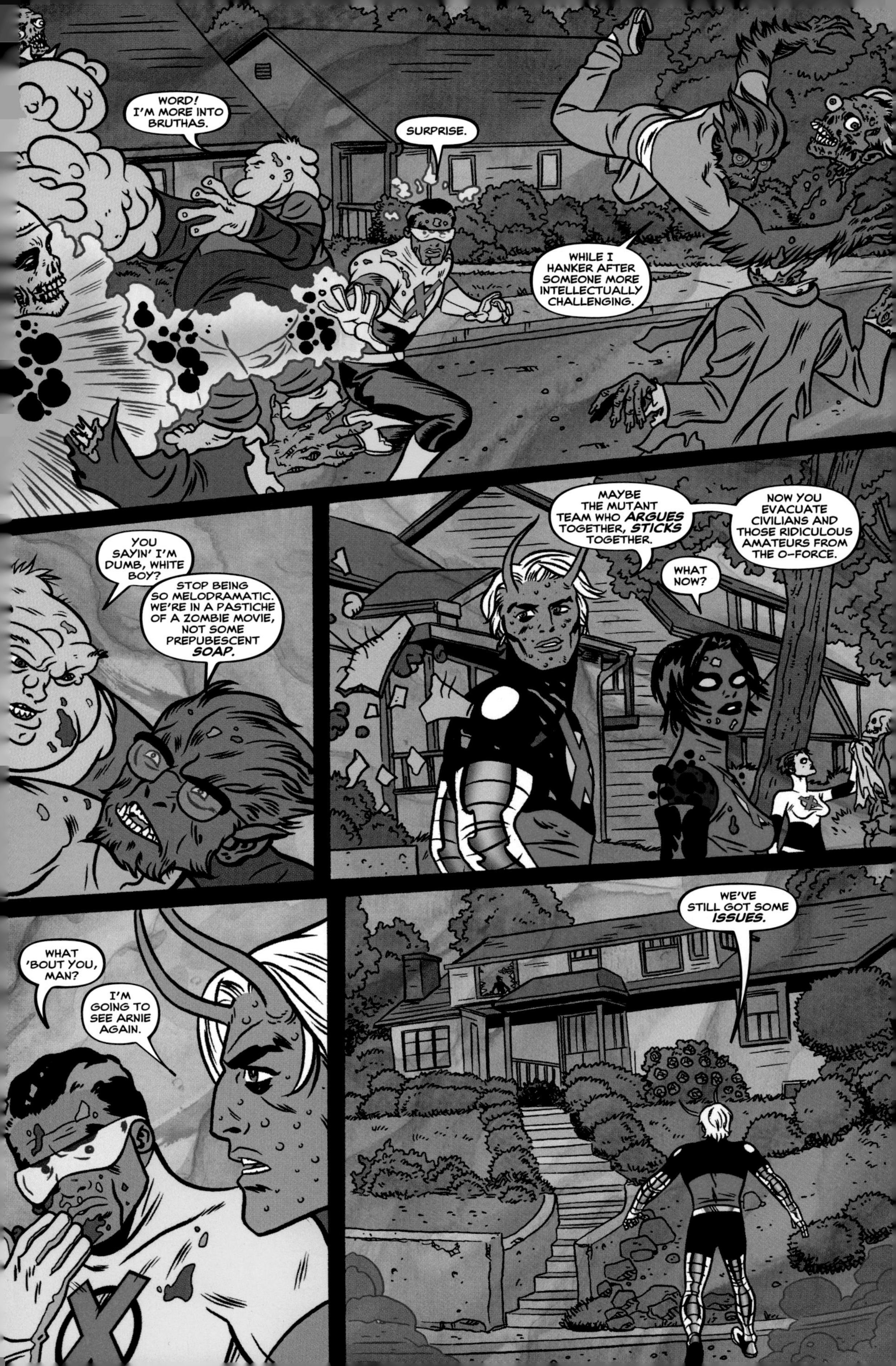
WORD! I'M MORE INTO BRUTHAS.
SURPRISE.
WHILE I HANKER AFTER SOMEONE MORE INTELLECTUALLY CHALLENGING.
YOU SAYIN' I'M DUMB, WHITE BOY?
STOP BEING SO MELODRAMATIC. WE'RE IN A PASTICHE OF A ZOMBIE MOVIE, NOT SOME PREPUBESCENT SOAP.
MAYBE THE MUTANT TEAM WHO ARGUES TOGETHER, STICKS TOGETHER.
NOW YOU EVACUATE CIVILIANS AND THOSE RIDICULOUS AMATEURS FROM THE O-FORCE.
WHAT NOW?
WHAT 'BOUT YOU, MAN?
I'M GOING TO SEE ARNIE AGAIN.
WE'VE STILL GOT SOME ISSUES.

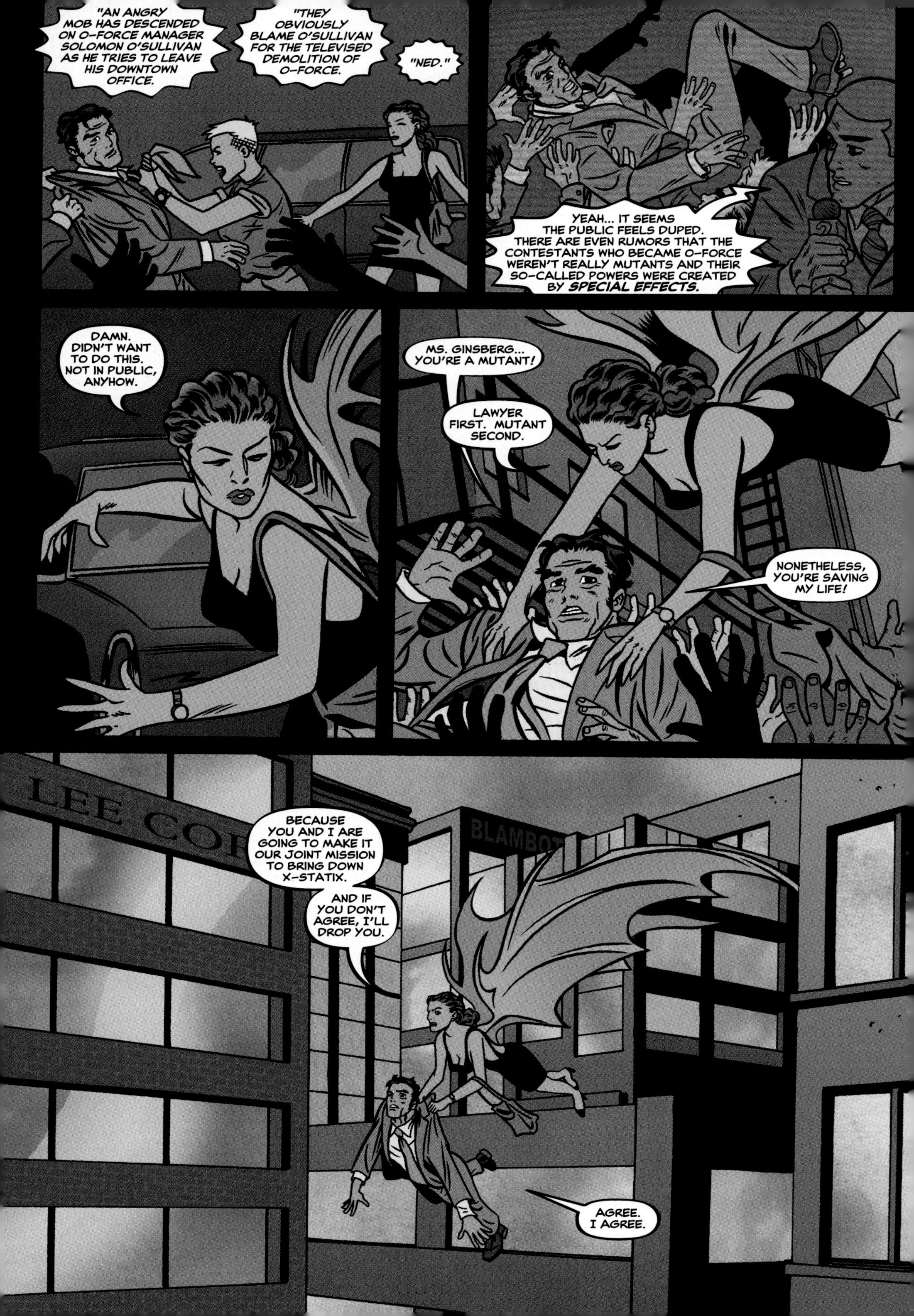
"AN ANGRY MOB HAS DESCENDED ON O-FORCE MANAGER SOLOMON O'SULLIVAN AS HE TRIES TO LEAVE HIS DOWNTOWN OFFICE.
"THEY OBVIOUSLY BLAME O'SULLIVAN FOR THE TELEVISED DEMOLITION OF O-FORCE.
"NED."
YEAH... IT SEEMS THE PUBLIC FEELS DUPED. THERE ARE EVEN RUMORS THAT THE CONTESTANTS WHO BECAME O-FORCE WEREN'T REALLY MUTANTS AND THEIR SO-CALLED POWERS WERE CREATED BY SPECIAL EFFECTS.
DAMN. DIDN'T WANT TO DO THIS. NOT IN PUBLIC, ANYHOW.
MS. GINSBERG... YOU'RE A MUTANT!
LAWYER FIRST. MUTANT SECOND.
NONETHELESS, YOU'RE SAVING MY LIFE!
LEE COR
BLAMBOT
BECAUSE YOU AND I ARE GOING TO MAKE IT OUR JOINT MISSION TO BRING DOWN X-STATIX.
AND IF YOU DON'T AGREE, I'LL DROP YOU.
AGREE. I AGREE.

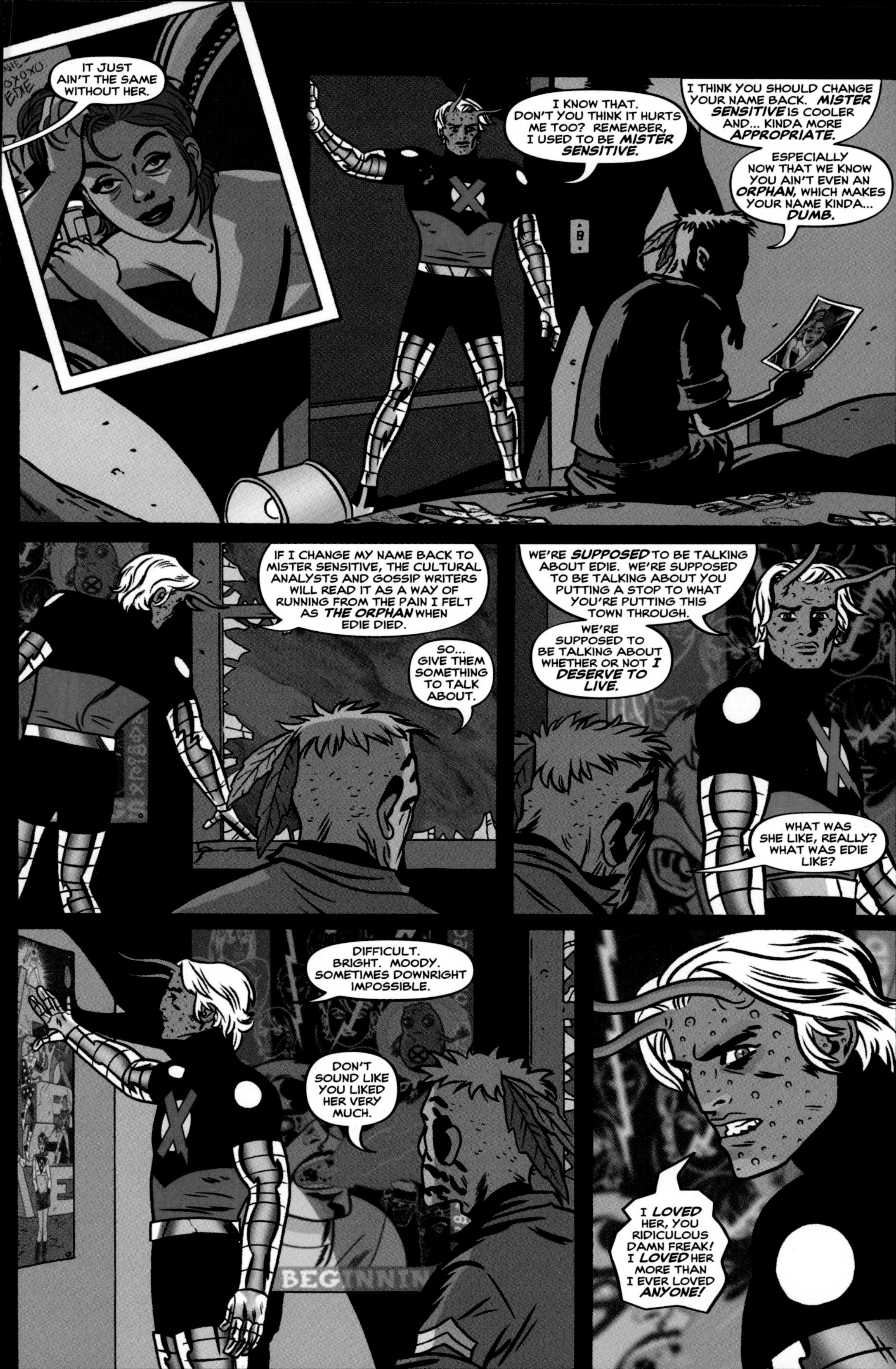

IT JUST AIN'T THE SAME WITHOUT HER.
I KNOW THAT. DON'T YOU THINK IT HURTS ME TOO? REMEMBER, I USED TO BE *MISTER SENSITIVE.*
I THINK YOU SHOULD CHANGE YOUR NAME BACK. *MISTER SENSITIVE* IS COOLER AND... KINDA MORE *APPROPRIATE.*
ESPECIALLY NOW THAT WE KNOW YOU AIN'T EVEN AN *ORPHAN,* WHICH MAKES YOUR NAME KINDA... *DUMB.*
IF I CHANGE MY NAME BACK TO MISTER SENSITIVE, THE CULTURAL ANALYSTS AND GOSSIP WRITERS WILL READ IT AS A WAY OF RUNNING FROM THE PAIN I FELT AS *THE ORPHAN* WHEN EDIE DIED.
SO... GIVE THEM SOMETHING TO TALK ABOUT.
WE'RE *SUPPOSED* TO BE TALKING ABOUT EDIE. WE'RE SUPPOSED TO BE TALKING ABOUT YOU PUTTING A STOP TO WHAT YOU'RE PUTTING THIS TOWN THROUGH.
WE'RE SUPPOSED TO BE TALKING ABOUT WHETHER OR NOT *I DESERVE TO LIVE.*
WHAT WAS SHE LIKE, REALLY? WHAT WAS EDIE LIKE?
DIFFICULT. BRIGHT. MOODY. SOMETIMES DOWNRIGHT IMPOSSIBLE.
DON'T SOUND LIKE YOU LIKED HER VERY MUCH.
BEGINNIN
I *LOVED* HER, YOU RIDICULOUS DAMN FREAK! I *LOVED* HER MORE THAN I EVER LOVED *ANYONE!*

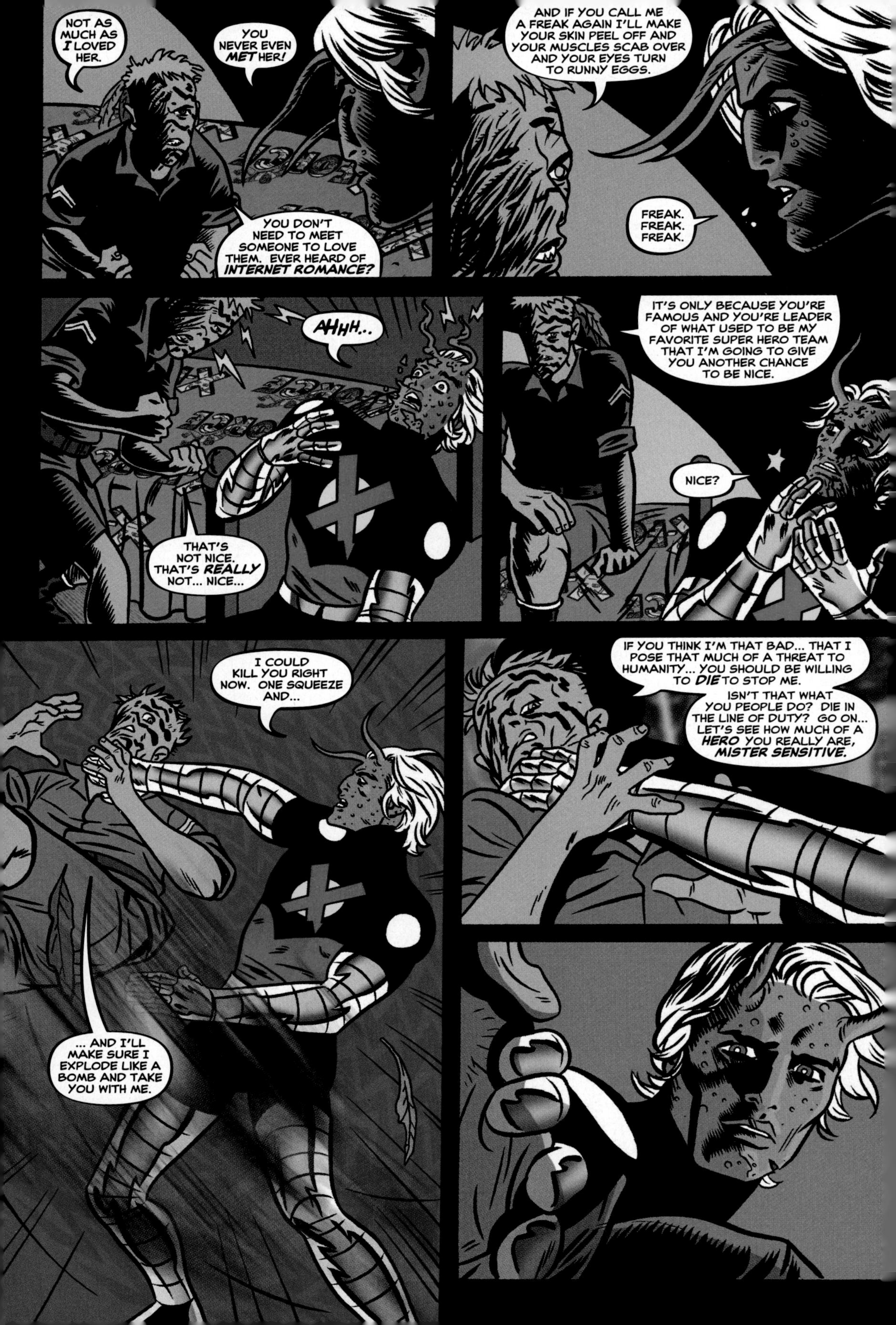

NOT AS MUCH AS I LOVED HER.
YOU NEVER EVEN MET HER!
YOU DON'T NEED TO MEET SOMEONE TO LOVE THEM. EVER HEARD OF INTERNET ROMANCE?
AND IF YOU CALL ME A FREAK AGAIN I'LL MAKE YOUR SKIN PEEL OFF AND YOUR MUSCLES SCAB OVER AND YOUR EYES TURN TO RUNNY EGGS.
FREAK. FREAK. FREAK.
AHHH...
THAT'S NOT NICE. THAT'S REALLY NOT... NICE...
IT'S ONLY BECAUSE YOU'RE FAMOUS AND YOU'RE LEADER OF WHAT USED TO BE MY FAVORITE SUPER HERO TEAM THAT I'M GOING TO GIVE YOU ANOTHER CHANCE TO BE NICE.
NICE?
I COULD KILL YOU RIGHT NOW. ONE SQUEEZE AND...
... AND I'LL MAKE SURE I EXPLODE LIKE A BOMB AND TAKE YOU WITH ME.
IF YOU THINK I'M THAT BAD... THAT I POSE THAT MUCH OF A THREAT TO HUMANITY... YOU SHOULD BE WILLING TO DIE TO STOP ME.
ISN'T THAT WHAT YOU PEOPLE DO? DIE IN THE LINE OF DUTY? GO ON... LET'S SEE HOW MUCH OF A HERO YOU REALLY ARE, MISTER SENSITIVE.

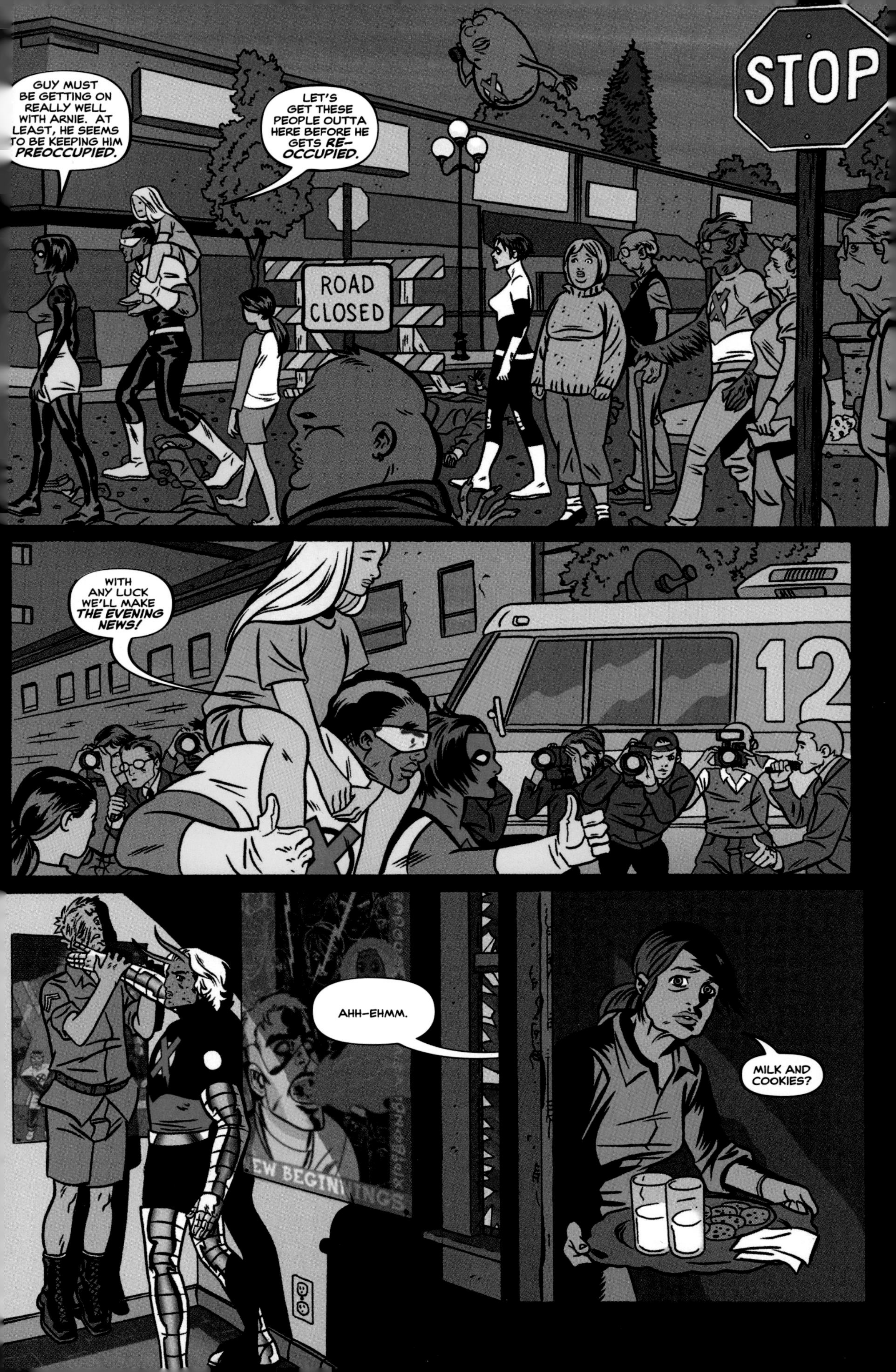
GUY MUST BE GETTING ON REALLY WELL WITH ARNIE. AT LEAST, HE SEEMS TO BE KEEPING HIM PREOCCUPIED.
LET'S GET THESE PEOPLE OUTTA HERE BEFORE HE GETS RE-OCCUPIED.
STOP
ROAD CLOSED
WITH ANY LUCK WE'LL MAKE THE EVENING NEWS!
12
AHH-EHMM.
MILK AND COOKIES?
EW BEGINNINGS

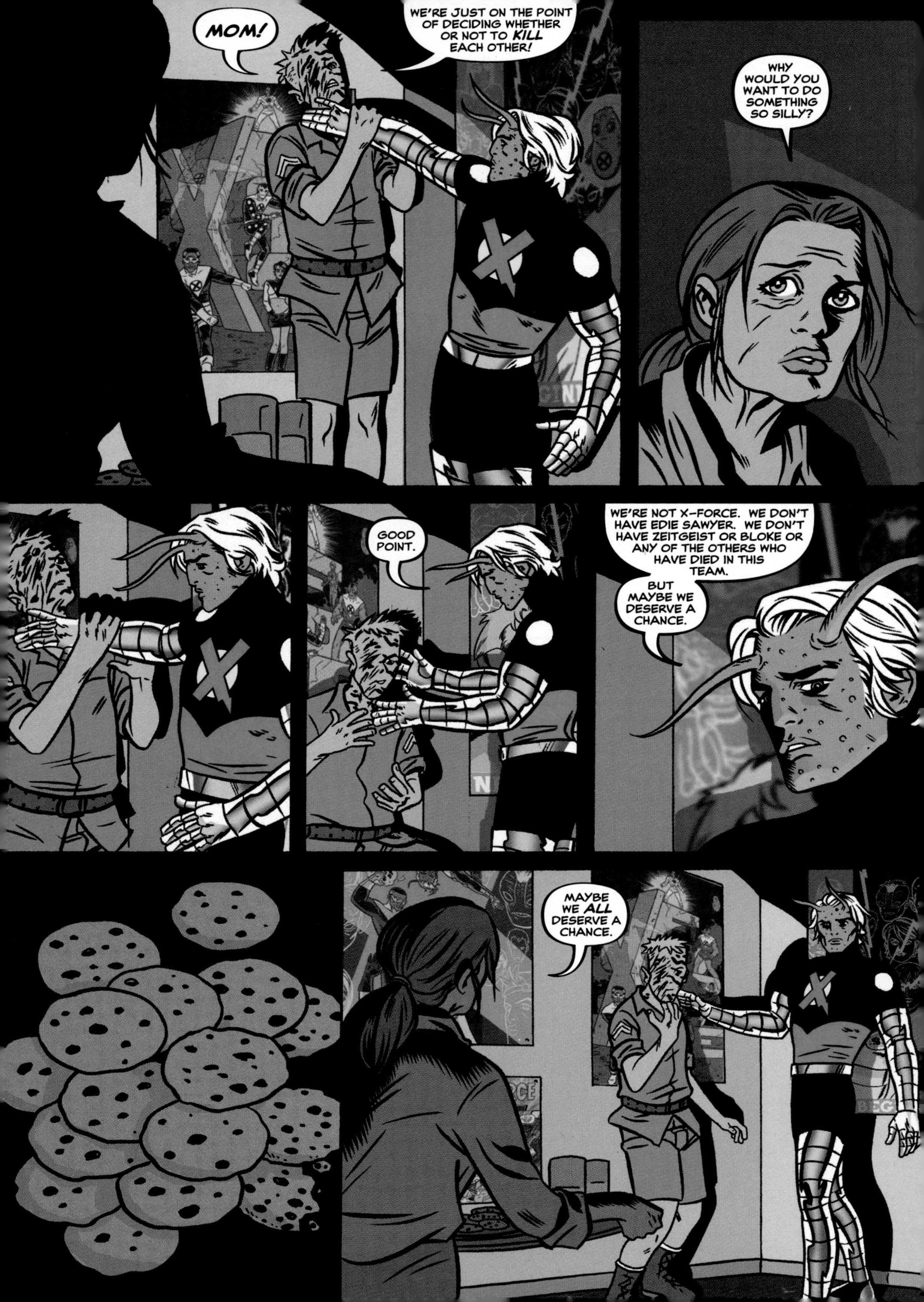
MOM!
WE'RE JUST ON THE POINT OF DECIDING WHETHER OR NOT TO KILL EACH OTHER!
WHY WOULD YOU WANT TO DO SOMETHING SO SILLY?
GOOD POINT.
WE'RE NOT X-FORCE. WE DON'T HAVE EDIE SAWYER. WE DON'T HAVE ZEITGEIST OR BLOKE OR ANY OF THE OTHERS WHO HAVE DIED IN THIS TEAM.
BUT MAYBE WE DESERVE A CHANCE.
MAYBE WE ALL DESERVE A CHANCE.

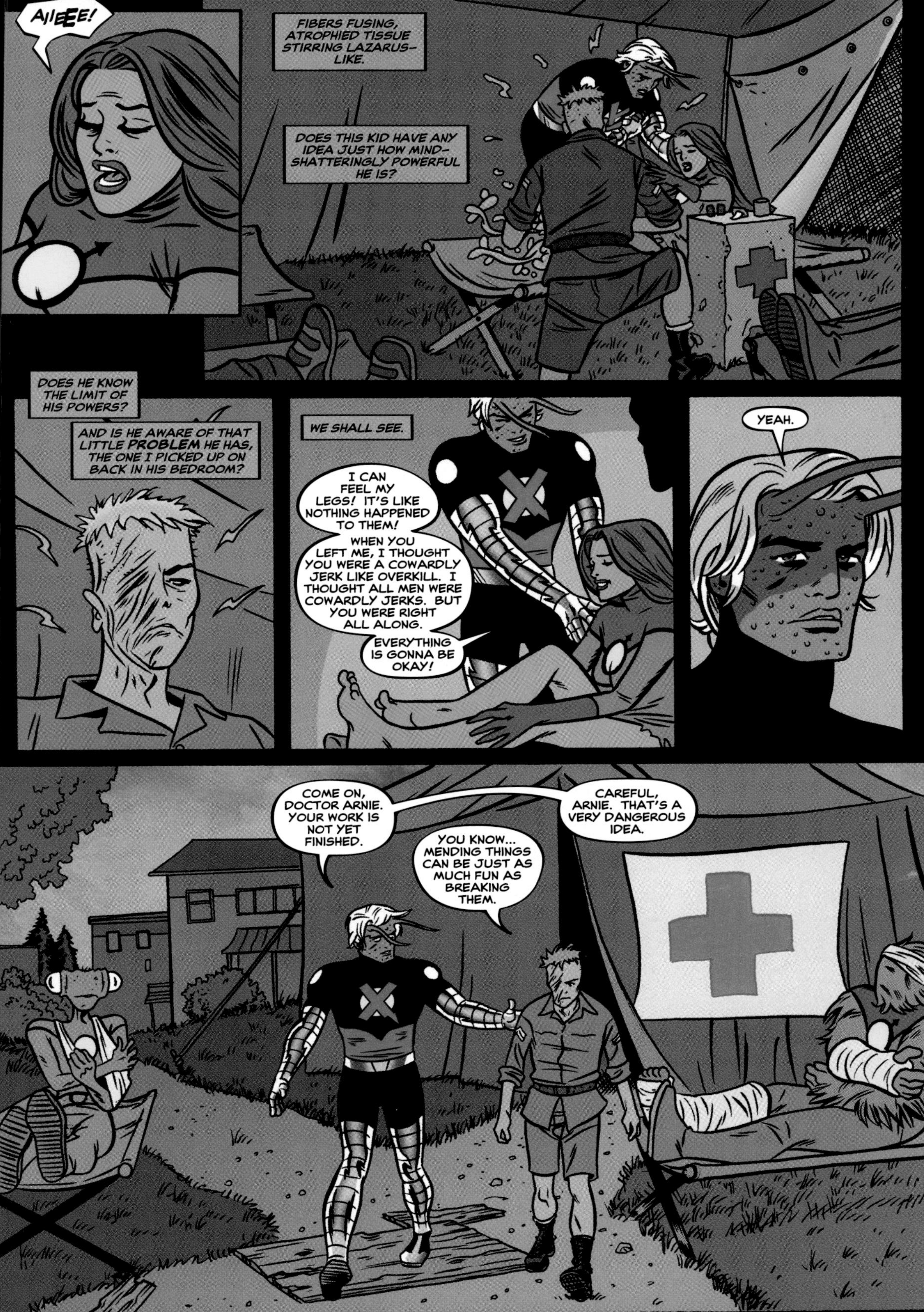
AIIEEE!
FIBERS FUSING, ATROPHIED TISSUE STIRRING LAZARUS-LIKE.
DOES THIS KID HAVE ANY IDEA JUST HOW MIND-SHATTERINGLY POWERFUL HE IS?
DOES HE KNOW THE LIMIT OF HIS POWERS?
AND IS HE AWARE OF THAT LITTLE PROBLEM HE HAS, THE ONE I PICKED UP ON BACK IN HIS BEDROOM?
WE SHALL SEE.
I CAN FEEL MY LEGS! IT'S LIKE NOTHING HAPPENED TO THEM!
WHEN YOU LEFT ME, I THOUGHT YOU WERE A COWARDLY JERK LIKE OVERKILL. I THOUGHT ALL MEN WERE COWARDLY JERKS. BUT YOU WERE RIGHT ALL ALONG.
EVERYTHING IS GONNA BE OKAY!
YEAH.
COME ON, DOCTOR ARNIE. YOUR WORK IS NOT YET FINISHED.
YOU KNOW... MENDING THINGS CAN BE JUST AS MUCH FUN AS BREAKING THEM.
CAREFUL, ARNIE. THAT'S A VERY DANGEROUS IDEA.

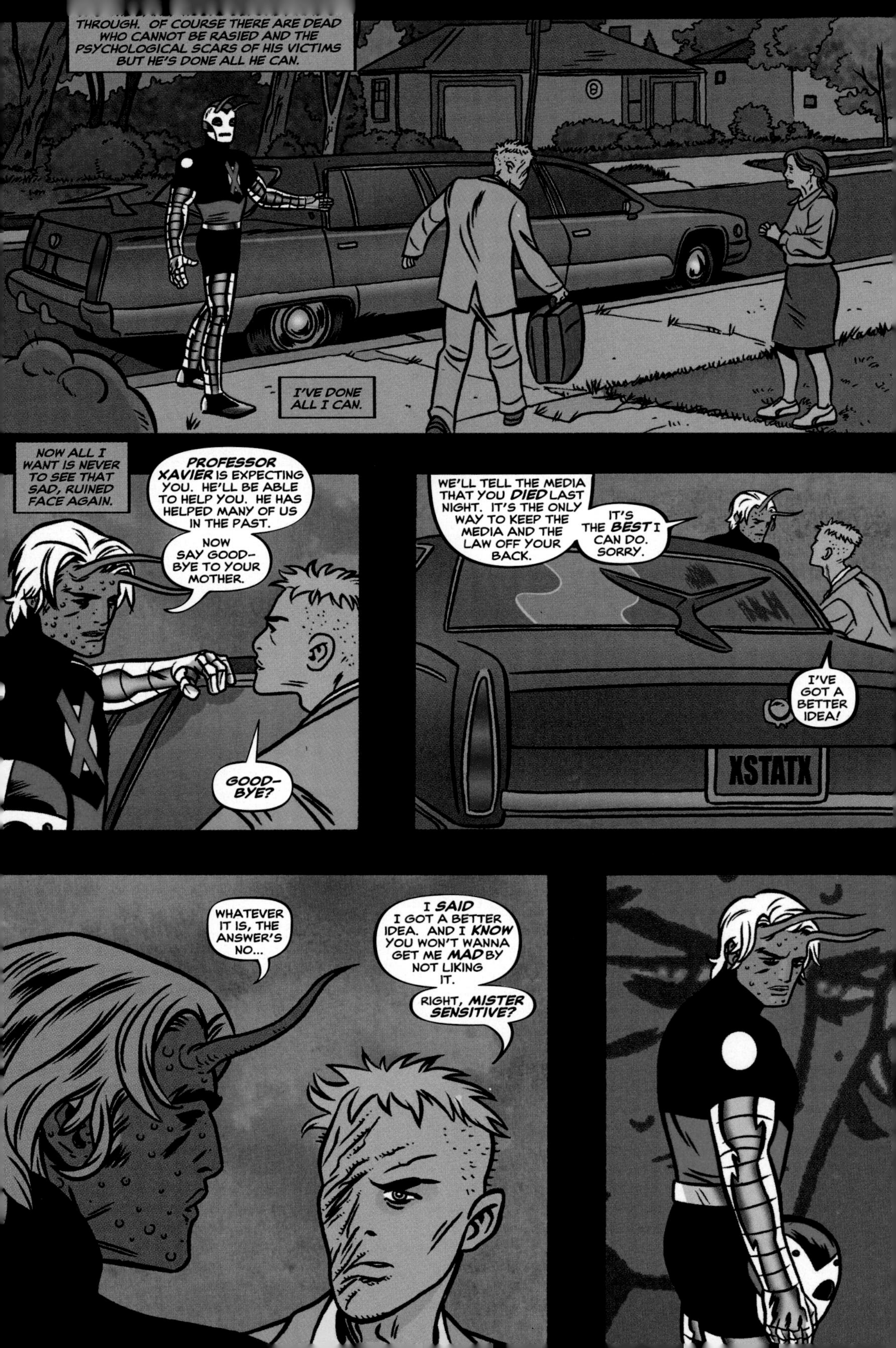
THROUGH. OF COURSE THERE ARE DEAD WHO CANNOT BE RASIED AND THE PSYCHOLOGICAL SCARS OF HIS VICTIMS BUT HE'S DONE ALL HE CAN.
I'VE DONE ALL I CAN.
NOW ALL I WANT IS NEVER TO SEE THAT SAD, RUINED FACE AGAIN.
PROFESSOR XAVIER IS EXPECTING YOU. HE'LL BE ABLE TO HELP YOU. HE HAS HELPED MANY OF US IN THE PAST.
NOW SAY GOOD-BYE TO YOUR MOTHER.
GOOD-BYE?
WE'LL TELL THE MEDIA THAT YOU DIED LAST NIGHT. IT'S THE ONLY WAY TO KEEP THE MEDIA AND THE LAW OFF YOUR BACK.
IT'S THE BEST I CAN DO. SORRY.
I'VE GOT A BETTER IDEA!
XSTATX
WHATEVER IT IS, THE ANSWER'S NO...
I SAID I GOT A BETTER IDEA. AND I KNOW YOU WON'T WANNA GET ME MAD BY NOT LIKING IT.
RIGHT, MISTER SENSITIVE?

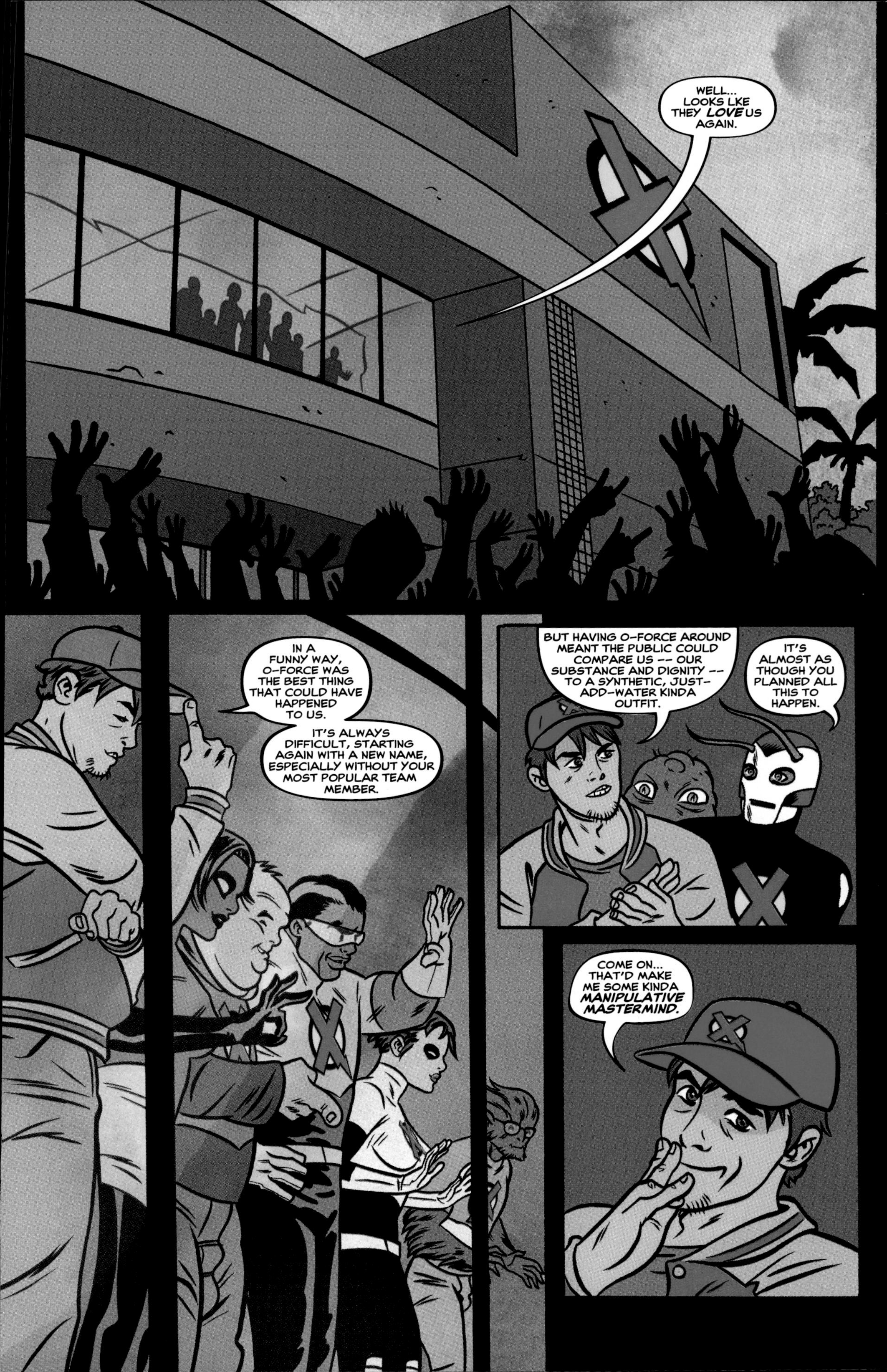
WELL... LOOKS LKE THEY *LOVE* US AGAIN.
IN A FUNNY WAY, O-FORCE WAS THE BEST THING THAT COULD HAVE HAPPENED TO US.
IT'S ALWAYS DIFFICULT, STARTING AGAIN WITH A NEW NAME, ESPECIALLY WITHOUT YOUR MOST POPULAR TEAM MEMBER.
BUT HAVING O-FORCE AROUND MEANT THE PUBLIC COULD COMPARE US -- OUR SUBSTANCE AND DIGNITY -- TO A SYNTHETIC, JUST-ADD-WATER KINDA OUTFIT.
IT'S ALMOST AS THOUGH YOU PLANNED ALL THIS TO HAPPEN.
COME ON... THAT'D MAKE ME SOME KINDA ***MANIPULATIVE MASTERMIND.***

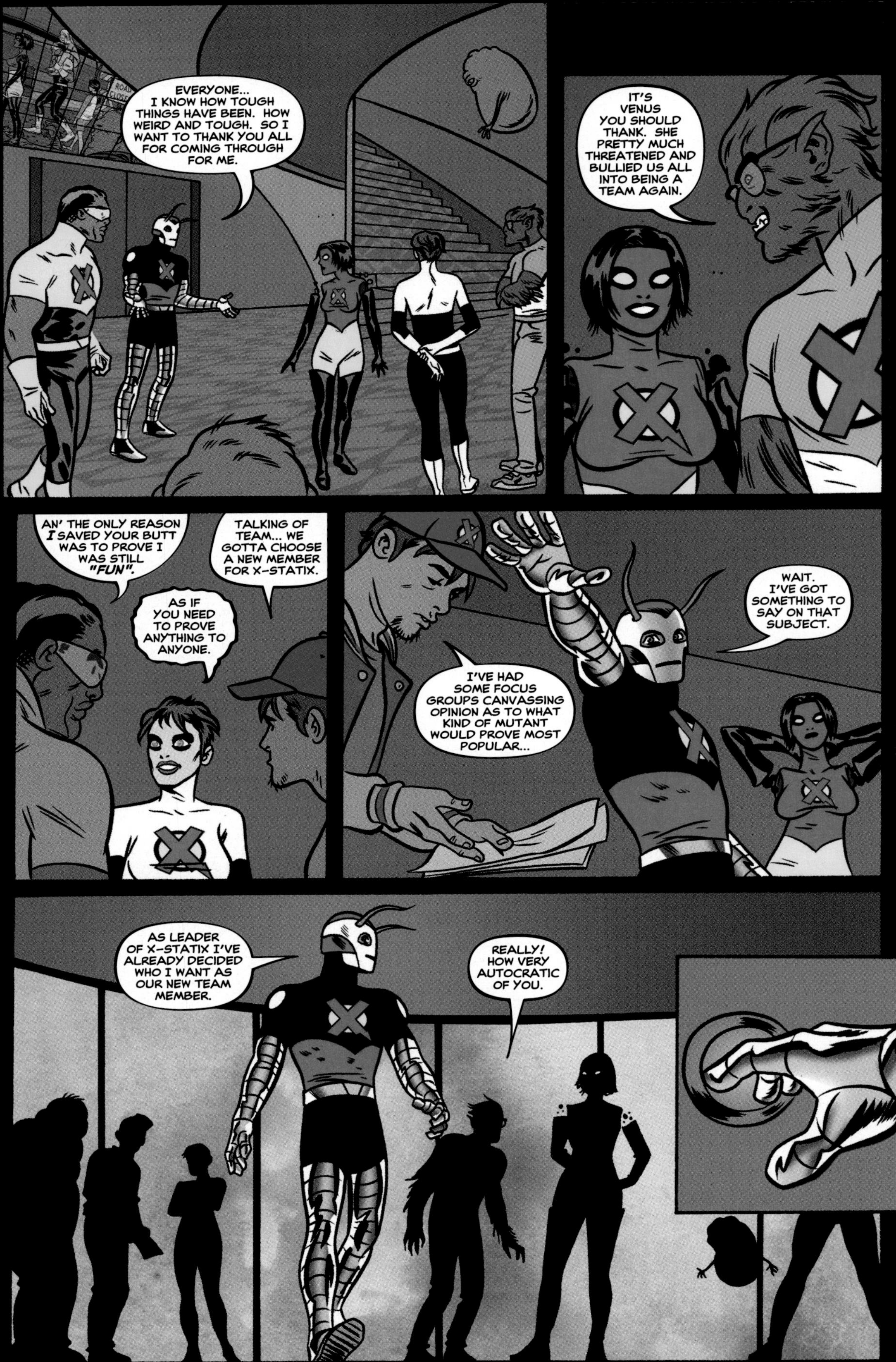
EVERYONE... I KNOW HOW TOUGH THINGS HAVE BEEN. HOW WEIRD AND TOUGH. SO I WANT TO THANK YOU ALL FOR COMING THROUGH FOR ME.
IT'S VENUS YOU SHOULD THANK. SHE PRETTY MUCH THREATENED AND BULLIED US ALL INTO BEING A TEAM AGAIN.
AN' THE ONLY REASON I SAVED YOUR BUTT WAS TO PROVE I WAS STILL "FUN".
AS IF YOU NEED TO PROVE ANYTHING TO ANYONE.
TALKING OF TEAM... WE GOTTA CHOOSE A NEW MEMBER FOR X-STATIX.
WAIT. I'VE GOT SOMETHING TO SAY ON THAT SUBJECT.
I'VE HAD SOME FOCUS GROUPS CANVASSING OPINION AS TO WHAT KIND OF MUTANT WOULD PROVE MOST POPULAR...
AS LEADER OF X-STATIX I'VE ALREADY DECIDED WHO I WANT AS OUR NEW TEAM MEMBER.
REALLY! HOW VERY AUTOCRATIC OF YOU.

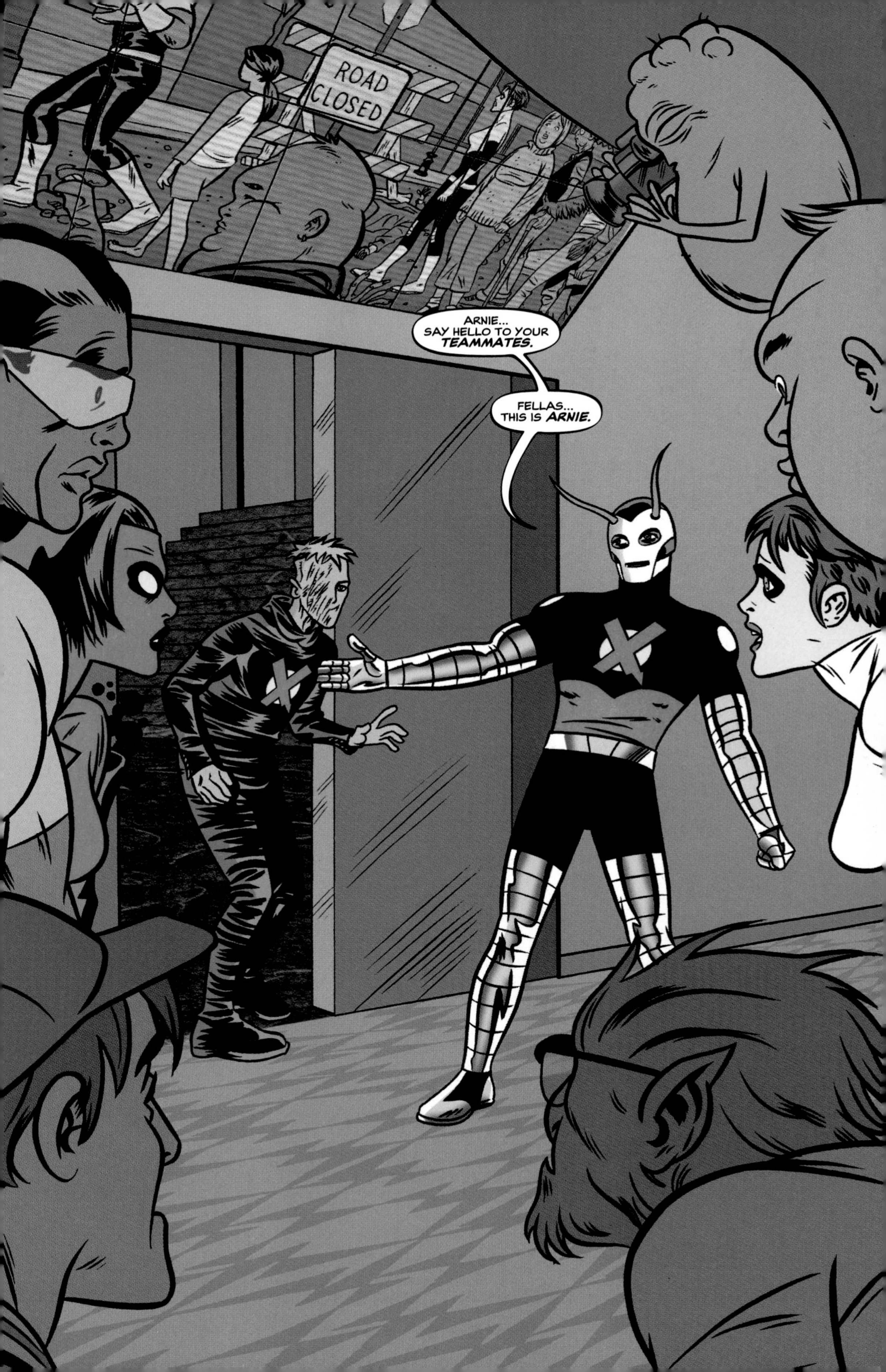
ROAD CLOSED
ARNIE... SAY HELLO TO YOUR TEAMMATES.
FELLAS... THIS IS ARNIE.

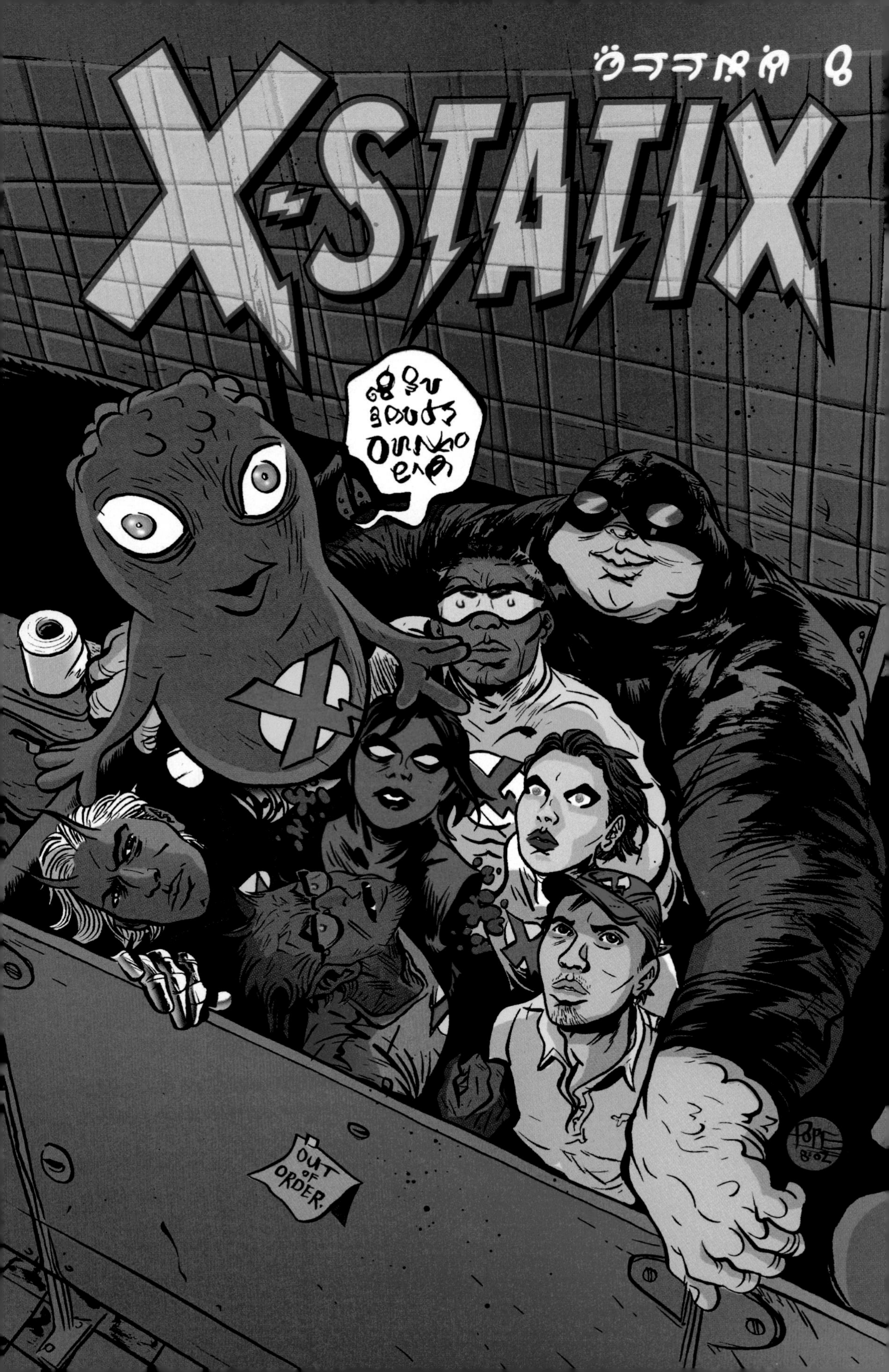
X-STATIX
OUT OF ORDER.
POPE 8.02

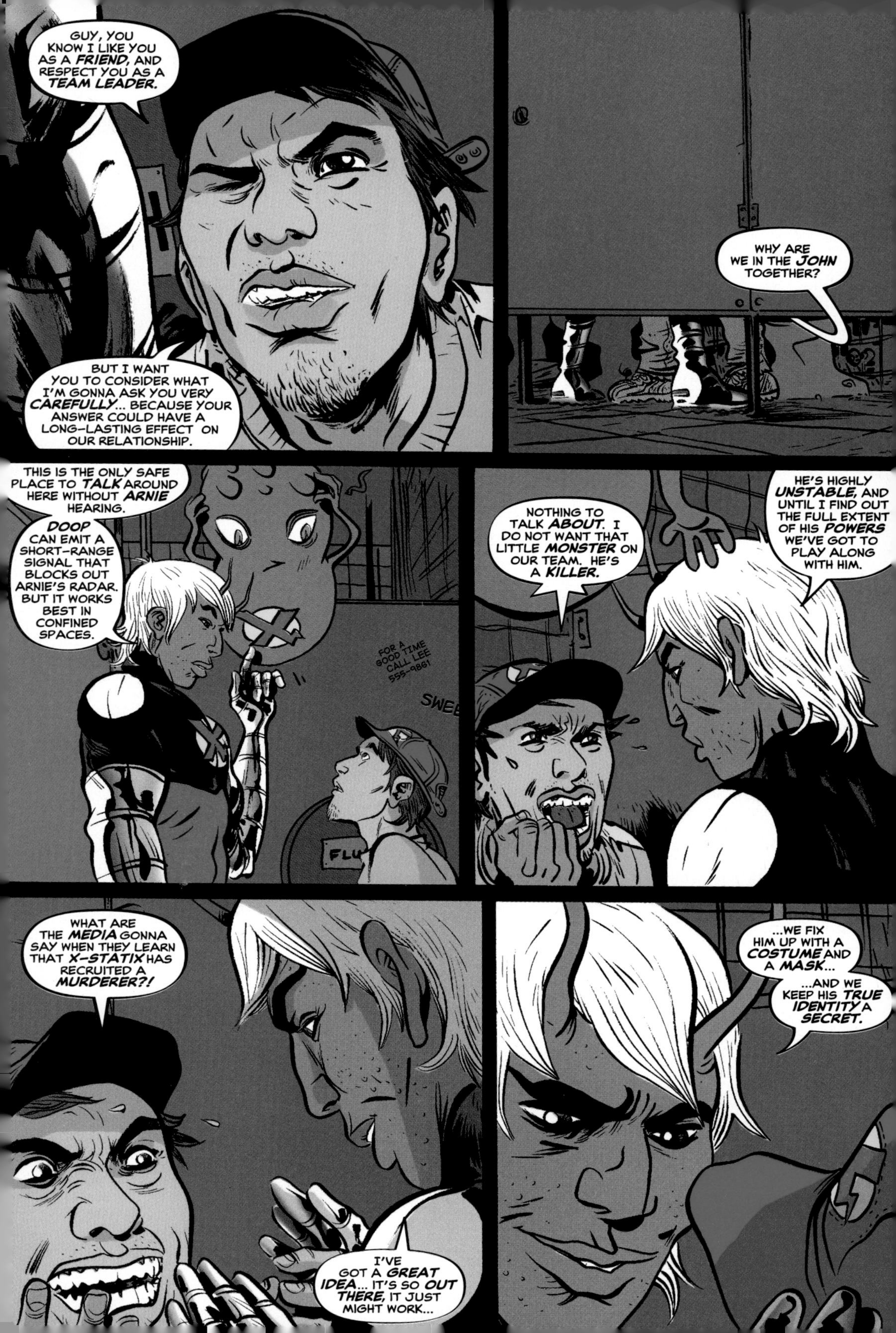
GUY, YOU KNOW I LIKE YOU AS A FRIEND, AND RESPECT YOU AS A TEAM LEADER.
BUT I WANT YOU TO CONSIDER WHAT I'M GONNA ASK YOU VERY CAREFULLY... BECAUSE YOUR ANSWER COULD HAVE A LONG-LASTING EFFECT ON OUR RELATIONSHIP.
WHY ARE WE IN THE JOHN TOGETHER?
THIS IS THE ONLY SAFE PLACE TO TALK AROUND HERE WITHOUT ARNIE HEARING.
DOOP CAN EMIT A SHORT-RANGE SIGNAL THAT BLOCKS OUT ARNIE'S RADAR. BUT IT WORKS BEST IN CONFINED SPACES.
FOR A GOOD TIME CALL LEE 555-9861
SWEE
FLU
NOTHING TO TALK ABOUT. I DO NOT WANT THAT LITTLE MONSTER ON OUR TEAM. HE'S A KILLER.
HE'S HIGHLY UNSTABLE, AND UNTIL I FIND OUT THE FULL EXTENT OF HIS POWERS WE'VE GOT TO PLAY ALONG WITH HIM.
WHAT ARE THE MEDIA GONNA SAY WHEN THEY LEARN THAT X-STATIX HAS RECRUITED A MURDERER?!
I'VE GOT A GREAT IDEA... IT'S SO OUT THERE, IT JUST MIGHT WORK...
...WE FIX HIM UP WITH A COSTUME AND A MASK...
...AND WE KEEP HIS TRUE IDENTITY A SECRET.

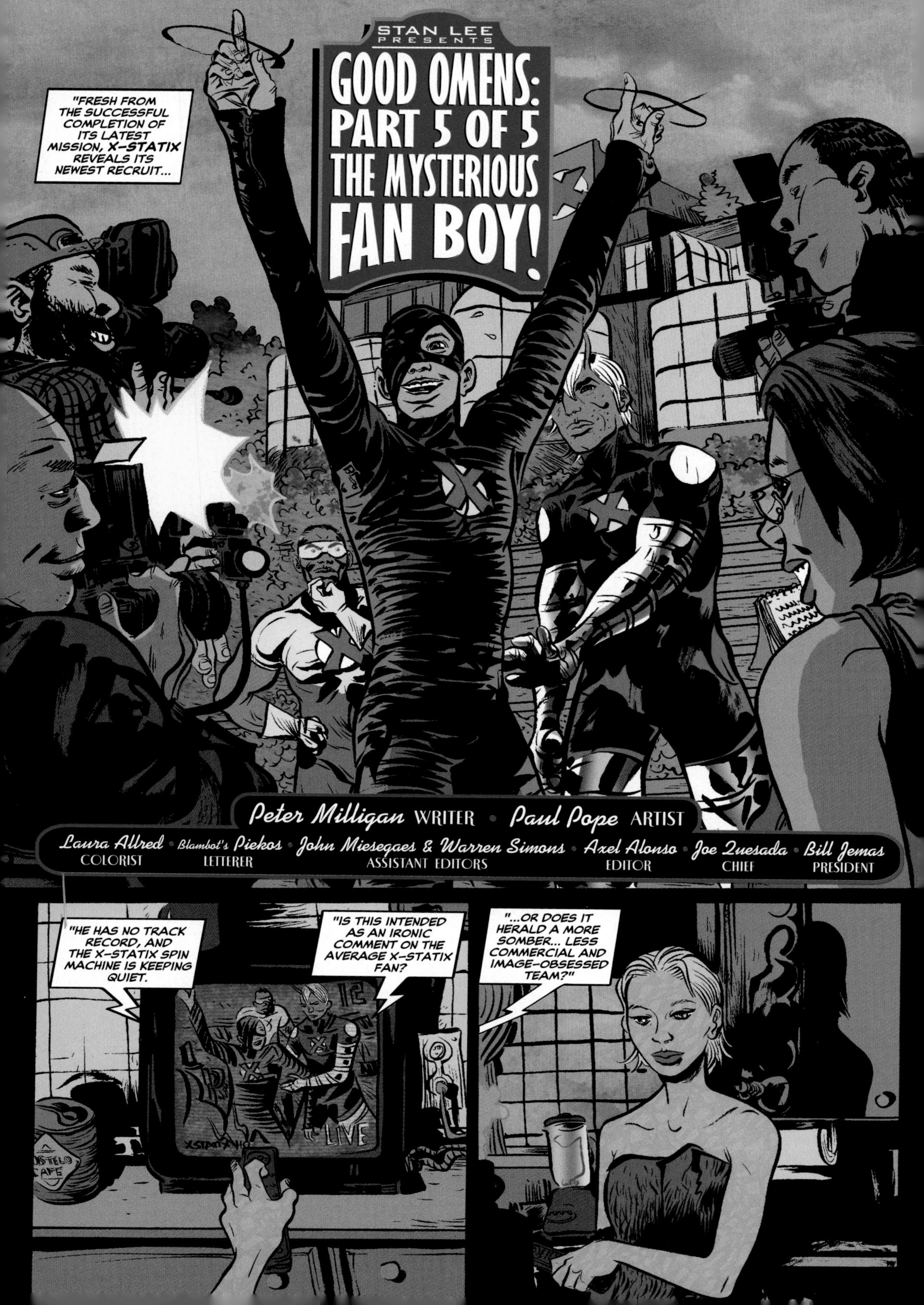
STAN LEE PRESENTS
GOOD OMENS: PART 5 OF 5
THE MYSTERIOUS FAN BOY!
"FRESH FROM THE SUCCESSFUL COMPLETION OF ITS LATEST MISSION, X-STATIX REVEALS ITS NEWEST RECRUIT...
Peter Milligan WRITER • Paul Pope ARTIST
Laura Allred COLORIST • Blambot's Piekos LETTERER • John Miesegaes & Warren Simons ASSISTANT EDITORS • Axel Alonso EDITOR • Joe Quesada CHIEF • Bill Jemas PRESIDENT
"HE HAS NO TRACK RECORD, AND THE X-STATIX SPIN MACHINE IS KEEPING QUIET.
"IS THIS INTENDED AS AN IRONIC COMMENT ON THE AVERAGE X-STATIX FAN?
"...OR DOES IT HERALD A MORE SOMBER... LESS COMMERCIAL AND IMAGE-OBSESSED TEAM?"
LIVE

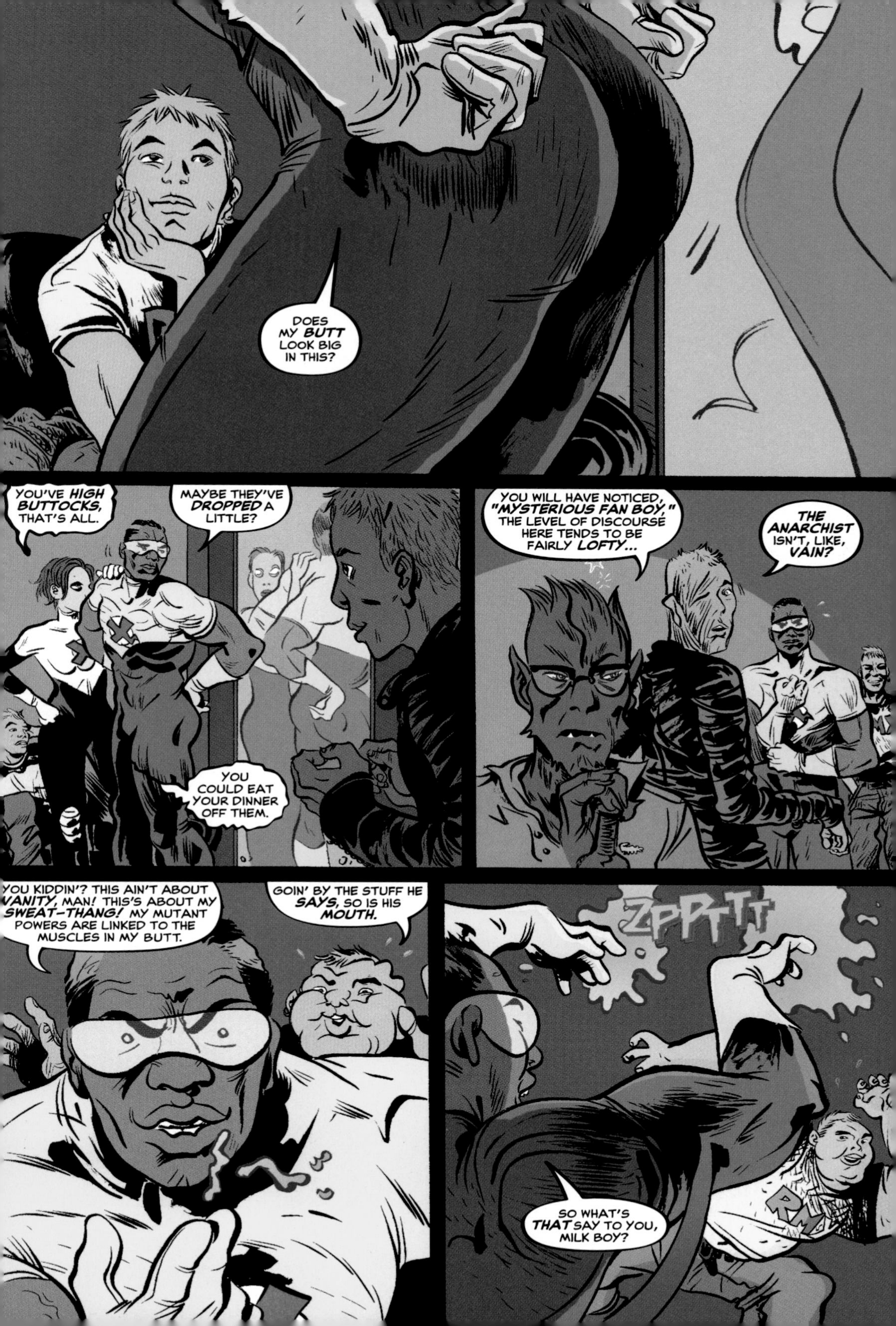
DOES MY BUTT LOOK BIG IN THIS?
YOU'VE HIGH BUTTOCKS, THAT'S ALL.
MAYBE THEY'VE DROPPED A LITTLE?
YOU COULD EAT YOUR DINNER OFF THEM.
YOU WILL HAVE NOTICED, "MYSTERIOUS FAN BOY," THE LEVEL OF DISCOURSE HERE TENDS TO BE FAIRLY LOFTY...
THE ANARCHIST ISN'T, LIKE, VAIN?
YOU KIDDIN'? THIS AIN'T ABOUT VANITY, MAN! THIS'S ABOUT MY SWEAT-THANG! MY MUTANT POWERS ARE LINKED TO THE MUSCLES IN MY BUTT.
GOIN' BY THE STUFF HE SAYS, SO IS HIS MOUTH.
ZPPTTT
SO WHAT'S THAT SAY TO YOU, MILK BOY?

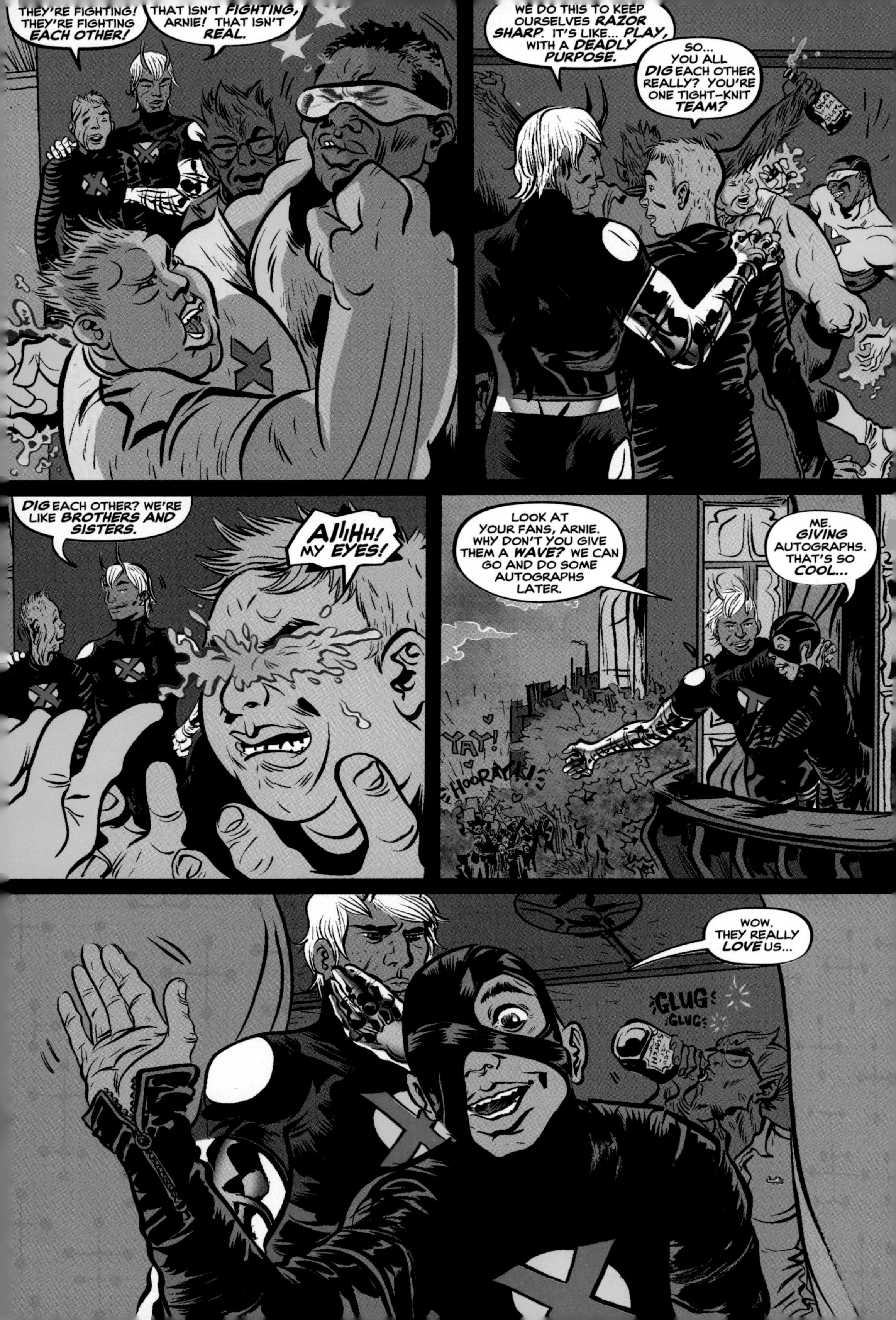
THEY'RE FIGHTING! THEY'RE FIGHTING EACH OTHER!
THAT ISN'T FIGHTING, ARNIE! THAT ISN'T REAL.
WE DO THIS TO KEEP OURSELVES RAZOR SHARP. IT'S LIKE... PLAY, WITH A DEADLY PURPOSE.
SO... YOU ALL DIG EACH OTHER REALLY? YOU'RE ONE TIGHT-KNIT TEAM?
DIG EACH OTHER? WE'RE LIKE BROTHERS AND SISTERS.
AIIIHH! MY EYES!
LOOK AT YOUR FANS, ARNIE. WHY DON'T YOU GIVE THEM A WAVE? WE CAN GO AND DO SOME AUTOGRAPHS LATER.
ME. GIVING AUTOGRAPHS. THAT'S SO COOL...
YAY!
HOORAY!
WOW. THEY REALLY LOVE US...
GLUG
GLUG

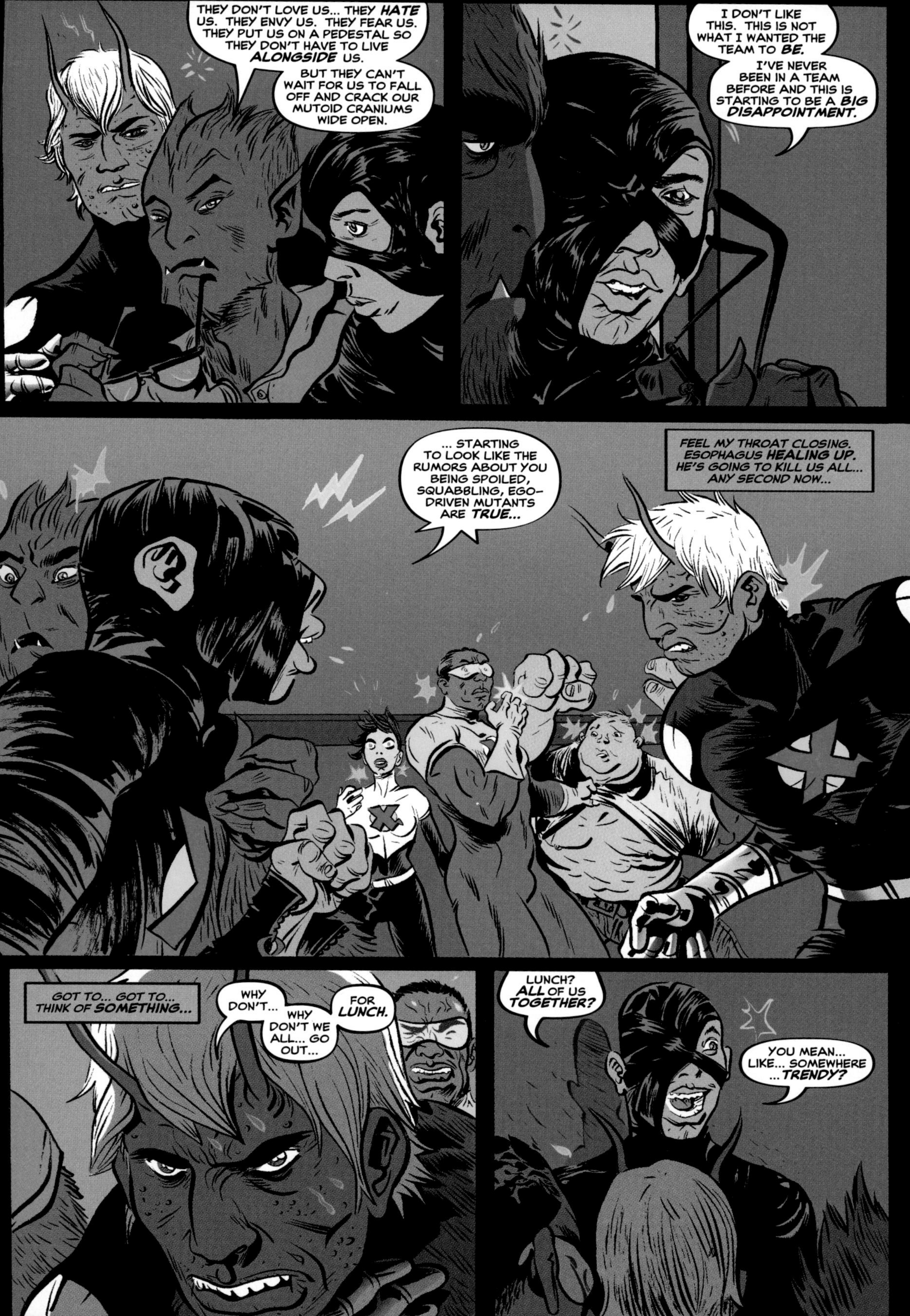
THEY DON'T LOVE US... THEY HATE US. THEY ENVY US. THEY FEAR US. THEY PUT US ON A PEDESTAL SO THEY DON'T HAVE TO LIVE ALONGSIDE US.
BUT THEY CAN'T WAIT FOR US TO FALL OFF AND CRACK OUR MUTOID CRANIUMS WIDE OPEN.
I DON'T LIKE THIS. THIS IS NOT WHAT I WANTED THE TEAM TO BE.
I'VE NEVER BEEN IN A TEAM BEFORE AND THIS IS STARTING TO BE A BIG DISAPPOINTMENT.
... STARTING TO LOOK LIKE THE RUMORS ABOUT YOU BEING SPOILED, SQUABBLING, EGO-DRIVEN MUTANTS ARE TRUE...
FEEL MY THROAT CLOSING. ESOPHAGUS HEALING UP. HE'S GOING TO KILL US ALL... ANY SECOND NOW...
GOT TO... GOT TO... THINK OF SOMETHING...
WHY DON'T...
WHY DON'T WE ALL... GO OUT...
FOR LUNCH.
LUNCH? ALL OF US TOGETHER?
YOU MEAN... LIKE... SOMEWHERE ...TRENDY?

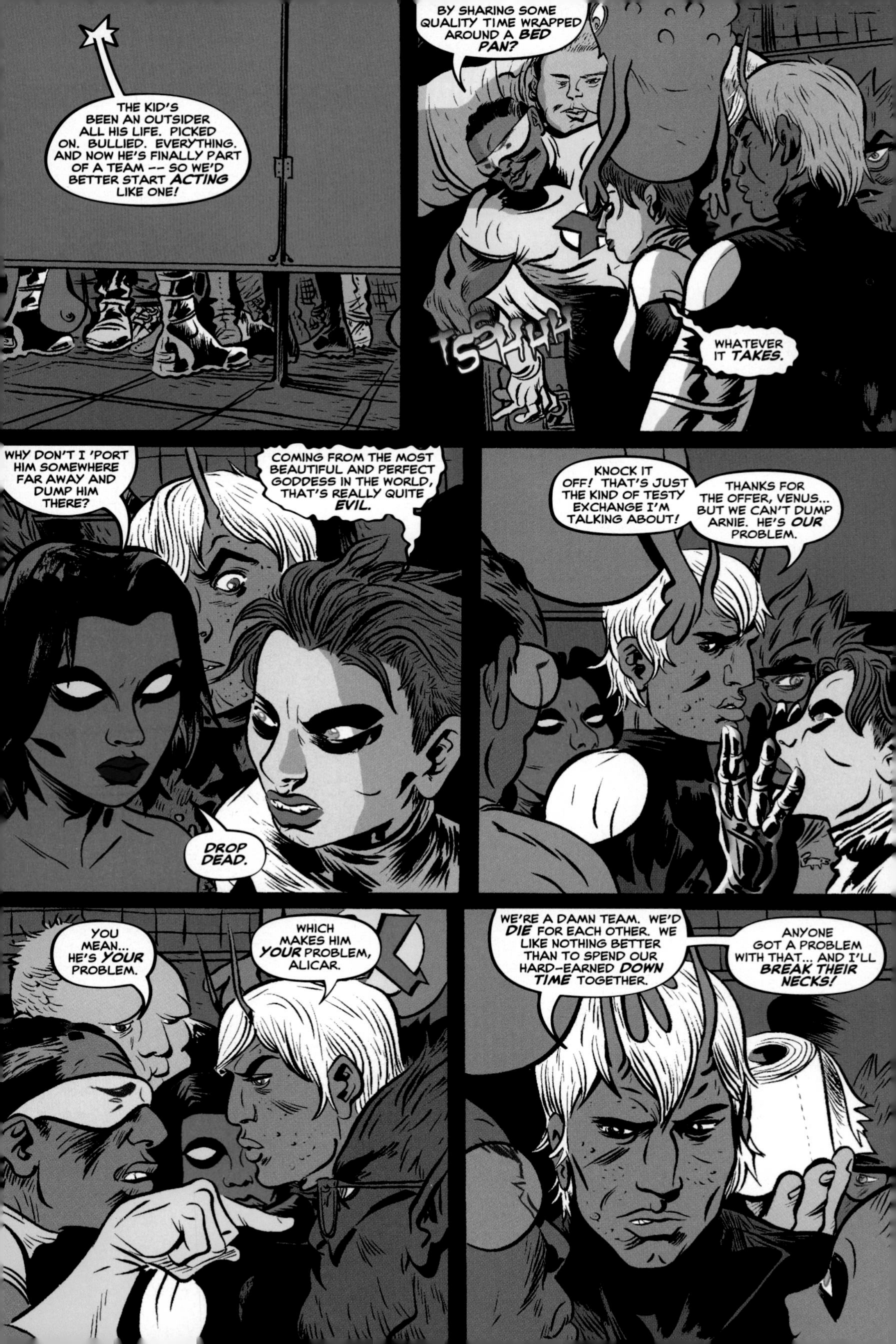

THE KID'S BEEN AN OUTSIDER ALL HIS LIFE. PICKED ON. BULLIED. EVERYTHING. AND NOW HE'S FINALLY PART OF A TEAM -- SO WE'D BETTER START ACTING LIKE ONE!
BY SHARING SOME QUALITY TIME WRAPPED AROUND A BED PAN?
TSSHHH
WHATEVER IT TAKES.
WHY DON'T I 'PORT HIM SOMEWHERE FAR AWAY AND DUMP HIM THERE?
COMING FROM THE MOST BEAUTIFUL AND PERFECT GODDESS IN THE WORLD, THAT'S REALLY QUITE EVIL.
DROP DEAD.
KNOCK IT OFF! THAT'S JUST THE KIND OF TESTY EXCHANGE I'M TALKING ABOUT!
THANKS FOR THE OFFER, VENUS... BUT WE CAN'T DUMP ARNIE. HE'S OUR PROBLEM.
YOU MEAN... HE'S YOUR PROBLEM.
WHICH MAKES HIM YOUR PROBLEM, ALICAR.
WE'RE A DAMN TEAM. WE'D DIE FOR EACH OTHER. WE LIKE NOTHING BETTER THAN TO SPEND OUR HARD-EARNED DOWN TIME TOGETHER.
ANYONE GOT A PROBLEM WITH THAT... AND I'LL BREAK THEIR NECKS!

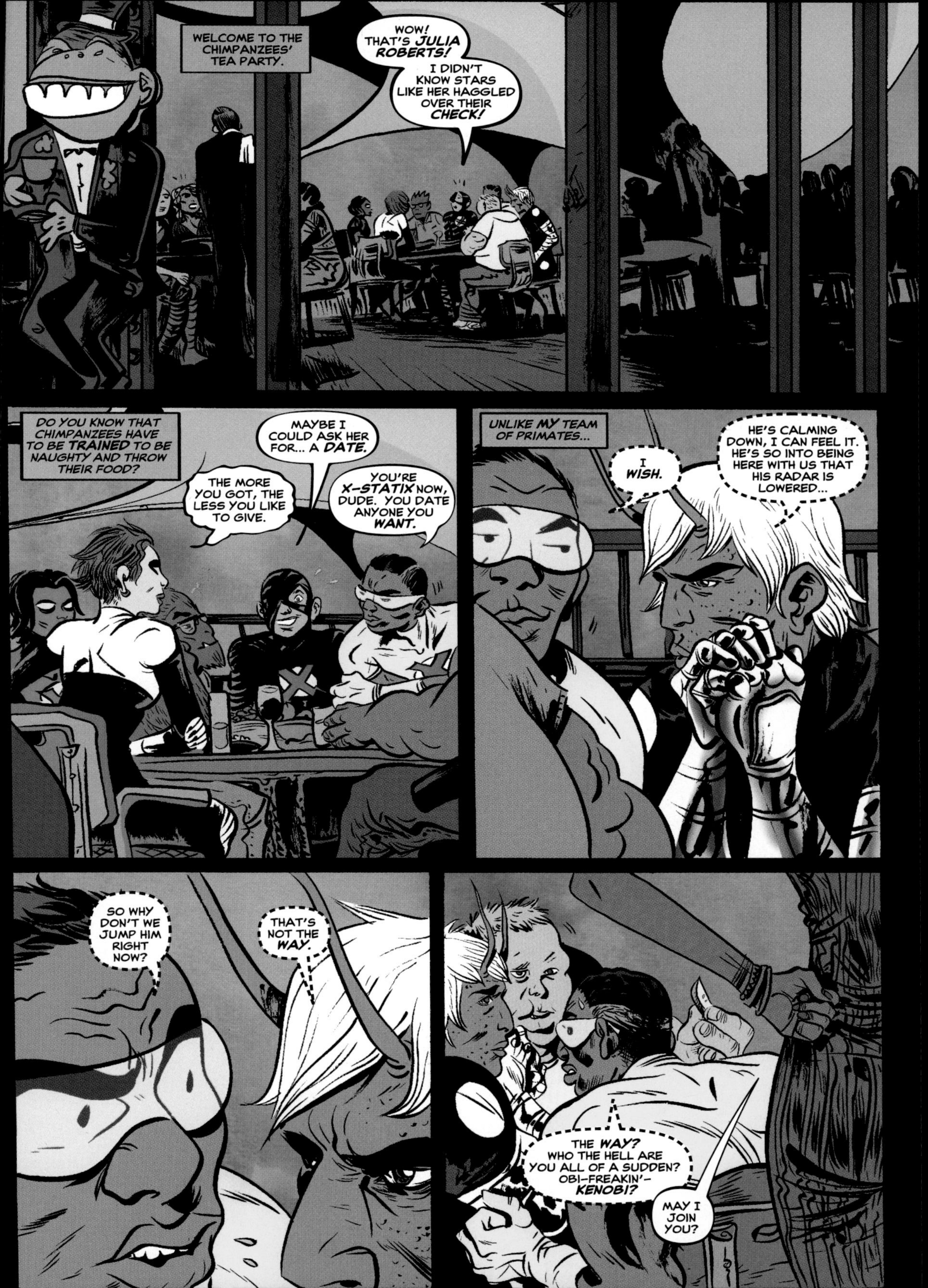
WELCOME TO THE CHIMPANZEES' TEA PARTY.
WOW! THAT'S JULIA ROBERTS! I DIDN'T KNOW STARS LIKE HER HAGGLED OVER THEIR CHECK!
DO YOU KNOW THAT CHIMPANZEES HAVE TO BE TRAINED TO BE NAUGHTY AND THROW THEIR FOOD?
MAYBE I COULD ASK HER FOR... A DATE.
THE MORE YOU GOT, THE LESS YOU LIKE TO GIVE.
YOU'RE X-STATIX NOW, DUDE. YOU DATE ANYONE YOU WANT.
UNLIKE MY TEAM OF PRIMATES...
I WISH.
HE'S CALMING DOWN, I CAN FEEL IT. HE'S SO INTO BEING HERE WITH US THAT HIS RADAR IS LOWERED...
SO WHY DON'T WE JUMP HIM RIGHT NOW?
THAT'S NOT THE WAY.
THE WAY? WHO THE HELL ARE YOU ALL OF A SUDDEN? OBI-FREAKIN'-KENOBI?
MAY I JOIN YOU?

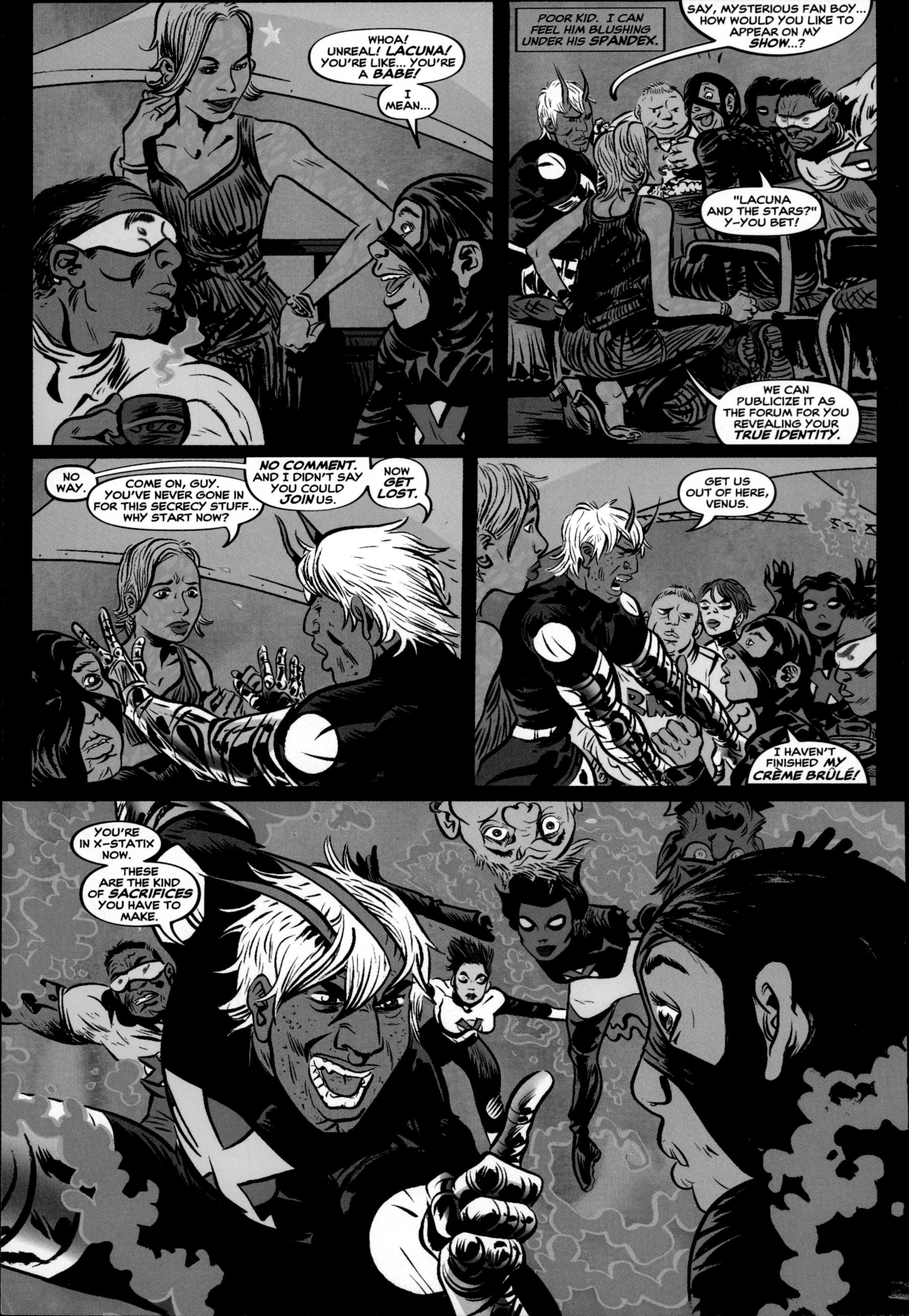
WHOA! UNREAL! LACUNA! YOU'RE LIKE... YOU'RE A BABE!
I MEAN...
POOR KID. I CAN FEEL HIM BLUSHING UNDER HIS SPANDEX.
SAY, MYSTERIOUS FAN BOY... HOW WOULD YOU LIKE TO APPEAR ON MY SHOW...?
"LACUNA AND THE STARS?" Y-YOU BET!
WE CAN PUBLICIZE IT AS THE FORUM FOR YOU REVEALING YOUR TRUE IDENTITY.
NO WAY.
COME ON, GUY. YOU'VE NEVER GONE IN FOR THIS SECRECY STUFF... WHY START NOW?
NO COMMENT. AND I DIDN'T SAY YOU COULD JOIN US.
NOW GET LOST.
GET US OUT OF HERE, VENUS.
I HAVEN'T FINISHED MY CRÈME BRÛLÉ!
YOU'RE IN X-STATIX NOW.
THESE ARE THE KIND OF SACRIFICES YOU HAVE TO MAKE.

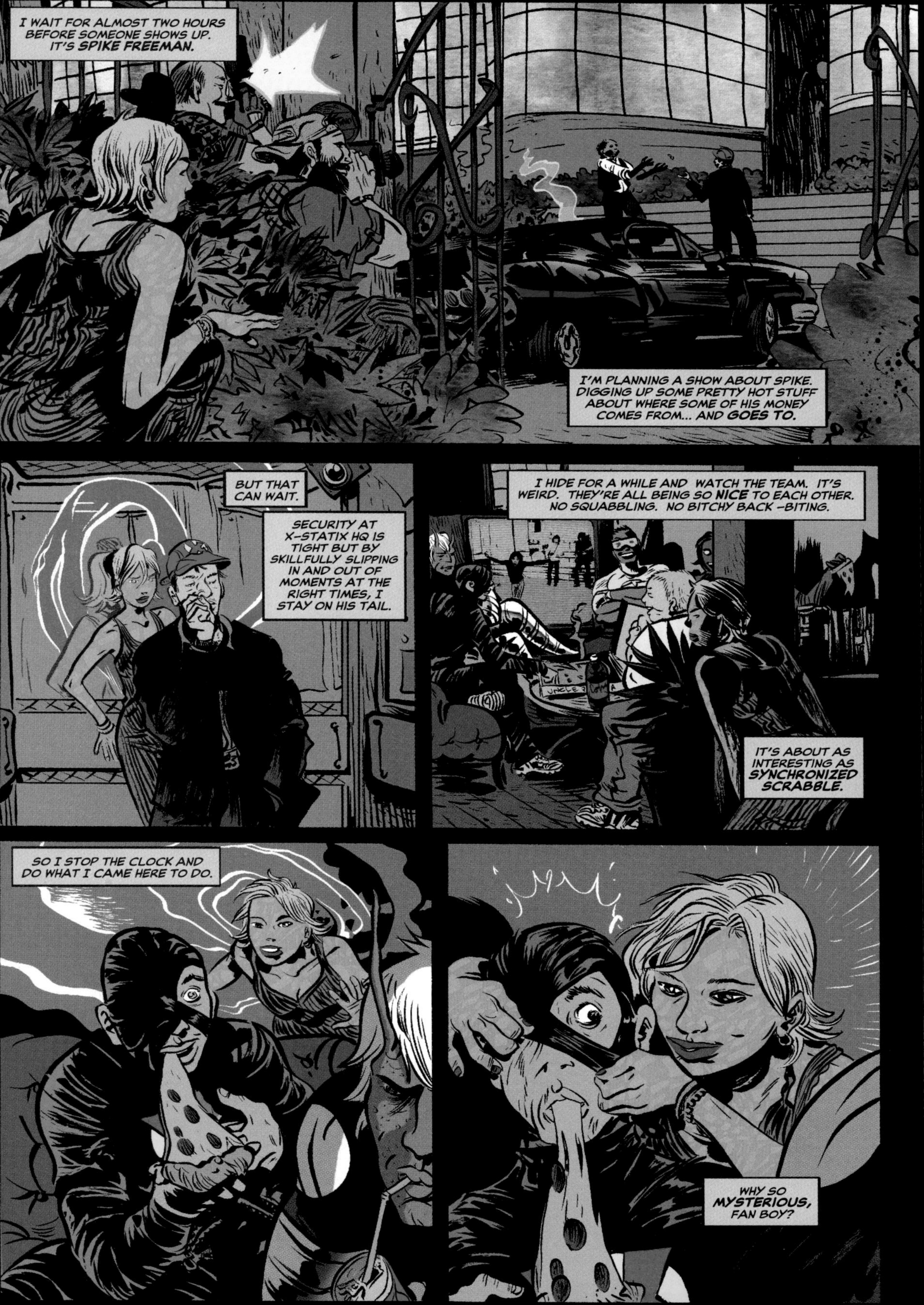
I WAIT FOR ALMOST TWO HOURS BEFORE SOMEONE SHOWS UP. IT'S SPIKE FREEMAN.
I'M PLANNING A SHOW ABOUT SPIKE. DIGGING UP SOME PRETTY HOT STUFF ABOUT WHERE SOME OF HIS MONEY COMES FROM... AND GOES TO.
BUT THAT CAN WAIT.
SECURITY AT X-STATIX HQ IS TIGHT BUT BY SKILLFULLY SLIPPING IN AND OUT OF MOMENTS AT THE RIGHT TIMES, I STAY ON HIS TAIL.
I HIDE FOR A WHILE AND WATCH THE TEAM. IT'S WEIRD. THEY'RE ALL BEING SO NICE TO EACH OTHER. NO SQUABBLING. NO BITCHY BACK-BITING.
IT'S ABOUT AS INTERESTING AS SYNCHRONIZED SCRABBLE.
SO I STOP THE CLOCK AND DO WHAT I CAME HERE TO DO.
WHY SO MYSTERIOUS, FAN BOY?

"...ARNIE LUNDBERG, CONTRARY TO WHAT X-STATIX HAD US BELIEVE... IS VERY MUCH ALIVE AND WELL... WEARING AN 'X'!"

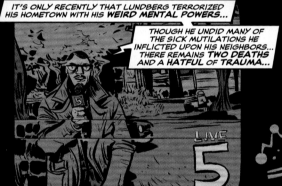

IT'S ONLY RECENTLY THAT LUNDBERG TERRORIZED HIS HOMETOWN WITH HIS *WEIRD MENTAL POWERS*...

THOUGH HE UNDID MANY OF THE SICK MUTILATIONS HE INFLICTED UPON HIS NEIGHBORS... THERE REMAINS *TWO DEATHS* AND A *HATFUL OF TRAUMA*...

LIVE 5

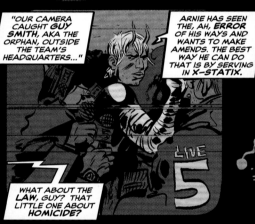

"OUR CAMERA CAUGHT *GUY SMITH*, AKA THE *ORPHAN*, OUTSIDE THE TEAM'S HEADQUARTERS..."

ARNIE HAS SEEN THE, AH, *ERROR* OF HIS WAYS AND WANTS TO MAKE AMENDS. THE BEST WAY HE CAN DO THAT IS BY SERVING IN *X-STATIX.*

WHAT ABOUT THE *LAW*, GUY? THAT LITTLE ONE ABOUT *HOMICIDE*?

LIVE 5

THE LAW DOESN'T COVER THINGS LIKE THIS.

YOU MEAN X-STATIX IS *ABOVE* THE LAW?

I DIDN'T SAY...

IF OSAMA BIN LADEN HAD *SUPER POWERS*, WOULD YOU CONSIDER HIM FOR YOUR TEAM?

LIVE 5

I...

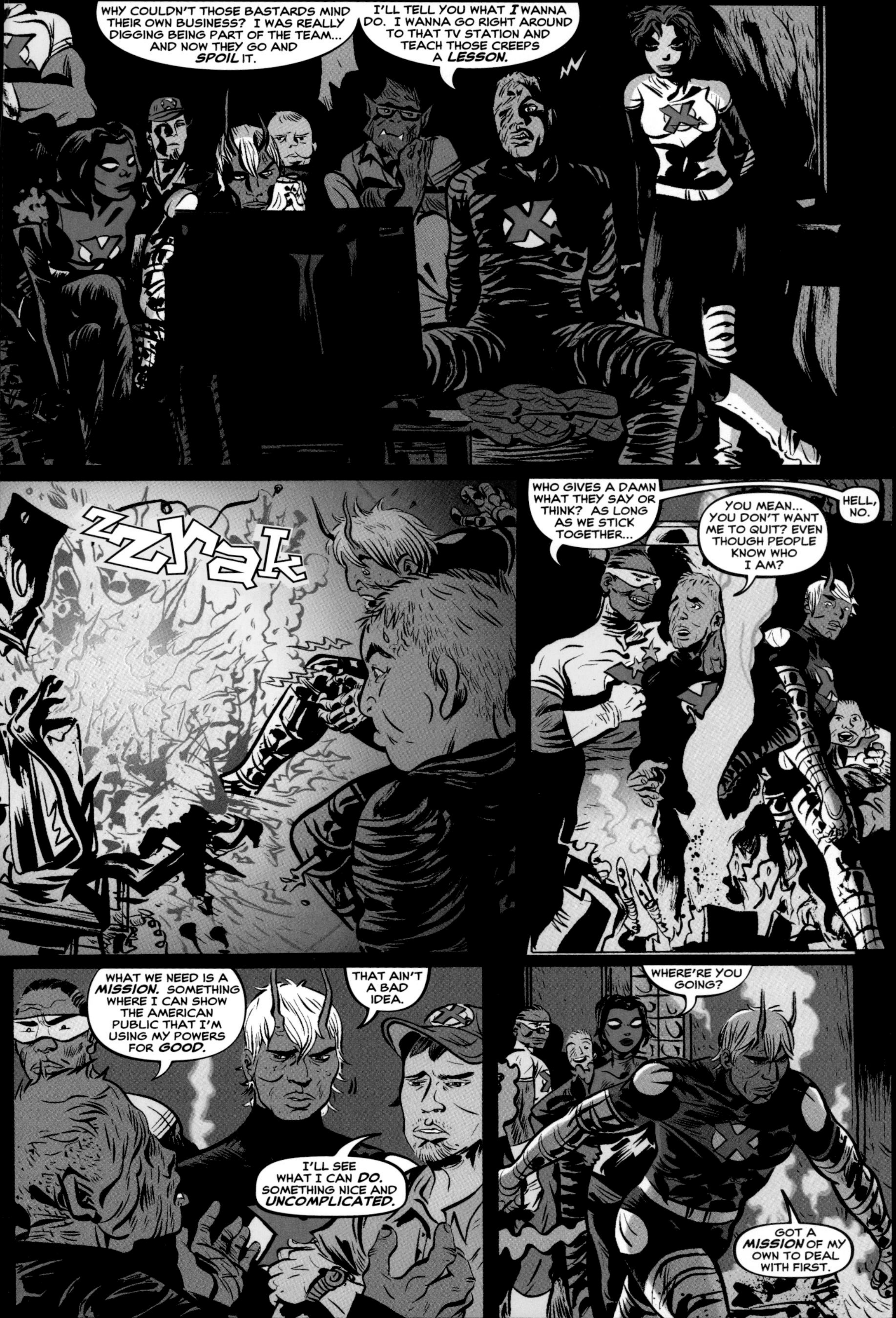

WHY COULDN'T THOSE BASTARDS MIND THEIR OWN BUSINESS? I WAS REALLY DIGGING BEING PART OF THE TEAM... AND NOW THEY GO AND *SPOIL* IT.
I'LL TELL YOU WHAT *I* WANNA DO. I WANNA GO RIGHT AROUND TO THAT TV STATION AND TEACH THOSE CREEPS A *LESSON.*
ZZRAK
WHO GIVES A DAMN WHAT THEY SAY OR THINK? AS LONG AS WE STICK TOGETHER...
YOU MEAN... YOU DON'T WANT ME TO QUIT? EVEN THOUGH PEOPLE KNOW WHO I AM?
HELL, NO.
WHAT WE NEED IS A *MISSION.* SOMETHING WHERE I CAN SHOW THE AMERICAN PUBLIC THAT I'M USING MY POWERS FOR *GOOD.*
THAT AIN'T A BAD IDEA.
I'LL SEE WHAT I CAN *DO.* SOMETHING NICE AND *UNCOMPLICATED.*
WHERE'RE YOU GOING?
GOT A *MISSION* OF MY OWN TO DEAL WITH FIRST.

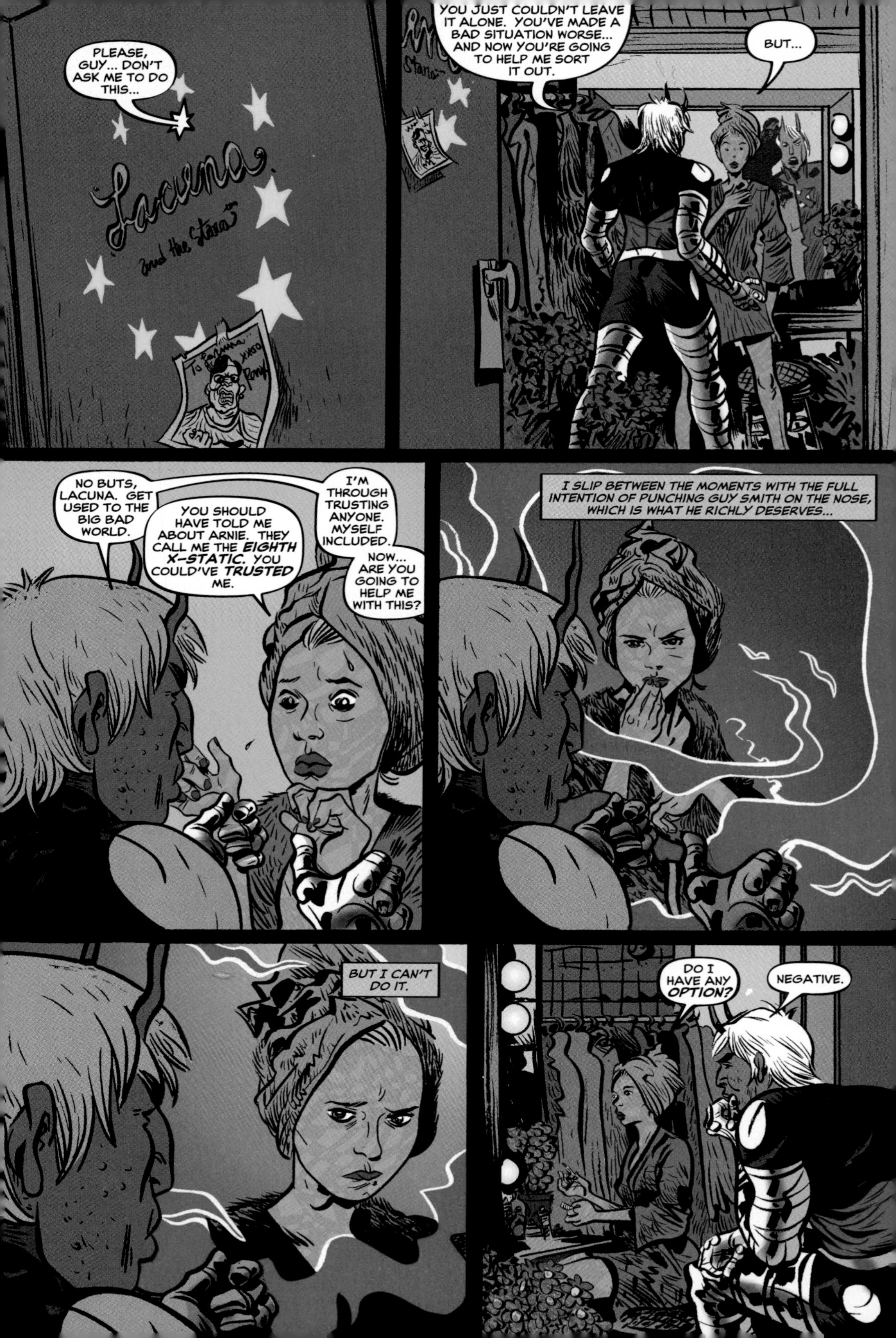
PLEASE, GUY... DON'T ASK ME TO DO THIS...
Lacuna and the Stars
YOU JUST COULDN'T LEAVE IT ALONE. YOU'VE MADE A BAD SITUATION WORSE... AND NOW YOU'RE GOING TO HELP ME SORT IT OUT.
BUT...
NO BUTS, LACUNA. GET USED TO THE BIG BAD WORLD.
I'M THROUGH TRUSTING ANYONE. MYSELF INCLUDED.
NOW... ARE YOU GOING TO HELP ME WITH THIS?
YOU SHOULD HAVE TOLD ME ABOUT ARNIE. THEY CALL ME THE EIGHTH X-STATIC. YOU COULD'VE TRUSTED ME.
I SLIP BETWEEN THE MOMENTS WITH THE FULL INTENTION OF PUNCHING GUY SMITH ON THE NOSE, WHICH IS WHAT HE RICHLY DESERVES...
BUT I CAN'T DO IT.
DO I HAVE ANY OPTION?
NEGATIVE.

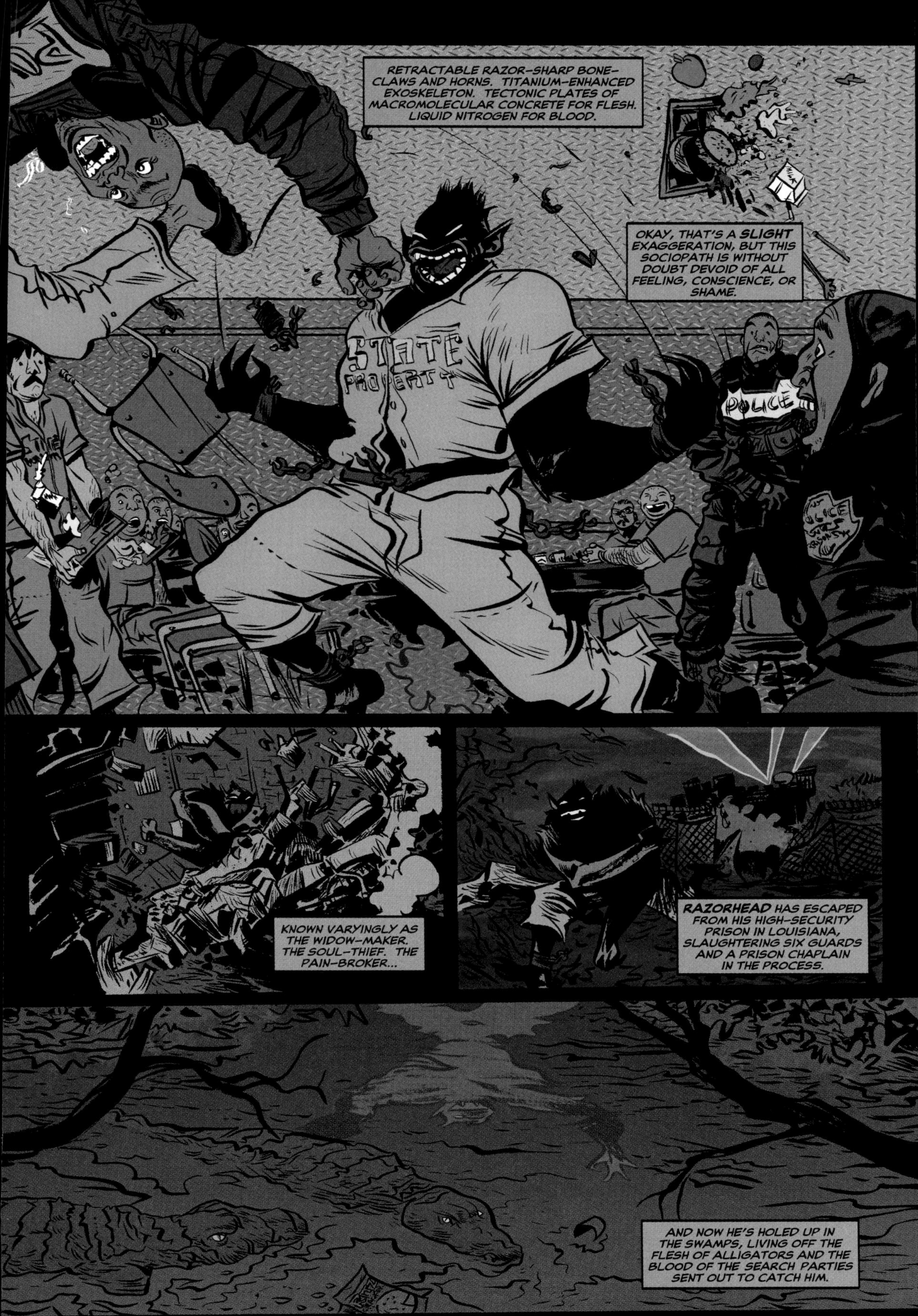
RETRACTABLE RAZOR-SHARP BONE-CLAWS AND HORNS. TITANIUM-ENHANCED EXOSKELETON. TECTONIC PLATES OF MACROMOLECULAR CONCRETE FOR FLESH. LIQUID NITROGEN FOR BLOOD.
OKAY, THAT'S A **SLIGHT** EXAGGERATION, BUT THIS SOCIOPATH IS WITHOUT DOUBT DEVOID OF ALL FEELING, CONSCIENCE, OR SHAME.
STATE PROPERTY
POLICE
KNOWN VARYINGLY AS THE WIDOW-MAKER. THE SOUL-THIEF. THE PAIN-BROKER...
RAZORHEAD HAS ESCAPED FROM HIS HIGH-SECURITY PRISON IN LOUISIANA, SLAUGHTERING SIX GUARDS AND A PRISON CHAPLAIN IN THE PROCESS.
AND NOW HE'S HOLED UP IN THE SWAMPS, LIVING OFF THE FLESH OF ALLIGATORS AND THE BLOOD OF THE SEARCH PARTIES SENT OUT TO CATCH HIM.

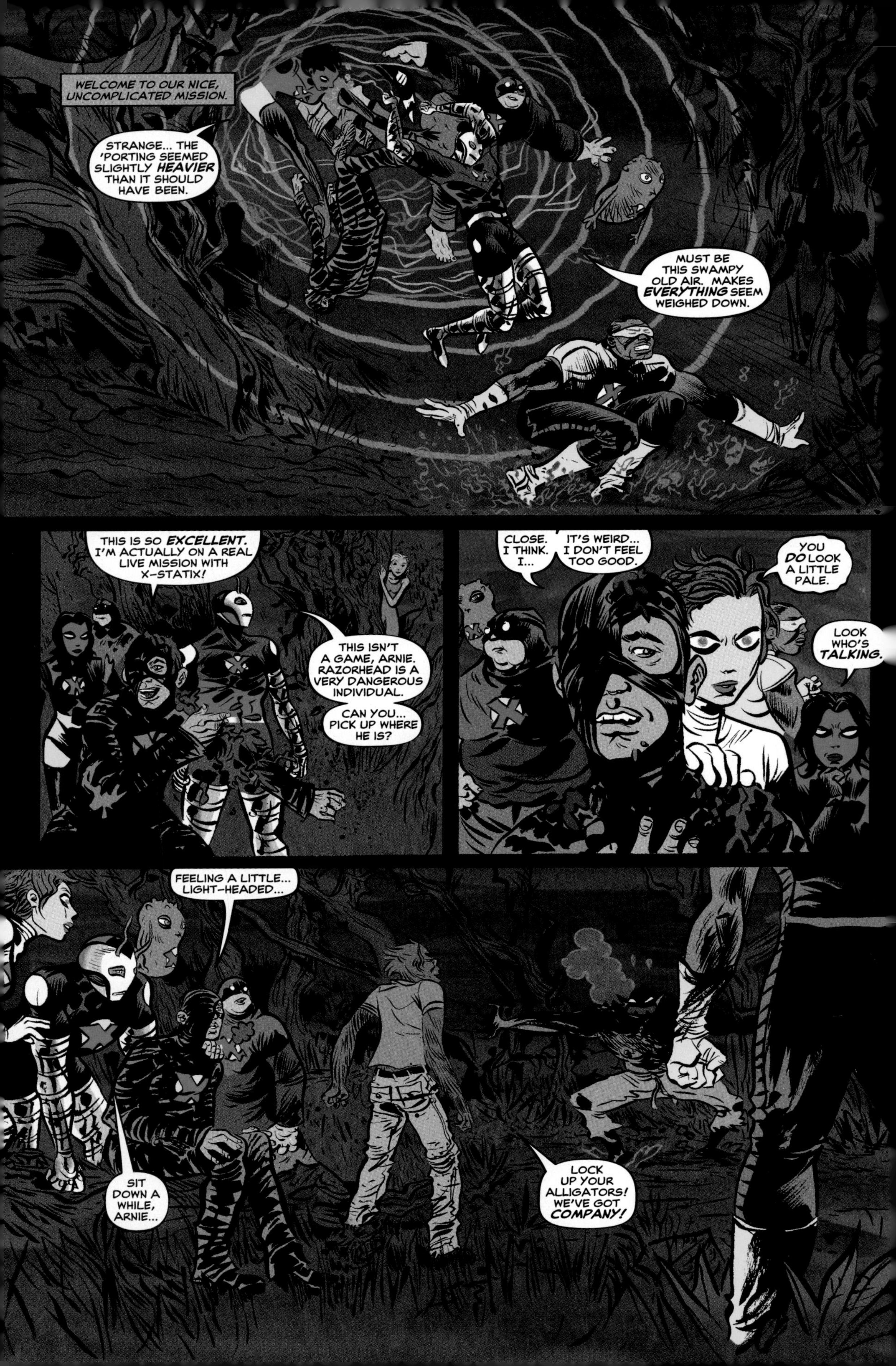

WELCOME TO OUR NICE, UNCOMPLICATED MISSION.
STRANGE... THE 'PORTING SEEMED SLIGHTLY HEAVIER THAN IT SHOULD HAVE BEEN.
MUST BE THIS SWAMPY OLD AIR. MAKES EVERYTHING SEEM WEIGHED DOWN.
THIS IS SO EXCELLENT. I'M ACTUALLY ON A REAL LIVE MISSION WITH X-STATIX!
THIS ISN'T A GAME, ARNIE. RAZORHEAD IS A VERY DANGEROUS INDIVIDUAL.
CAN YOU... PICK UP WHERE HE IS?
CLOSE. I THINK. I...
IT'S WEIRD... I DON'T FEEL TOO GOOD.
YOU DO LOOK A LITTLE PALE.
LOOK WHO'S TALKING.
FEELING A LITTLE... LIGHT-HEADED...
SIT DOWN A WHILE, ARNIE...
LOCK UP YOUR ALLIGATORS! WE'VE GOT COMPANY!

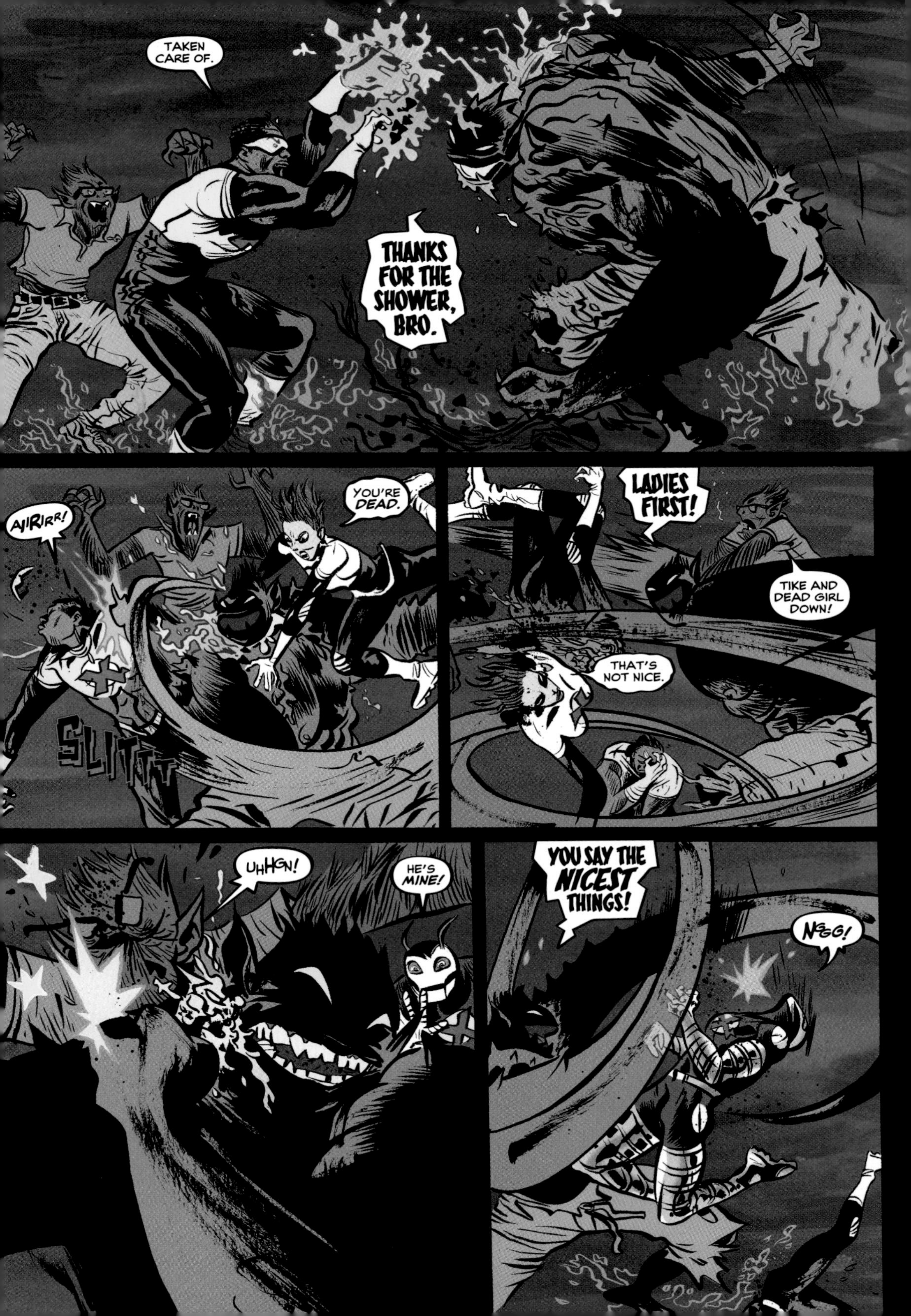

TAKEN CARE OF.
THANKS FOR THE SHOWER, BRO.
AIIRIRR!
YOU'RE DEAD.
SLITTT
LADIES FIRST!
TIKE AND DEAD GIRL DOWN!
THAT'S NOT NICE.
UHHGN!
HE'S MINE!
YOU SAY THE NICEST THINGS!
NGGG!

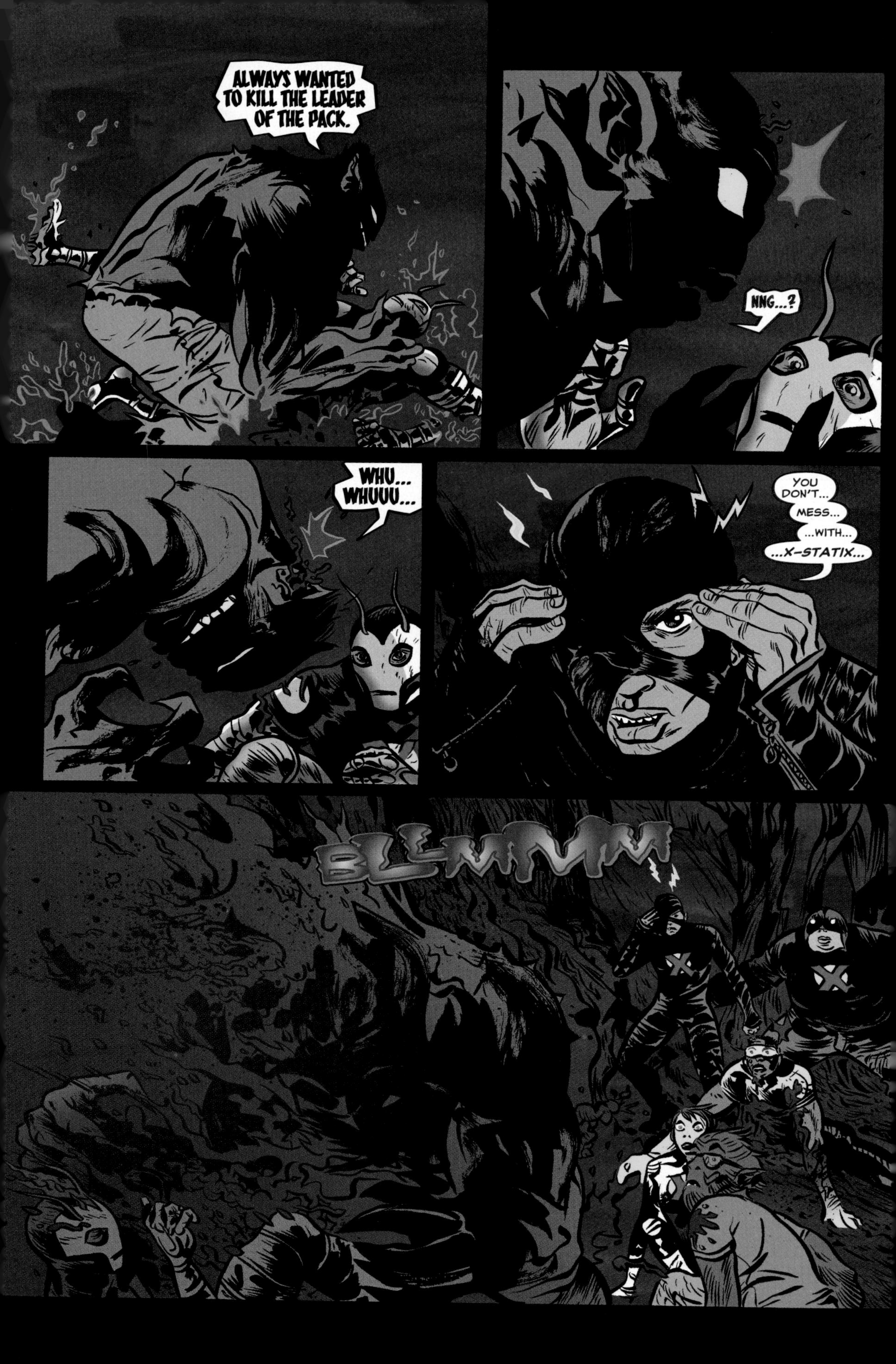
ALWAYS WANTED TO KILL THE LEADER OF THE PACK.
NNG...?
WHU... WHUUU...
YOU DON'T... MESS... ...WITH... ...X-STATIX...
BLMMM

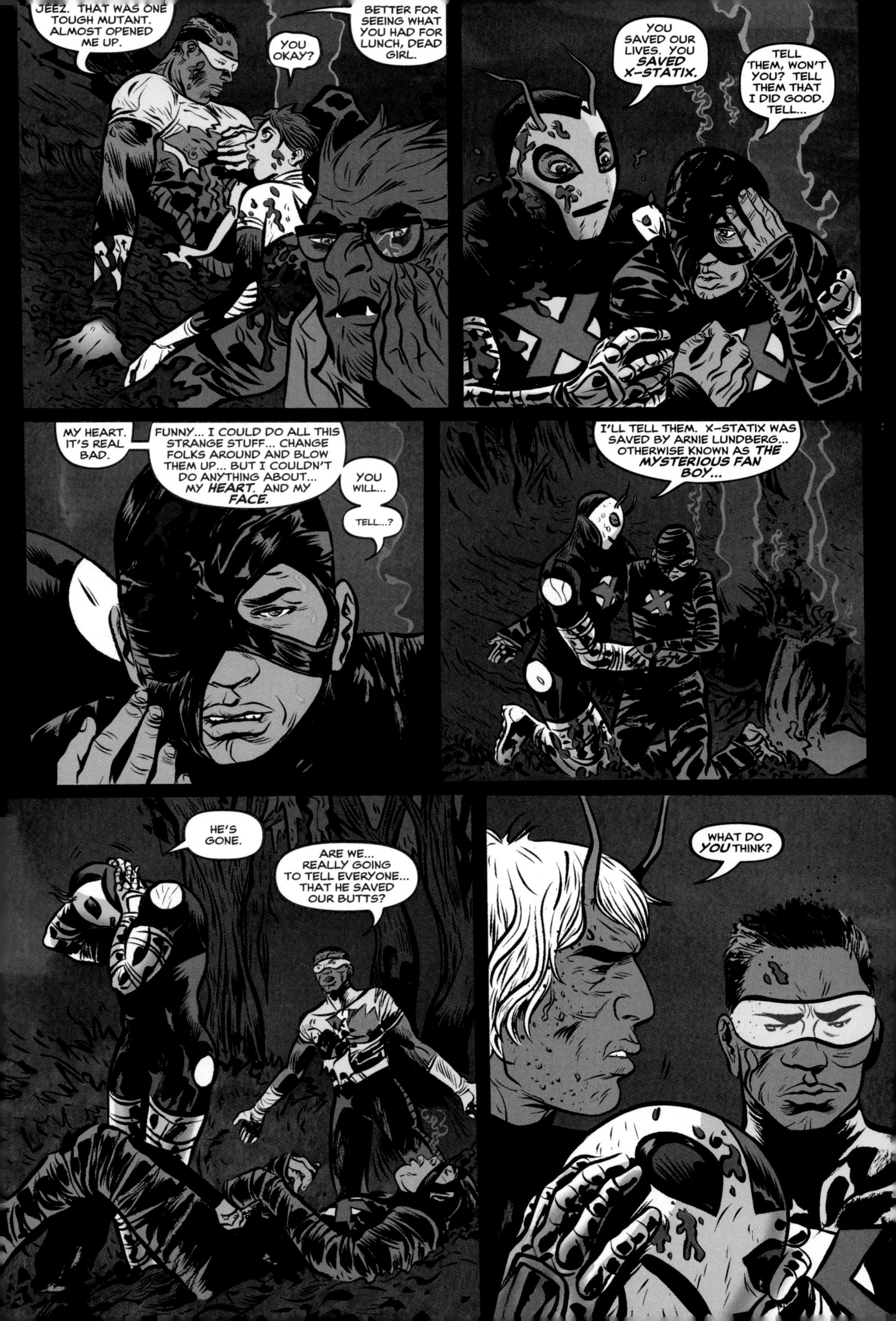
JEEZ. THAT WAS ONE TOUGH MUTANT. ALMOST OPENED ME UP.
YOU OKAY?
BETTER FOR SEEING WHAT YOU HAD FOR LUNCH, DEAD GIRL.
YOU SAVED OUR LIVES. YOU SAVED X-STATIX.
TELL THEM, WON'T YOU? TELL THEM THAT I DID GOOD. TELL...
MY HEART. IT'S REAL BAD.
FUNNY... I COULD DO ALL THIS STRANGE STUFF... CHANGE FOLKS AROUND AND BLOW THEM UP... BUT I COULDN'T DO ANYTHING ABOUT... MY HEART. AND MY FACE.
YOU WILL...
TELL...?
I'LL TELL THEM. X-STATIX WAS SAVED BY ARNIE LUNDBERG... OTHERWISE KNOWN AS THE MYSTERIOUS FAN BOY...
HE'S GONE.
ARE WE... REALLY GOING TO TELL EVERYONE... THAT HE SAVED OUR BUTTS?
WHAT DO YOU THINK?

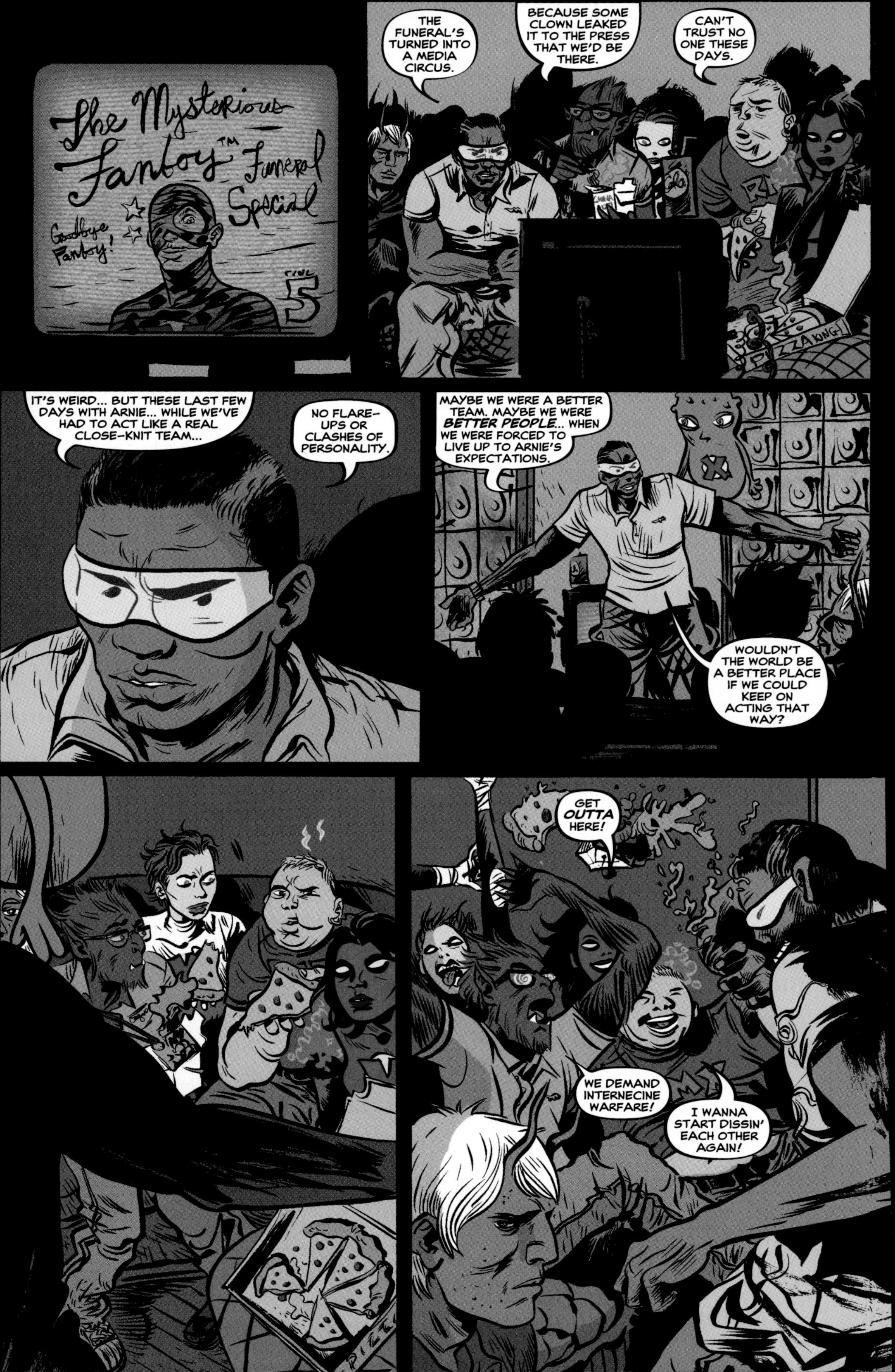
The Mysterious Fanboy™ Funeral Special
Goodbye Fanboy!
5
THE FUNERAL'S TURNED INTO A MEDIA CIRCUS.
BECAUSE SOME CLOWN LEAKED IT TO THE PRESS THAT WE'D BE THERE.
CAN'T TRUST NO ONE THESE DAYS.
PIZZA KING!
IT'S WEIRD... BUT THESE LAST FEW DAYS WITH ARNIE... WHILE WE'VE HAD TO ACT LIKE A REAL CLOSE-KNIT TEAM...
NO FLARE-UPS OR CLASHES OF PERSONALITY.
MAYBE WE WERE A BETTER TEAM. MAYBE WE WERE BETTER PEOPLE... WHEN WE WERE FORCED TO LIVE UP TO ARNIE'S EXPECTATIONS.
WOULDN'T THE WORLD BE A BETTER PLACE IF WE COULD KEEP ON ACTING THAT WAY?
GET OUTTA HERE!
WE DEMAND INTERNECINE WARFARE!
I WANNA START DISSIN' EACH OTHER AGAIN!

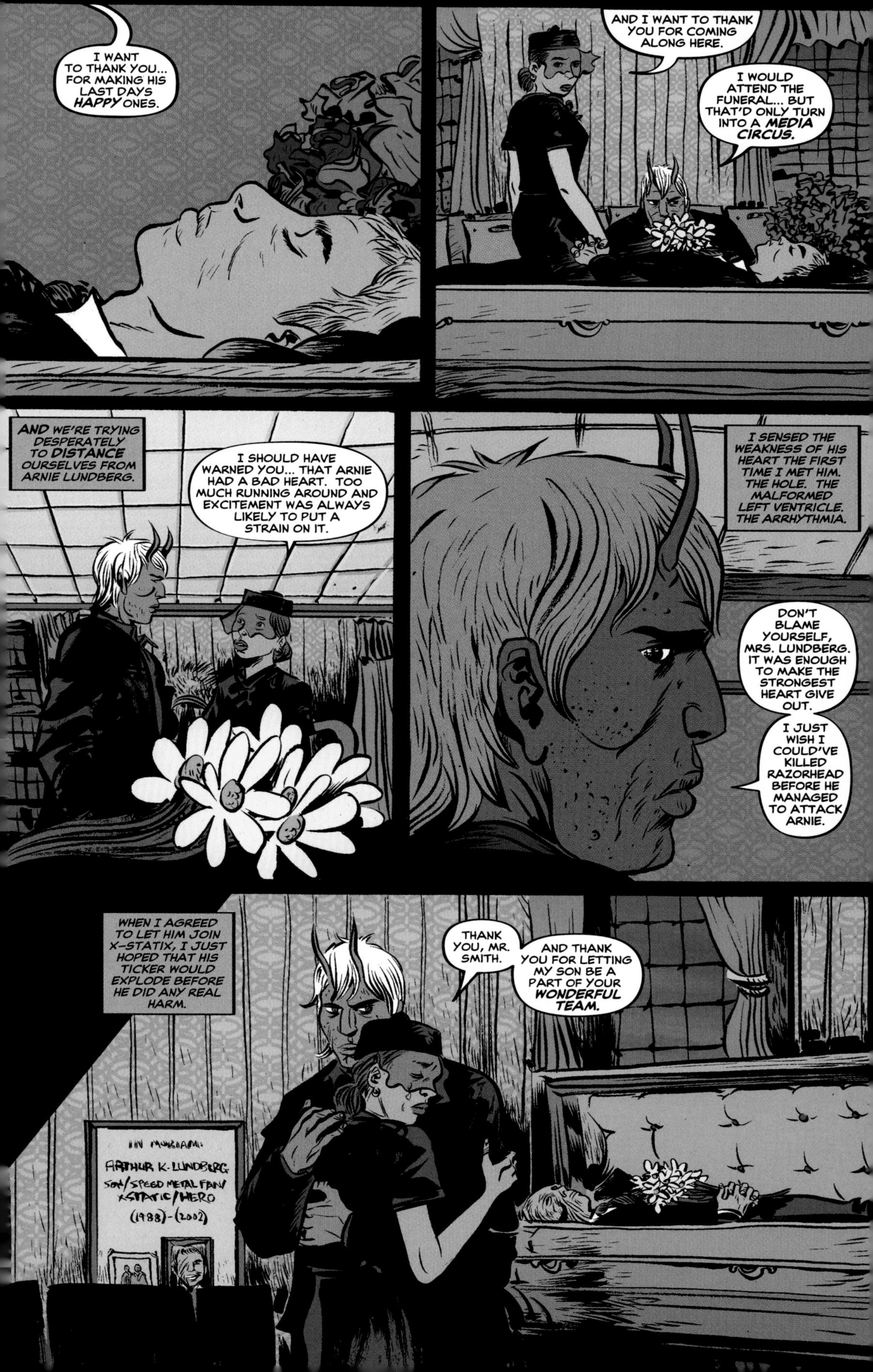
I WANT TO THANK YOU... FOR MAKING HIS LAST DAYS HAPPY ONES.
AND I WANT TO THANK YOU FOR COMING ALONG HERE.
I WOULD ATTEND THE FUNERAL... BUT THAT'D ONLY TURN INTO A MEDIA CIRCUS.
AND WE'RE TRYING DESPERATELY TO DISTANCE OURSELVES FROM ARNIE LUNDBERG.
I SHOULD HAVE WARNED YOU... THAT ARNIE HAD A BAD HEART. TOO MUCH RUNNING AROUND AND EXCITEMENT WAS ALWAYS LIKELY TO PUT A STRAIN ON IT.
I SENSED THE WEAKNESS OF HIS HEART THE FIRST TIME I MET HIM. THE HOLE. THE MALFORMED LEFT VENTRICLE. THE ARRHYTHMIA.
DON'T BLAME YOURSELF, MRS. LUNDBERG. IT WAS ENOUGH TO MAKE THE STRONGEST HEART GIVE OUT.
I JUST WISH I COULD'VE KILLED RAZORHEAD BEFORE HE MANAGED TO ATTACK ARNIE.
WHEN I AGREED TO LET HIM JOIN X-STATIX, I JUST HOPED THAT HIS TICKER WOULD EXPLODE BEFORE HE DID ANY REAL HARM.
THANK YOU, MR. SMITH.
AND THANK YOU FOR LETTING MY SON BE A PART OF YOUR WONDERFUL TEAM.
IN MEMORIAM:
ARTHUR K. LUNDBERG
SON/SPEED METAL FAN/
X-STATIC/HERO
(1988)-(2002)

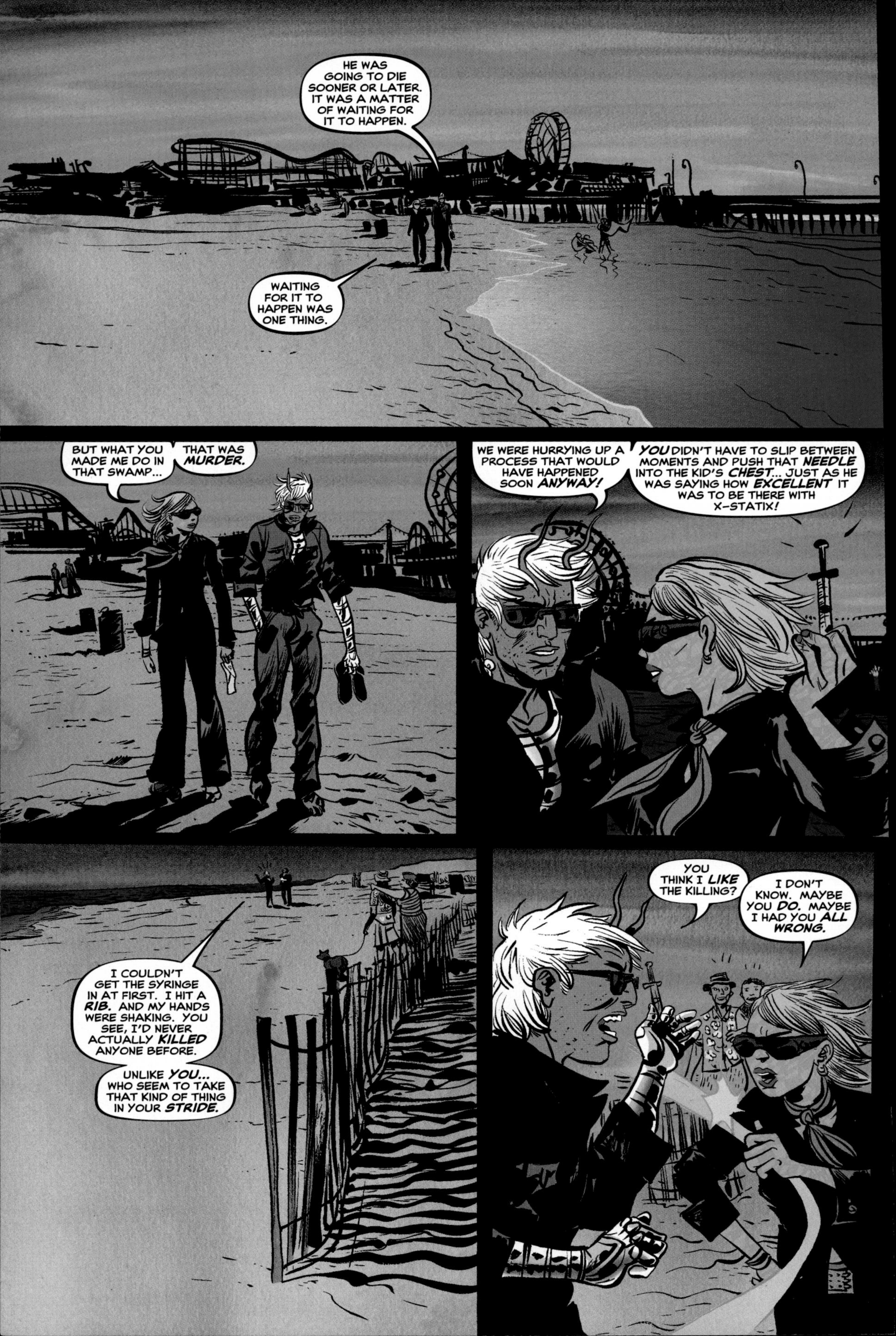
HE WAS GOING TO DIE SOONER OR LATER. IT WAS A MATTER OF WAITING FOR IT TO HAPPEN.
WAITING FOR IT TO HAPPEN WAS ONE THING.
BUT WHAT YOU MADE ME DO IN THAT SWAMP...
THAT WAS MURDER.
WE WERE HURRYING UP A PROCESS THAT WOULD HAVE HAPPENED SOON ANYWAY!
YOU DIDN'T HAVE TO SLIP BETWEEN MOMENTS AND PUSH THAT NEEDLE INTO THE KID'S CHEST... JUST AS HE WAS SAYING HOW EXCELLENT IT WAS TO BE THERE WITH X-STATIX!
I COULDN'T GET THE SYRINGE IN AT FIRST. I HIT A RIB. AND MY HANDS WERE SHAKING. YOU SEE, I'D NEVER ACTUALLY KILLED ANYONE BEFORE.
UNLIKE YOU... WHO SEEM TO TAKE THAT KIND OF THING IN YOUR STRIDE.
YOU THINK I LIKE THE KILLING?
I DON'T KNOW. MAYBE YOU DO. MAYBE I HAD YOU ALL WRONG.

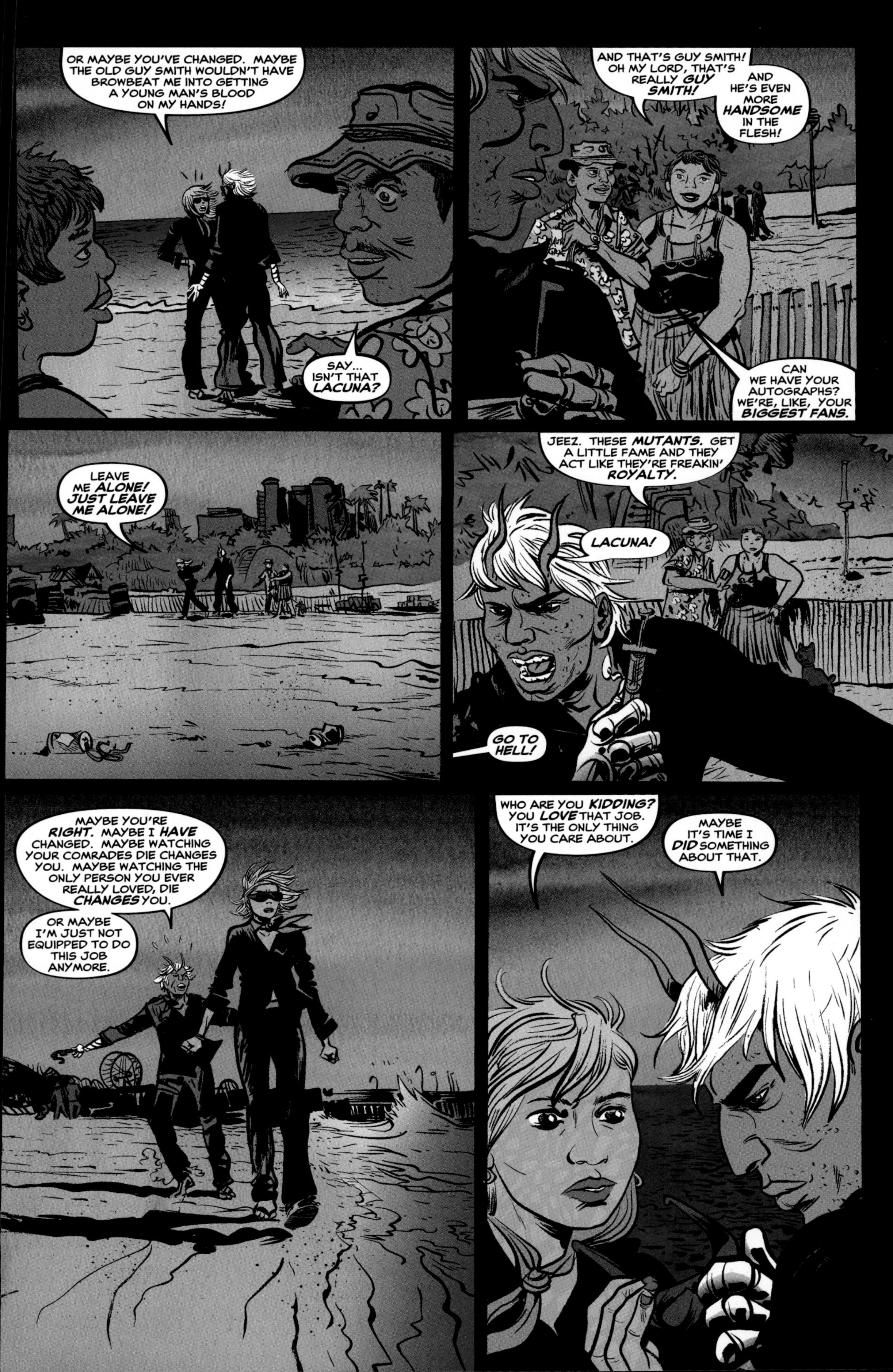

OR MAYBE YOU'VE CHANGED. MAYBE THE OLD GUY SMITH WOULDN'T HAVE BROWBEAT ME INTO GETTING A YOUNG MAN'S BLOOD ON MY HANDS!
SAY... ISN'T THAT LACUNA?
AND THAT'S GUY SMITH! OH MY LORD, THAT'S REALLY GUY SMITH!
AND HE'S EVEN MORE HANDSOME IN THE FLESH!
CAN WE HAVE YOUR AUTOGRAPHS? WE'RE, LIKE, YOUR BIGGEST FANS.
LEAVE ME ALONE! JUST LEAVE ME ALONE!
JEEZ. THESE MUTANTS. GET A LITTLE FAME AND THEY ACT LIKE THEY'RE FREAKIN' ROYALTY.
LACUNA!
GO TO HELL!
MAYBE YOU'RE RIGHT. MAYBE I HAVE CHANGED. MAYBE WATCHING YOUR COMRADES DIE CHANGES YOU. MAYBE WATCHING THE ONLY PERSON YOU EVER REALLY LOVED, DIE CHANGES YOU.
OR MAYBE I'M JUST NOT EQUIPPED TO DO THIS JOB ANYMORE.
WHO ARE YOU KIDDING? YOU LOVE THAT JOB. IT'S THE ONLY THING YOU CARE ABOUT.
MAYBE IT'S TIME I DID SOMETHING ABOUT THAT.

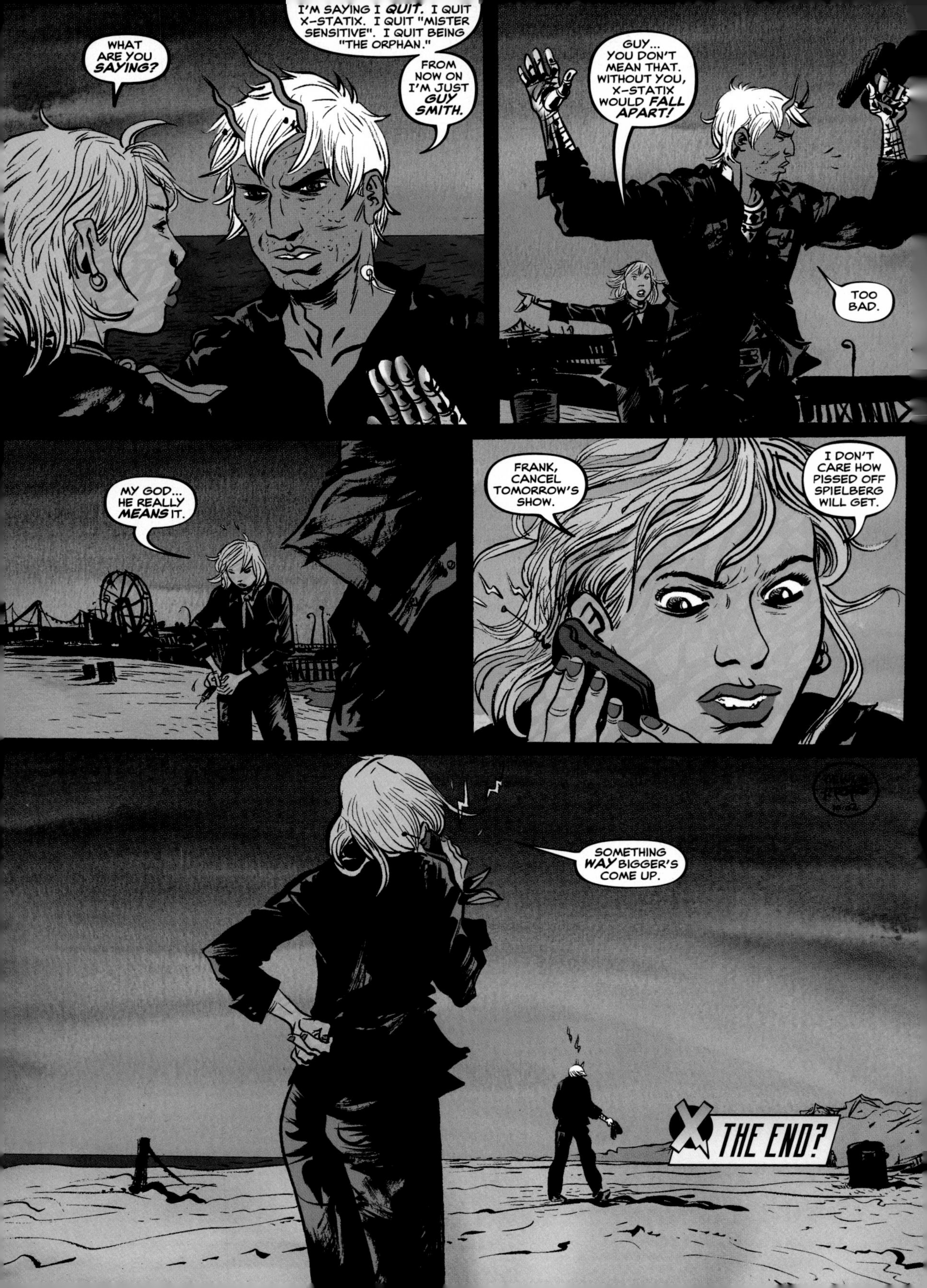
WHAT ARE YOU SAYING?
I'M SAYING I QUIT. I QUIT X-STATIX. I QUIT "MISTER SENSITIVE". I QUIT BEING "THE ORPHAN."
FROM NOW ON I'M JUST GUY SMITH.
GUY... YOU DON'T MEAN THAT. WITHOUT YOU, X-STATIX WOULD FALL APART!
TOO BAD.
MY GOD... HE REALLY MEANS IT.
FRANK, CANCEL TOMORROW'S SHOW.
I DON'T CARE HOW PISSED OFF SPIELBERG WILL GET.
SOMETHING WAY BIGGER'S COME UP.
THE END?

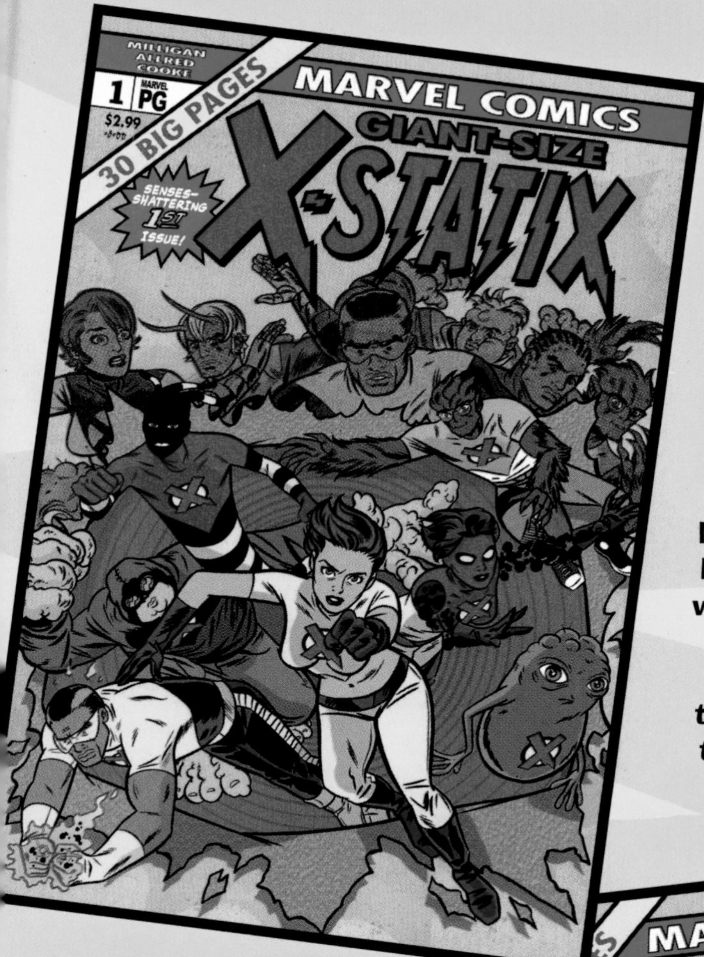
MILLIGAN
ALLRED
COOKE
1
MARVEL
PG
$2.99
30 BIG PAGES
MARVEL COMICS
GIANT-SIZE
X-STATIX
SENSES-SHATTERING 1ST ISSUE!

Not even *X-Statix* artist Mike Allred can predict who will live and who will die. Covering all his bases, Mike created these alternate versions to the *X-Statix #1* cover.

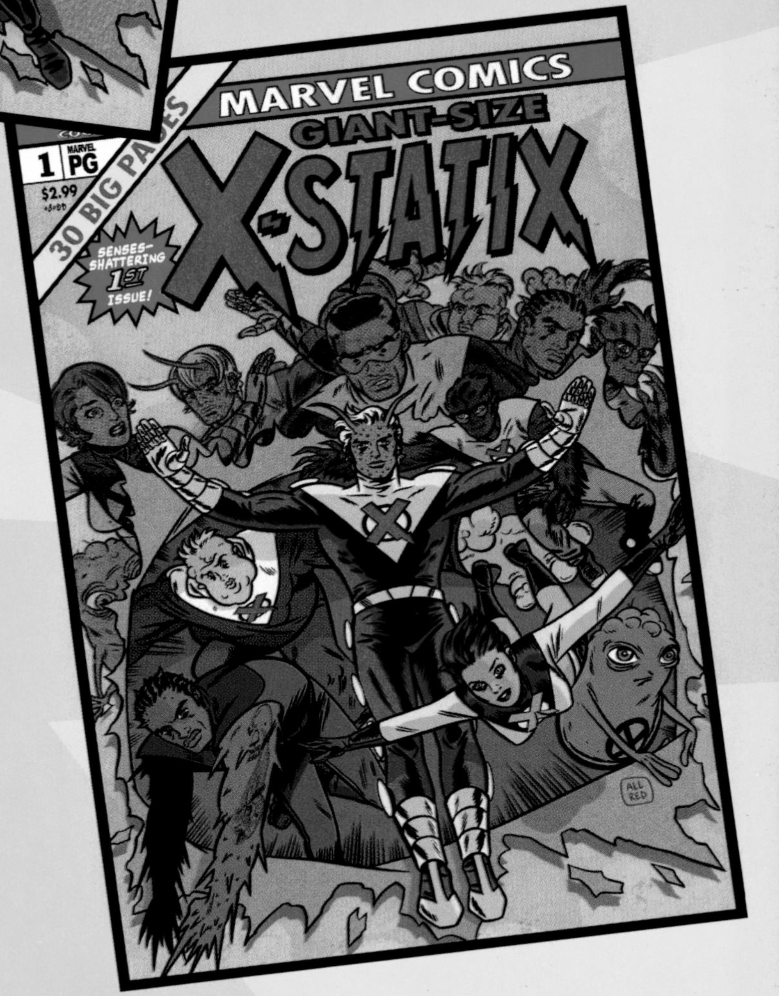
1
MARVEL
PG
$2.99
30 BIG PAGES
MARVEL COMICS
GIANT-SIZE
X-STATIX
SENSES-SHATTERING 1ST ISSUE!
ALL RED

Darwyn Cooke's sketches for

CORKSCREW

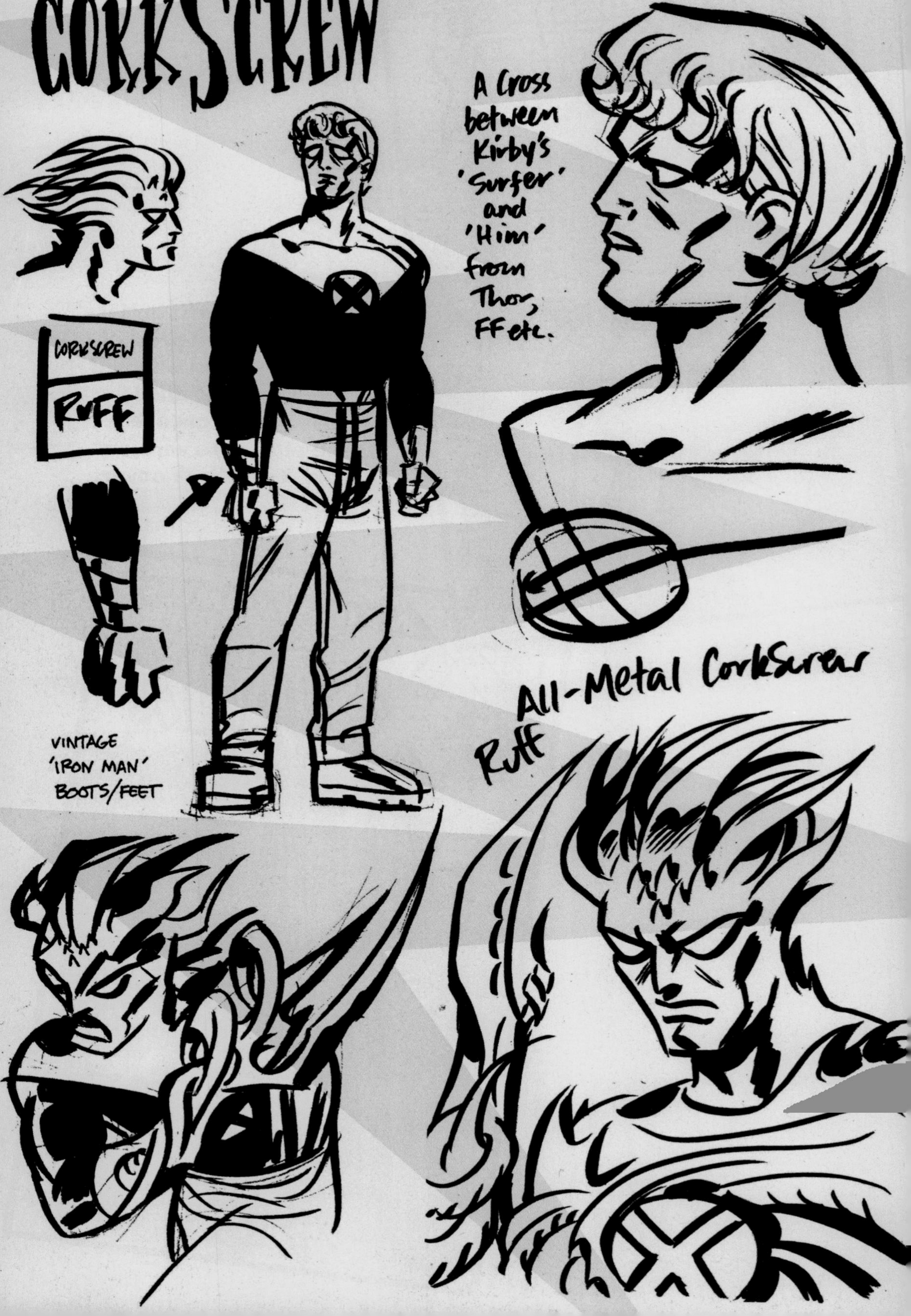
A Cross between Kirby's 'Surfer' and 'Him' from Thor, FF etc.
CORKSCREW
RUFF
VINTAGE 'IRON MAN' BOOTS/FEET
All-Metal CorkScrew Ruff